LACAN AND NARRATION

LACAN AND NARRATION
The Psychoanalytic Difference in Narrative Theory

Edited by Robert Con Davis

The Johns Hopkins University Press
Baltimore and London

© 1983 by The Johns Hopkins University Press
All rights reserved
Printed in the United States of America
Originally published, 1983
Second printing, 1985

The Johns Hopkins University Press
701 West 40th Street
Baltimore, Maryland 21211
The Johns Hopkins Press Ltd, London

Library of Congress Cataloging in Publication Data
Main entry under title:
Lacan and narration.
    "Originally published in December 1983 as a special
number of MLN, volume 98, no. 5"—T.p. verso.
    Bibliography: p. 1054
    1. Narration (Rhetoric)—Addresses, essays, lectures.
2. Lacan, Jacques, 1901-   —Addresses, essays,
lectures.   I. Davis, Robert Con, 1948-   .
PN212.L3   1984   809'.923   84-47946
ISBN 0-8018-2414-1

Contents

Contributors

Régis Durand teaches at the Université des Lettres et des Sciences Humaines de Lille III. He has written extensively on American literature and psychoanalysis. In 1980 he published *Melville, Signes et Métaphores* (L'Age d'Homme).

Ronald Schleifer teaches at The University of Oklahoma where he is the editor of *Genre*. He has published widely on modern literature and criticism. Recently he co-translated (with Daniele McDowell and Alan R. Velie) and wrote the introduction for A. J. Greimas' *Structural Semantics* (Nebraska 1983).

Beryl Schlossman completed a doctorate (troisième cycle) in Paris with Julia Kristeva and teaches at The Johns Hopkins University, where she is a candidate for a Ph.D.; her *Joyce's Catholic Comedy of Manners* (Wisconsin) is in press.

Juliet Flower MacCannell teaches at the University of California at Irvine. In addition to many essays on French literature and contemporary criticism, she is the co-author (with Dean MacCannell) of *Time of the Sign* (Indiana 1982).

Jerry Aline Flieger teaches French, critical theory, and women's studies at Rutgers University. She has published extensively on psychoanalysis and modern criticism in *Diacritics, SubStance,* and *French Forum* and is the author of a forthcoming book on the comic mode in twentieth-century French literature.

Jeffrey Mehlman teaches at Boston University and is a distinguished Freudian theorist of contemporary criticism. His works include *Legacies of Anti-Semitism in France* (Minnesota 1983), *Revolution and Repetition: Marx/Hugo/Balzac* (California 1977), and *A Structural Study of Autobiography: Proust, Leiris, Sartre, and Lévi-Strauss* (Cornell 1974).

Robert Con Davis teaches American literature and critical theory at The University of Oklahoma. He has published widely on contemporary criticism and edited and contributed to *The Fictional Father: Lacanian Readings of the Text* (Massachusetts 1981).

Richard Macksey teaches in the Humanities Center of The Johns Hopkins University. An editor of *MLN* and a comparatist, his publications include *The Structuralist Controversy* (Johns Hopkins 1970, 1972), *Velocities of Change* (Johns Hopkins 1974), *Richard Wright* (Prentice-Hall 1984), and a special number of *Genre, The World as Text* (1984).

Shoshana Felman teaches at Yale University and is a major contributor to psychoanalytic and literary theory. Among her many publications are *La Folie et la chose littéraire* (Seuil 1978), *Le Scandale du corps parlant* (Seuil 1980), and *Literature and Psychoanalysis* (Johns Hopkins 1982).

Encore

Il faut que vous vous mettiez tout de même
à lire un peu des auteurs—je ne dirai pas de
votre temps, je ne dirai pas de lire Philippe
Sollers, il est illisible, comme moi d'ailleurs—
mais vous pouvez lire Joyce par example.
Vous verrez là comment le langage se per-
fectionne quand il sait jouer avec l'écriture.
—Jacques Lacan, *Encore, Le Séminaire XX,* p. 37

The essays collected in this MLN Beiheft were originally published as the first section of the December 1983 special issue of *MLN: Comparative Literature,* Volume 98, Number 5. Robert Con Davis served as the Guest Editor. In order to contain production costs we have retained the original pagination (pages 843–1063). We are grateful to the sponsorship noted in the preface, which made publication of this volume possible.

The art work for the cover was designed by Ellen King. Jacques Lacan's gloss for our window ("The best image to sum up the unconscious is exactly Baltimore in the early morning") may be found on page 845.

RICHARD MACKSEY
MLN

Lacan and Narration: The Psychoanalytic Difference in Narrative Theory

"Sur un terrain en friche": Liminal Note

Richard Macksey

> La découverte de Freud, c'est la redécou-
> verte, sur un terrain en friche, de la raison.
> J. Lacan, *Le Séminaire*, livre I

Jacques Lacan was one of the great mythographers of our time.
Through design and accident he also managed to become one of
our major contemporary myths. Like any mythic hero, he came to
define the intricate braids of Parisian cultural politics, the dramatic
splits and sutures of the psychoanalytic movement, both by his
presence and by his absence. He fought under the banners of
classical reason and uncompromising orthodoxy, yet once entered
on the field he possessed an uncanny power to unleash violence
and revolutionary fervor. In resuming the Myth of the Master he
contrived to put radically into question the possibility of discipleship. The "difficulties" of Lacan—contingent, modal, tactical, and
ontologic—are legendary, yet he managed to penetrate and col-
onize the most alien and resistant reaches of our shattered culture.
Relentless in his criticism of the professional, political, and cultural
establishments of the United States, which came to represent for
him *grosso modo* the discourse of the Other, he ultimately effected
a series of dramatic conversions there that have altered the vectors
of American literary disciplines, film studies, social psychology,
and even psychoanalytic practice.

Jacques Lacan's first American epiphany can be dated precisely:
he agreed to attend an international symposium entitled "The Lan-

guages of Criticism and the Sciences of Man," convened under the auspices of the Johns Hopkins Humanities Center, during the week of October 18-21, 1966. Other francophone participants in what was familiarly styled "the structuralist controversy," included Roland Barthes, Jacques Derrida, René Girard, Lucien Goldmann, Jean Hyppolite, Charles Morazé, Georges Poulet, Nicolas Ruwet, Tzvetan Todorov, and Jean-Pierre Vernant. If the terrain for this first trans-Atlantic epiphany was unlikely, the gallery of potential co-stars was even stranger, since with the exception of Hyppolite there were few allies of the Ecole freudienne de Paris on the scene. Lacan was, however, to share an evening program with one of his better known interpreters, Guy Rosolato. (By the time the dust settled from the explosion elicited by Lacan's presentation, Dr. Rosolato's paper had to be rescheduled for the following day.) Most of the American participants in the symposium came from provinces of literary studies, philosophy, and the social sciences still quite alien to Lacan's thought and were consequently hardly prepared for either the intellectual or the histrionic dimensions of the event. The alien terrain chosen by Lacan for his embassy was not, however, totally circumscribed by what he was apt to call "the discourse of the University": Eugenio Donato had been offering seminars at Hopkins for several years devoted to Lévi-Strauss and Lacan, while Anthony Wilden, then a graduate student, had just completed the first draft of his translation and commentary of the "Discours de Rome" ("Fonction et champ de la parole et du langage en psychanalyse") that he was to publish eighteen months later as *The Language of the Self: The Function of Language in Psychoanalysis.* (Not content with the prospects for confrontation patent in the Hopkins symposium, Lacan also requested an opportunity to speak to the professional psychiatric community in Baltimore. At the end of the same week he consequently addressed the traumatized staff of the Enoch and Sheppard Pratt Hospital on the notorious subject of the length of the analytic session.)

To the consternation of his American friends, Lacan insisted on delivering his communication to the symposium ("Of Structure as an Inmixing of an Otherness Prerequisite to Any Subject Whatever") in English, a language that was to him utterly other. (This tactic had the amusing effect of seducing his anglophone auditors into addressing *him* during the heated discussion in approximations of French.) Early in his address, however, he supplied the gloss for the cover illustration of this special supplement to *M L N* on "Lacan and Narration":

> When I prepared this little talk for you, it was early in the morning. I could see Baltimore through the window and it was a very interesting moment, because it was not quite daylight and a neon sign indicated to me every minute the change of time; and naturally there was heavy traffic; and I remarked to myself that exactly all that I could see, except for some trees in the distance, was the result of thoughts, actively thinking thoughts, where the function played by the subjects was not completely obvious—perhaps only transmission organs. In any case, the so-called *Dasein*, as a definition of the subject, was there in this rather intermittent or fading—or perhaps "irrealizing"—spectator. The best image to sum up the unconscious is exactly Baltimore in the early morning. (from the tapes of the symposium, lightly edited)

The window of our cover opens on this 1966 confrontation between psychoanalysis and the unconscious in "another country." But it also suggests the way in which literature has subversively taught us to confront psychoanalysis: what seems innocently to be a question of vision is also, in the threat to comfortable notions of interiority explicit in the status of the unconscious, profoundly a matter of the occlusion of vision. Shoshana Felman in the introduction to her collection *Literature and Psychoanalysis* (Baltimore: The Johns Hopkins University Press, 1980, p. 10) supplies an economical gloss to this disruptive turn of events:

> We would like to suggest that, in the same way that psychoanalysis points to the unconscious of literature, *literature, in its turn, is the unconscious of psychoanalysis;* that the unthought-out shadow in psychoanalytic *theory* is precisely its own involvement with literature; that literature *in* psychoanalysis functions precisely as its *"unthought"*: as the condition of possibility *and* the self-subversive blind spot of psychoanalytical *thought*.

Paradoxically, Lacan's journey to the underworld of American culture in 1966 led to an initial proselytizing not of psychoanalytic practitioners but of literary critics, and this foreign appropriation took the form of a bold theft. But then Lacan consistently taught that all knowledge in the psychoanalytic process must appear under the sign of Hermes as an act of larceny. It was not merely as an affront to Marie Bonaparte, as Stuart Schneiderman has observed, that Lacan chose to open his *Ecrits* with his most literary and larcenous text, "Le Séminaire sur 'La Lettre volée.' "

The framing of the window on the essays collected here is, then, the question of the possibility of a narrative theory purloined from the linguistic model of Lacan's psychoanalytic theory. Whether as the generative motor or the parabolic elaboration of desire, the recognition of the structural kinship of literary narrative and clinical case history is at least as old as Freud. In fact, one of the distinctive inventions of the nineteenth century was the development of the case history as a mode of inquiry in many fields—medicine, anthropology, sociology, history; and this was concurrent with the rise of a new literary genre of realist fiction also modeled on the case history, with its consuming interest in the subject and its increasing stress on a "scientific" methodology, its concern with interpreting "pathologies" and "nosologies." A closely related literary phenomenon was the coincident rise of an allied genre—the detective story—whose riddling roots reach back to the Oedipus narrative. The modern detective story was, of course, initially secure in its emphases on the ordering of empiric evidence, the reciprocal relations of reason and intuition, and its "realistic" assumptions about human behavior and social institutions. (The argument could be made that Poe is the founder of both the detective story and the case history as peculiarly modern forms.) It remained, however, for Freud to fuse these two modes in a clinical practice and at the same time to put into question the naive compact between the author and reader, between the analyst and analysand. It was one of the distinctive achievements of Lacan, in rethinking Freud, to unsettle further the status and the place of the subject, to demonstrate the triangular structure of the Symbolic figurations that organize these fictions and compacts. And in his reconstitution of the subject, enlisting concepts such as the radical revision of Ernest Jones's *aphanisis,* situated at the very line of cleavage (of the terrain of the subject and of disciplines), he forged, as Régis Durand argues, a remarkable instrument for charting the minimalist ambitions of post-modern fiction.

But the reading of literary narration with Lacan also invites, as Shoshana Felman observed above, a privileged mode of interrogating the "self-subversive blind spot" of psychoanalytic thought itself. In her essay that concludes this collection she considers further the vitally implicated functions of *myth* and *science* that constitute the Freudian-Lacanian enterprise—and the necessity in practice of reliving its beginnings. Freud finds in reading the myth of Oedipus the confirmation of his theory, the unconscious nature of desire, while Lacan in his parallel reading uncovers the validation of his practice, the articulation of the structural homology between language and desire. And clinically for Lacan, as she also

reminds us, it is not a question of what a story *means* but of what
it *does*. In order for the myth to act, there must be a commitment
to the conditions of narrative. But science, including the "science
of psychoanalysis," is always, as Felman reminds us, in immanent
danger of forgetting, of repudiating its mythic origins. And it is
only when psychoanalysis has lost hold of its generative mythic
origins that commitment fails and the agents to the drama lose
the power to act. Perhaps Oedipus should have the last words,
since they can stand for both the mythographer and the myth:
μηδεὶς κρατείτω τῆς ἐμῆς ψυχῆς ποτε. (*Oed. Col.* 1207)

Robert Con Davis, Guest Editor for this supplement on Lacan
and Narration, teaches American literature and critical theory at
the University of Oklahoma, Norman. He has published widely on
both literary and psychoanalytic topics and is the editor of an earlier
collection of essays exploring the relations between textual strategies and symbolic processes, *The Fictional Father: Lacanian Readings
of the Text* (Amherst: The University of Massachusetts Press, 1981).
He was the organizer of a session at the 1982 M L A meeting in
Los Angeles "Jacques Lacan's Impact on Narrative Theory") at
which MacCannell, Macksey, and Schleifer presented papers.

The Editors are happy to acknowledge timely financial support
for this *M L N* supplement from the Office of Research Admin-
istration of the University of Oklahoma and two anonymous do-
nors.

RICHARD MACKSEY

Introduction: Lacan and Narration

❧

Robert Con Davis

I

Jacques Lacan as narrative theorist? A Lacanian narratology? The answer to both questions, as this collection advances generally, is a qualified yes. Jacques Lacan's concern with the Freudian subject suggests a position in regard to narration—an approach, even (with some elaboration) a narratology. It is an approach derivable from his view—his central insight into psychoanalysis—that *l'inconscient est structuré comme un langage.* It says simply that narration, too, operates like a language, is a language, and manifests linguistic operations in various ways. Narration exists, finally, within the context of an unconscious "discourse," within the bounds of what Lacan calls the "discourse of the Other." Since the early 1970s, though earlier in France, literary theorists have busily sought to understand this central insight of Jacques Lacan's rethinking of psychoanalysis—in a sense to reverse it, not to disprove it necessarily, but to grasp how language in literary texts is constituted, buoyed up, permeated, and decentered by the unconscious. The aim has been to understand (reversing Lacan's statement) how *"literature,"* in Shoshana Felman's words, *". . . is the unconscious of psychoanalysis."*[1] In this regard, the studies of this collection, focused as they are on narration, mark another step, possibly an advance, in the literary appropriation of Lacan. This collection as a whole experiments in the situating of narration as an effect (or product) of the unconscious—narration (in a sense) as *already Lacanian* even before or apart from, even in spite of, Lacan.

Indeed, the theoretical melding of *l'inconscient* and *le langage*—psychoanalysis and linguistics—does take place *before* Lacan, as Lacan himself insists, in Freud, particularly in *The Interpretation of Dreams* (1900), *The Psychopathology of Everyday Life* (1901), *Jokes and*

Their Relation to the Unconscious (1905), and many of the metapsy-
chology pieces. Freud, unlike Lacan, did not have access to Ferdinand de Saussure's formulation of semiotics on which modern
linguistics is based (the *Cours de linguistique générale* was not published until 1916, sixteen years after *The Interpretation of Dreams*).
But, as Lacan shows, Freud was simultaneously "discovering" the
sign and semiotics for psychology just as Saussure was doing so for
linguistics. In that Freud's major work on dreams "appeared long
before the formalizations of linguistics," Lacan argues even that
psychoanalysis "paved the way [for linguistics] by the sheer weight
of its truth."[2]

This "discovery" of semiotics can be seen in a passage in *The
Interpretation of Dreams*, a central Freudian "scene of writing" that
Lacan discusses, where Freud describes two different modes of
narrative interpretation. In this passage Freud gives a sample
dream about a "house with a boat on its roof, a single letter of the
alphabet, [and] the figure of a running man whose head has been
conjured away."[3] Now as he might interpret it, or as Lacan might,
this brief narration is actually *about* semiotics. We see this in the
placement of a house with too much of a top (a head) in relation
to its contrary, to the image of a running man "whose head has
been conjured away." The images form a binary opposition. There
is an excess of presence in the boat-head, and there is a stark and
inappropriate absence in the man's missing head. In this contrast,
further, is a theatrically distinct opposition between presence and
absence, the condition of difference in a binary system that makes
a sign (and semiotics) possible. That is, what stands apart from and
yet represents a semiotic difference is the possibility of representation itself, the signifying possibility (as represented in the dream)
of "a single letter of the alphabet." This signifying capability, further, exacts a human cost in that the subject of language is signified
within and, simultaneously, is alienated from language—hence the
man's symbolic castration in being headless. The dream's figures
or elements—Lacan calls them "sliding signifiers"—thus move over
certain "positions" in the dream in a kind of articulation structured
in language and, through interpretation, actually *about* language.
That is, they inhabit the "binarity" of language and semiotics.
Freud speaks, as does Lacan, in several registers simultaneously—
in both his commentary and choice of an example so that his discourse foregrounds the structurality of language and semiotics.

    Thus, Freud's main interest in this "scene of writing" is interpretation itself, the principles by which we read the dream as essentially a picture, at one extreme, or as a narrative, at another. His first approach to the dream focuses on the *"manifest* content" (p. 277) of the narrative details as if they are in a "pictographic script" (p. 277) where all of the pieces are present simultaneously for inspection as in a "picture-puzzle, a rebus" (p. 277). In this pictographic approach the disjunctive quality of the picture— "house with a boat on the roof," etc.—creates a problem for interpretation. The dream elements, dislocated from a familiar context and yet fixed in place, have no significance except possibly as icons with preexistent and fixed meanings. If they are icons, the dream narrative may be read as an intelligible picture-story, a deciphered rebus with its meaning available on its surface. For the second mode, instead of being a picture, the dream functions like a language governed by, as Freud says, "syntactic laws" (p. 277). In this approach, by contrast, the dream elements are not seen, at least not exclusively, as if in a picture or as inherently meaningful. Rather, now they are arbitrary "signifiers" occupying "positions" in discourse with no intrinsic or assigned meaning. In this "linguistic" approach, Freud explains, we "replace each separate element by a syllable or word that can be represented by that element in some way or another" (p. 278). This kind of interpretation, in other words, takes place through the substitution of one element for another according to certain narrative codes. Crucial here is the interchangeability, the substitutability, of dream elements— signifiers—which can hold particular places in the dream. The dream is an interpretable text only according to the possible substitutions of elements. While in Freud's pictographic approach particular dream elements are meaningful (or lacking in meaning) as they are locked in a particular pattern, in the linguistic approach dream elements lack inherent meaning but can stand in for (be replaced by) other elements within a certain structure or set of possibilities.

In view of the choices—the interpretive dilemma—that Freud sets up in this discussion, we must say that Lacan chooses to go the second way of interpretation, that of language and linguistics—of, as Lacan says, "writing rather than of mime."[4] The apparent simplicity of such a choice, however, is misleading in the extreme. Freud's pictographic approach, on closer examination, actually contains important aspects of the linguistic approach and so cannot be completely discarded. If the dream elements are not icons,

Freud's picture-dream is reduced to being a structure of juxta-posed elements. Since the particular elements themselves are without meaning, what is left are the combinatory possibilities of dislocated and yet co-present elements—contiguous and/or simul-taneously adjacent to each other. In the second or linguistic ap-proach, Freud emphatically does not attribute inherent meaning to the dream elements; he does say that their relative positions, their existence in a system of differences, affect another process, that of elements being selected to go in the dream initially and to replace other elements as interpretation takes place, especially to replace the "original" (or manifest) elements that would otherwise form a pictograph. In short, the pictographic approach, as Freud describes it, emphasizes combinatory possibilities; the linguistic ap-proach, as we are using the term here, indicates a selective process of one element substituting for another. In both approaches, ele-ments in a series are placed in different relationships, but in being so placed they are also being selected and then substituted so as to represent any number of combinatory possibilities.

This is the distinction of postSaussurean linguistics in which "combination" emphasizes purely relational concepts such as syntax, concepts inconceivable, however, apart from the selective (or paradigmatic) possibilities of words and word parts, such as morphemes, available in language as a whole. Roman Jakobson insists that—to point up the interdependence of combination/se-lection as a single system of discourse—necessarily in any one "ut-terance (message) is a COMBINATION [syntagmatic dimension] of constituent parts (sentences, words, phonemes, etc.) SELECTED [paradigmatically] from the repository of all possible constituent parts (the code)."[5] Thus, while Freud for his own purposes sepa-rates these analyses into two approaches to narrative, insofar as they represent syntagmatic and paradigmatic analyses they are in-terdependent and imply each other. Pictography and linguistics, Freud's commentary aside, are not finally different modes of anal-ysis.

And yet, and perhaps this is Freud's real point, such extremes of analysis—especially for narration—do exist usefully as ideals. We surely can imagine a narrative criticism that, merely tending toward the ideal (the "lure," as Lacan says) of naturally meaningful pictographic inscription, would emphasize spatial form in narra-tion. This approach, of course, actually exists in the narrative tra-dition associated with modernist fiction and spatial form (for ex-

ample, in much criticism of Virginia Woolf's fiction). Joseph Frank
imagines "modern" narrative structure as somehow escaping temporality, yielding its intended content when narrative elements are
arranged as adjacent and copresent in the semblance of a picture,
an organization Frank calls a nontemporal unity. Here narrative
form resides inherently in the pattern of individual elements which
are presented metonymically as if in a still life. At another extreme,
we can imagine narration as tending toward being an operation of
substitution; that is, narration is created as elements, signifiers,
stand in for other elements in a sequence, the selective process that
Roman Jakobson identifies as metaphoric. This possibility, too, is
a reality; there is the tradition of modern narrative interpretation
inspired by Ferdinand de Saussure, Vladimir Propp, and Marcelo
Mauss, developed by Claude Lévi-Strauss, A. J. Greimas, and the
structuralists, and which continues on to Lacan and the post-struc-
turalists—a tradition of narration as language process, not a pictograph, but a linguistic system of substitutions and alterations in
time. Freud's discussion of the dream is, in fact, a rough but reli-
able map of two main areas of narrative theory—pictographic and
linguistic—that have existed and dominated literary criticism since
1900. It is Lacan's contribution to all of this to show that the operation of the unconscious, encompassing the extremes of what
Freud calls pictographic and linguistic analyses, is itself a linguistic
process and to bring this insight intensely to bear in the psychoanalytic critique of the subject as inscribed in language.

Lacan's interpretive choice, then, is not linguistics over pictography, or selection over combination—choices not available theoretically. It is, rather, a move to show the explicitly linguistic structure of the subject within an unconscious discourse. By "subject"
Lacan means both the agency of knowing *and* the site at which this
agency functions, has form, and is meaningful. Lacan's view here
has implications for the narrative terms we have been using: what
Freud calls the manifest content of a dream (or narration)—the
pictograph—does not stand alone as a privileged structure. It is
already a repetition, the result of a previous interpretation, of an
interpretive process—Freud's "dream work"—that already having
taken place (and fated always to be a repetition) has produced the
pictographic representation of a dream thought. Lacanian analysis
takes this manifest content, this monument to a previous interpretation, and—treating it as one phase of interpretation—places it
(in importance) on naration's margin, decentered, as a part and

just one effect of the unconscious process involving metonymy and metaphor. As manifest content, this "literal" story or plot is "real," just as it is "real" when it displays the traces—"gaps" in meaning or "lapses" of logic—that represent the unconscious system that produced it.

In this way, the so-called manifest content (really an "old" interpretation) is resubjected in interpretation to the same process of combination *and* selection, metonymy and metaphor, that produced the manifest content in the dream work initially. Narrative interpretation actually mimics and repeats the dream work analytically, as if to give the message back to its sender "in an inverted form" in narration.[6] The actual dream work began with unconscious desires and dream thoughts and moved the thoughts through displacement (metonymy) and condensation (metaphor). Lacan's analysis of narration, as Lacan's readings of *Hamlet* and "The Purloined Letter" show, begins with language, the product of a previous interpretation, and proceeds to rediscover—by giving attention to certain "gaps" or "lapses," the indications of the unconscious process—the Other discourse that previously produced the so-called manifest text. In this way, narrative interpretation from a Lacanian viewpoint in fact does reverse Lacan's statement (as Lacan himself reverses it) about the unconscious and language and finds the unconscious structure of language, which, in turn, is structured like a language, which, in turn—and so on. Freud's dream narrative, then, as Lacan might say, is *structured like a subject* in that it has the unconscious structure of language.

What is narration à la Lacan? It is certainly the work of the signifier as it can be known in its metaphoric and metonymic operations, the fortunes of the signifier, its history, in relation to its own repressed origin in unconscious discourse. Narration—irremediably diachronic *and* synchronic—repeats and represents unconscious discourse in the only way the unconscious can be known: as a sequence of opportunities for linguistic substitution and (re)combination. The potential for continuity and unity in such sequences makes possible the "gaps" or "lapses" that indicate the "Other" scene of signification, the repressed scene of writing not a part of manifest narration but which (like a buoy, or series of buoys) holds it up and enables it to exist at all. In this formulation we are already assuming three fundamental propositions that characterize—though will not limit—a Lacanian concern with narration: 1.) Narration is structured like a (subject in) language. This places Lacan in a tradition of narrative theory with a linguistic orientation. 2.) Narration's manifest content is a product of the unconscious discourse that is both the precondition of narration and the site of its appearance. This says essentially that the subject of narration, what gives it form and meaning, will always be other than what is signified *in* narration, or what is signifiable *as* narration. 3.) Last, the unconscious discourse of language and its processes are revealed in the "gaps" or "lapses" (inconsistencies, failures of speech and signification, etc.) that appear in a narrative's manifest text. This final proposition situates narrative interpretation, too, as a movement, a trajectory, a contingent effect, within the larger (unconscious) discourse of the Other.

In practice, a Lacanian narratology based on these propositions is likely to be a triple reading: of the manifest text, of the unconscious discourse that buoys up the manifest text, and then of the reconstituted (repositioned) manifest text—a new interpretation. The *text* read here obviously is neither the New Critical, positivistic text—ambiguous and ironic but absolutely knowable—nor is it a rebus in which one reads and finds whatever one wants. To the question, "is there a text in this classroom?" we can answer yes; the Lacanian text is definitely *there,* but it is exclusively text-as-textual-production. This narrative text differs from Jakobson's structuralist one in that Jakobson's communication model of sender/receiver (addresser/addressee) is absorbed by Lacan's formulation of a split subject and a set of "positions" existing *within* narration—not necessarily between sender and receiver. This shift—marking an important shift from structuralist to poststructuralist modes of thought—occurs largely because "the conception of language as communication," as Rosalind Coward and John Ellis explain, "tends to obscure the way in which language sets up the positions of 'I' and 'you' that are necessary for communication to take place at all."[7] The key phrasing here is "sets up the positions of 'I' and 'you'"—that is, "sets up" positions through structuration within the subject and within narration itself, in time. And, finally, the Lacanian text differs from the deconstructionist (problematic) text, to which it bears a resemblance, in that the "positions" of narration ("I" and "you," for example) are anchored, held down, by Freudian desire, which enforces a curb on the infinite textual regress opened by *différance.* The "signifier"—subject to desire, as Lacan states—"stops the otherwise endless movement (*glissement*) of the signification."[8] Hence the Lacanian text—to Derrida's out-

raged dismay[9]—may speak its own "truth"—the Other's "truth,"
what Jacqueline Rose calls "the truth of the unconscious [that] is
only ever that moment of fundamental division through which the
subject entered into language and sexuality, and the constant
failing of position within both."[10] Thus, there is no knowable subject in Lacan's text or in Derrida's (no Other of the Other); Lacanalysis and deconstruction do not differ here. But the desire of
the Other—not part of the Derridean program—positions and
limits the free play of signification through the continual resub-
jection of the signifier (the subject) to the Other's desire, through
the continual "passage into the semiotic triangle of Oedipus."[11]

II

One can scarely contemplate this collection's studies of narration
à la Lacan without being mindful of the famous "difficulty" of
reading Lacan's own narration, his *écrits*—a "difficulty" vaguely
embarrassing (for us at least) and more often spoken than written
about. He is at times maddeningly elliptical, playful, and (at his
worst and best) polyphonic in his pronouncements. As George
Steiner says about similarly "difficult" writers, it can seem as
though "at certain levels, we are not meant to understand *at all,*
and our interpretation, indeed our reading itself is an intrusion."
"For whom"—and here Steiner could be interrogating Lacan's
texts—"was the Master composing his cryptograms?"[12] Why *should*
reading Lacan be this difficult? Where and what is the difficulty?

Steiner sheds light on four different types of difficulty (*contingent, modal, tactical,* and *ontological*) that are relevant—especially
ontological difficulty—to the task of reading Lacan's discourse. *Contingent* difficulties, in brief, are those problems we might have with
the obscurity of Lacan's text, possibly psychoanalytical, linguistic,
and philosophical terms that we, as Steiner says, "need to look up."
Either we look up "primary process," "foreclosure," and "aphanisis" and understand them, or we do not. And since Lacan is highly
allusive and steeped in the debates of psychoanalysis and twentieth-
century thought in general, the difficulty here is a formidable one.
Next, *modal* difficulty, rather than being an obscurity in the text,
is a problem of receptivity for the reader in regard to a text's mode
of presentation. Lacan's major publications, mostly transcripts of
lectures, are addressed to us as students who are supposedly in
diligent pursuit of this Master's teachings (imagine the audacity of

entitling one's own book simply *Écrits!*). This magisterial mode can pose problems of tone and can generate resistance enough to become a great obstacle in reading. Then, *tactical* difficulty, strangely enough, is created by Lacan's strategies for communicating efficiently and powerfully. In his discourse Lacan may explain a point about the "gaze" quite fully and then refuse to expound on a related concept, or suddenly break off all explanation. This practice, like his erratically short therapy sessions, is intended to prompt his listeners to a deep and direct engagement with psychoanalysis, to bring them face-to-face with "real" (impossibly continuous) discourse. The potential for such strategies to succeed is a great difficulty when they fail or only partially succeed.

These difficulties—enough to be fatal to a single reading—are certainly common enough and are ultimately (though at times it may seem otherwise) surmountable. The greatest difficulty in reading Lacan, and the far more interesting one to contemplate, is *ontological*, the "difficulty," as Steiner writes, that breaks "the contract of ultimate or preponderant intelligibility between poet and reader, between text and meaning."[13] "Difficulties of this category," he continues, "cannot be looked up" because ". . . they confront us with blank questions about the nature of human speech [and] about the status of significance."[14] In other words, an *ontological* difficulty arises—that is, the contract may break between writer and reader, text and meaning—when a text posits (in Thomas Kuhn's terminology) a whole new paradigm of understanding entailing a new grasp of phenomena, their relations, and the horizon of possibility that moves up behind them. This "difficulty," though not inherently insurmountable, can be an absolute obstacle to understanding.

The ontological difficulty here is that Lacan as a postSaussurean psychoanalyst offers a paradigm of possibilities which seemingly scandalize common sense, especially as seen in the tradition of American Freudian thought. Lacan's project, for example, is worlds away from the psychoanalytic criticism that Frederick C. Crews rejected in *Out of My System* (1975), Freudian criticism developed between 1900 and the 1960s as a distinctly formalizing and allegorizing tendency. The prior movement, strongly akin to New Criticism, existentialism, and archetypal interpretation, flourished during what may be called the Age of the Critic, an age of expert critical strategies formulated under the authority of T. S. Eliot, the southern Fugitives, I. A. Richards, and Northrop Frye.

Lacan's Freud, by contrast, is read in quite different company, intertextually (in Julia Kristeva's sense and in the popular meaning of "influence") with Ferdinand de Saussure, Martin Heidegger, Claude Lévi-Strauss, and Maurice Merleau-Ponty during our own Age of the Reader. It has connections with deconstruction, reader-response criticism, and feminism—to a critical era under the strong sway of Jacques Derrida, Geoffrey Hartman, J. Hillis Miller, Stanley Fish, Julia Kristeva, and Lacan himself.

Most scandalizing about Lacan's paradigm, and this goes to the heart of ontological difficulty, is a figure that can be described rather simply, that of a division, a *split*. For Lacan the pervasive figure of the split indicates a fundamental division in psychic life, in selfhood, and even within the things we know. In literary studies, it is a permanent division within the text and narration. Lacan's model of narrative, accordingly, is not that of a unified thing but of a split process, a two-fold process that swings metronome-like from side to side between product and production (manifest text and unconscious discourse), back and forth, and never reaches a point of stability or wholeness. This narrative model poses a serious threat to the empirically-based tradition of interpretation as a transparent and focusable lens, an open subjectivity, through which a detached investigator peers into a stable (possibly pictographic) narrative structure.[15] Positioned in a different paradigm, Lacan's concept of narration *and* of narrative interpretation rests squarely on an ontological fault line, the radical split of a subject irretrievably unwhole—the subject of what Lacan calls *aphanisis*. Lacanian analysis, in this regard, is difficult because it is revolutionary (literally so) in its promotion of this paradigm.

Lacan's greatest "difficulty," then, in Steiner's sense—and for which we need feel no embarrassment—is precisely here: since the subject (narration), for Lacan, is marked by this irrevocable split, what we are accustomed to calling unity and wholeness in form and seeing as concepts centrally important to narration and interpretation are unceremoniously ousted. But these concepts do not just vanish; we still have some reason to speak of wholeness and unity. Such concepts are relegated, however, to the status of being (in Jacques-Alain Miller's term) a mere "suturing" over of the fundamental split with the various commitments (threads) of ideology, the inevitable ideological bias that we bring to any one approach to the subject in a narration in hopes of promoting a view of meaningful significance and wholeness. In shifts such as these (dislocating and potentially painful)—in which sense and nonsense, the central and the marginal, are seen to switch places—we stand witness as the lines of understanding (as if seeking a new haunting) palpably move from one paradigm to the other, from a world in which they (already) made sense to a world in which they are (just now) making sense. This revolution of the subject's status, and the resultant shift in the way we understand narration, poses an ontological difficulty of the highest order. This difficulty, more than any other, is what the essays of this collection seek to address, not to solve, but merely to cast in the open.

NOTES

1 "To Open the Question," *Yale French Studies* 55/56(1977):10.

2 "The agency of the letter in the unconscious," in *Écrits: A Selection,* trans. Alan Sheridan (New York: W.W. Norton and Co., Inc., 1977), p. 162.

3 *The Interpretation of Dreams. Standard Edition,* Vol. IV, trans. and ed. James Strachey (London: The Hogarth Press, 1981), pp. 277-278.

4 "The agency of the letter in the unconscious," in *Écrits: A Selection,* p. 161.

5 "The Twofold Character of Language," in Roman Jakobson and Morris Halle, *Fundamentals of Language* (The Hague, Paris: Mouton, 1971), p. 75.

6 "The function and field of speech and language in psychoanalysis," in *Écrits: A Selection,* p. 85.

7 *Language and Materialism: Developments in Semiology and the Theory of the Subject* (London, Henley and Boston: Routledge and Kegan Paul, 1977), p. 79.

8 "The subversion of the subject and the dialectic of desire in the Freudian unconscious," in *Écrits: A Selection,* p. 303.

9 See Jacques Derrida, "The Purveyor of Truth," trans. W. Domingo, J. Hulbert, M. Ron, and M.-R. Logan, *Yale French Studies* 52(1975):31-113.

10 "Introduction—II," in Jacques Lacan and the *école freudienne, Feminine Sexuality,* eds. Juliet Mitchell and Jacqueline Rose, trans. Jacqueline Rose (New York and London: W.W. Norton and Co., 1982), p. 53.

11 Gayatri Chakravorty Spivak, "The Letter as Cutting Edge," *Yale French Studies* 55/56(1977):222.

12 "On Difficulty," in *On Difficulty and Other Essays* (New York and Oxford: Oxford Univ. Press, 1978), p. 45.

13 "On Difficulty, p. 40.

14 "On Difficulty," p. 41.

15 It is not suprising that the threat of Lacan's "return to Freud"—a return to concern with the unconscious system that engenders psychic life and virtually makes subject and text possible in the first place—is meeting tremendous resistance in practice and theory in America and England, possibly more than was met by deconstruction's emergence during the same period. A well-informed critic such as Edward Said, for example, worries that projects such as Lacan's "return to Freud" will only establish "a [new] canon whose legitimacy is maintained with loyal devotion." "A new canon," he continues, "means also a new past or a new history and, less happily, a new parochialism" (*The World, the Text,*

and the Critic. Cambridge, Mass.: Harvard Univ. Press, 1983, p. 143). Michael Ryan announces that Lacan is only superficially a "maverick" in psychoanalysis and is really a "clever fundamentalist, rather conservative, clearly antimarxist, roundly antifeminist, and theocratic" (*Marxism and Deconstruction: A Critical Introduction.* Baltimore: The Johns Hopkins Univ. Press, 1982, p. 104). Curious here, though, is the sharp edge—the near frenzy—of such resistance in the face of strong evidence to the contrary. The influence of Lacan's critique of the subject, very simply, now runs quite deep in the very areas mentioned, in Marxist, feminist, and deconstructive criticism; the work of Stephen Heath, Louis Althusser, Fredric Jameson, Juliet Mitchell, Jane Gallop, Jacqueline Rose, Diane Sadoff, Peggy Kamuf, Barbara Johnson, John T. Irwin, among others, testifies to this rather decisively. Juliet Mitchell suggested in 1974 that psychoanalysis in particular tends to generate such opposition: "though the criticism *seems* to be over specific issues," its aim is the "whole intellectual framework of psychoanalysis," particularly the dimension of the unconscious that Lacan has insisted on so fervently (*Psycho-Analysis and Feminism.* New York: Vintage Books, 1974, p. 5). Mitchell's suggestion recalls Freud's notion that psychoanalysis often takes hold theoretically most firmly where it is initially most strongly resisted; such resistance, Freud implies, is a sign of unconscious recognition and a defense—simultaneously an expression and a disavowal of desire. This process of acceptance appears to be taking place in America and England.

On *Aphanisis:* A Note on the Dramaturgy of the Subject in Narrative Analysis

Régis Durand

The only advantage a psychoanalyst is allowed to take from his position—assuming that it is recognized as such—is to remember with Freud that on his subject the artist always precedes him, and that he has no business acting the psychologist where the artist blazes the trail for him (J. Lacan, "Hommage fait à Marguerite Duras, du ravissement de Lol V. Stein," *Marguerite Duras,* Paris: Albatros, 1975) (transl. mine)

You will also understand that, if I have spoken to you of the unconscious as of something that opens and closes, it is because its essence is to mark that time by which, from the fact of being born with the signifier, the subject is born divided. The subject is this emergence which, just before, as subject, was nothing, but which, having scarcely appeared, solidifies into a signifier (J. Lacan, *The Four Fundamental Concepts of Psycho-Analysis,* ed. by J-A. Miller, transl. Alan Sheridan, New York: Norton, 1978)

I

I shall focus on a very limited aspect of what I take to be Lacan's major contribution to narrative theory. This contribution is mostly indirect—it is not necessarily to be found, that is, in Lacan's few comments on literary texts. Rather it concerns what I am calling a dramaturgy of the subject. I think it is possible to say that this dramaturgy, because it too is a narrative, bears some relation to narratives as such (a relation pointed out by Lacan himself when he remarks that "truth always manifests itself in a structure of fiction"). This dramaturgy might be dealt with historically. One could for instance take a particular text—say *Hamlet*—and see how it has served as a vehicle for different versions of the theory, from Freud via Jones, Lacan, to André Green and many others. Or it could be studied synchronically, as a particular area of a complex system which bears on many other aspects.

While I shall do neither, I shall focus on a particular concept, *aphanisis,* with the interesting characteristic of having both diachronic dynamism (since it describes a disappearance, a vanishing point, and since also it already has a long history), and systemic relevance (it is central to Lacan's description of the constitution of the subject). At the same time, it is situated at such a point (in its precarious life as a concept) of cleavage, on the very borderline between psychoanalytic and literary theory, that it acquires an almost performative quality, manifesting as it does the processes of interaction and transformation taking place.

The methodological problems inherent in the application of psychoanalytic theory have been extensively dealt with elsewhere, and it is not my intention to go into them again. In displacing certain concepts from their original *locus,* we may be distorting and metaphorizing them beyond recognition. At the same time, this metaphorical gesture is in the logic of Lacanian theory itself, which for the last ten years at least has become a broad cultural phenomenon, no longer restricted to the formation of analysts in training, but ranging over widely different fields.[1] So that the situation, at present, for one who would turn or return to Lacanian theory for a specific purpose—say, a re-vision of narrative theory—is a fairly uncomfortable one. On the one hand, it may appear to be a questionable deflection of the original theory; on the other, it may appear to be part of an (already ebbing?) cultural trend—never a pleasant prospect.

The question here, however, is more limited: have we developed, can we develop, concepts or approaches based on Lacanian theory, which contribute in a significant manner to the study of narrative? The answer, of course, has to be ambivalent: yes, there *have* been some innovative attempts; notions such as the Imaginary and the

Symbolic, suture, repression, the Gaze, have proved of interest for the study of literary narrative. At the same time, their usefulness has been nothing like the impact of Lacanian theory on film studies. Fredric Jameson, in one of his programmatic observations, has clearly outlined the problem:

> What is wanted is not only an instrument of analysis which will maintain the incommensurability of the subject with its narrative representations—or in other words between the Imaginary and the Symbolic in general—but also one which will articulate the discontinuities within the subject's various "representatives" themselves, not only those that Benveniste has taught us to observe between the first and second pronouns on the one hand and the third on the other, but also, and above all, that, stressed by Lacan, between the nominative and the accusative forms of the first person itself. *To a certain degree, the theoretical problem of the status of the subject in narrative analysis is itself a reflection of the historical attempt of modernistic practice to eliminate the old-fashioned subject from the literary text.* My own feeling is that you cannot deny the possibility of an adequate representation of the subject in narrative on the one hand, and then continue the search for a more satisfactory category for such representation on the other.[2]

The passage I have italicized addresses itself to one of the major difficulties in articulating Lacanian theory with narrative analysis.[3] To simplify: on the one hand, narrative analysis concerns itself with the way a subject represents itself or is represented through various agencies (characters, story, textuality in general); on the other hand, Lacanian theory, too, postulates the disappearance of "the old-fashioned subject." The question, then, is whether there can be a degree of congruence between what would seem to be a knotting of conflicting impulses: the impulse in "modernistic practice" to eliminate the "old-fashioned subject"; the attempt in narrative analysis to recapture the subject (*a* subject) through ever more complex categories; and finally Lacanian theory developing a new theory of the subject.

In some ways, Lacan's version of the subject would appear to have similarities, in more than a purely syllogistic way, with "modernistic" practice (I take "modernistic" to refer here to the mode of writing of High Modernism, say of the first forty years of the twentieth century, although the distinction, if one is to be made at all, between "modernist" and "modernistic" totally escapes me. At any rate, I take it to refer to the way the writing of Joyce, Faulkner, Virginia Woolf, through the subversion of story line, character,

point of view, etc. "ironizes" the "old-fashioned" subject out of existence). Indeed, there are moments when Lacan's description of
the "subversion" of the subject, of its complex strategies of rup-
tures and displacements, reads like a compendium of "modernistic" narrative and discursive strategies: mirror reflections, feints,
snares, a glimmer that fades out, a stutter, an enunciation that
renounces itself, a discourse that denounces itself, etc. . . . : this is
a theatre of deceptions, doublings, fadings, theory as theatre, as
"a structure of fiction."[4] At the same time, it is clear that Lacan's
theory of the subject cannot be reduced to this colorful and enigmatic masquerade. Behind this lies another narrative, that of the
subject "born divided." The "modernistic" fiction of the elusive
deceitful subject conceals the much more implacable logic of the
division and dispersal of the subject, its "intersubjective distribution," its scattering into different fictional roles (or "moments")
which signify only its "lack of being as a subject of enunciation."[5]
This dramaturgy of the subject owes little to modernism. In this
version, it becomes impossible to say what the subject is, no matter
with what luxury of deception and trickery. The theory itself becomes an intertext, a commentary and a re-writing of Freud's
aphoristic version of origins: *Wo es war, soll Ich werden.* . . . The
subject is a passage, "a pulsation," the mere effect of the sliding of
the signifier ("which represents a subject for another signifier").
Whenever we are tempted to pause on a description of the subject
as *epiphany* ("this emergence")—a temptation ministered to, if not
induced by, modernist texts—, a second beat follows: a loss, a disappearance, an *aphanisis.* Lacan takes the example of the *lamella* in
order to stress the analogy between the subject and the most primitive forms of life, the amoeba but also the drive, the libido as "pure
life instinct," "that is to say, immortal life, or irrepressible life, life
that has need of no organ, simplified indestructible life."[6] The
emergence of the subject, then, is that fleeting primordial relation
which comes before the theatre of identity and even of sexual roles,
when the subject has relations only with his Other, the principle
of his own disappearance:

> The relation with the Other is precisely that which, for us, brings out
> what is represented by the lamella—not sexed polarity, the relation
> between masculine and feminine, but the relation between the living
> subject and that which he loses by having to pass, for his reproduction,
> through the sexual cycle.

> In this way I explain the essential affinity of every drive with the zone of death, and reconcile the two sides of the drive—which at one and the same time, makes present sexuality in the unconscious and represents, in its essence, death. (*Four Concepts*, 199)

That is why I would like now to dwell a little on a notion which has had little success so far (in psychoanalytic as well as in narrative theory), but which seems to me of crucial importance, that of *aphanisis*.

II

The term itself, according to Laplanche and Pontalis, was introduced by Ernest Jones in a 1927 essay, bearing on "Early Developments of Female Sexuality."[7] According to Jones, *aphanisis*, which is taken by him to mean the disappearance of all sexual desire, is the object of a fear common to both sexes and more profound than the fear of castration. But whereas Freud (and Lacan after him) centered the sexual development of the child (male or female) on castration and the dominance of the Phallus, Jones sees the development of the female child as more specific and her sexuality as clearly differentiated. The common denominator, then, between male and female sexuality is not to be found in the castration complex but, as it were, "before," in a deeper fear, that of *aphanisis*.

It is understandable that this notion should have seemed totally unacceptable to Lacan and his followers, inasmuch as it challenges the primacy of castration in the constitution of the subject. Moustapha Safouan calls it "inconceivable" and adds: "No wonder it has never had any follow-up in analytic literature, including Jones's own later writings. It is in contradiction with the definition of need as well as with that of the unconscious" (*op. cit.*, p. 56, my translation). Without going into the technicalities of the debate, it seems possible to summarize it as follows. Jones's theory relies on natural order, on the anatomical difference between the sexes, with the host of cultural stereotypes that accompany it (such as male-active, female-passive, for instance). Starting from there, two different scenarios of the confrontation of the subject with his/her desire are seen to develop. The inevitable frustration of desire gives rise to a fear that desire should disappear as such. Guilt then becomes a rampart against desires which are doomed to remain unsatisfied. A superego is born, which will thrive on all subsequent moral disapprobation from outside.

This dramaturgy of sexual roles is of course in complete contradiction with Lacan's narrative of the emergence of the unconscious and of the subject. Yet Lacan (as was the case with the theory
of symbolism entertained by the same Ernest Jones) pays homage
to a rich intuition and promptly enrolls it into the service of his
own theory. In the chapter entitled "Alienation" in *The Four Fundamental Concepts of Psychoanalysis*, Lacan is trying to establish the
fact that "everything emerges from the structure of the signifier,"
and in particular the subject. Lacan insists on the distinction between the sign ("which represents something for someone") and
the signifier ("that which represents a subject for another signifier"). The whole development must be quoted at this point:

> The signifier, producing itself in the field of the other, makes manifest
> the subject of its signification. But it functions as a signifier only to
> reduce the subject in question to being no more than a signifier, to
> petrify the subject in the same movement in which it calls the subject
> to function, to speak, as subject. There, strictly speaking, is the temporal
> pulsation in which is established that which is the characteristic of the
> departure of the unconscious as such—the closing.
>   One analyst felt this at another level and tried to signify it in a term
> that was new, and which has never been exploited since in the field of
> analysis—*aphanisis*, disappearance. Ernest Jones, who invented it mis-
> took it for something rather absurd, the fear of seeing desire disappear.
> Now, *aphanisis* is to be situated in a more radical way at the level at
> which the subject manifests himself in his movement of disappearance
> that I have described as lethal. In a quite different way I have called
> this movement the *fading* of the subject. (*op.cit.*, 207-208)

In the space of a few lines, the sleight-of-hand is accomplished,
Jones is both dismissed and cannibalized, discarded and appro-
priated as an interesting signifier pressed into the service of Lacan's masterly and intransigent logic of alienation and disappearance. The ground of *aphanisis* has been shifted from biological and
"natural" order to that of the signifier and of dialectic (alienation):
"There is no subject without, somewhere, *aphanisis* of the subject,
and it is in this alienation, in this fundamental division, that the
dialectic of the subject is established" (*id.*, 221). This dialectic,
though, is non-Hegelian: it is non-reciprocal and non-totalizing.
In it, "a lack engendered from the previous time [. . .] serves to
reply to the lack raised by the following time" (*id.*, 215). Hence this
very precise statement of the whole process:

> The subject appears first in the Other, in so far as the first signifier,
> the unitary signifier, emerges in the field of the Other and represents

the subject for another signifier, which other signifier has as its effect
the *aphanisis* of the subject. Hence the division of the subject—when the
subject appears somewhere as meaning, he is manifested elsewhere as
"fading," as disappearance. (*id.*, 218)

It is easy to see how this version of the subject as emergence/
disappearance, as coming to life in aphanisic paradox, is conso-
nant with contemporary texts. It is, in fact, one of the very few
theoretical discourses that seems to me to have relevance to them
(and which perhaps meets for the first time André Green's accurate observation that "there seems to be a sort of *avoidance* on the
part of psychoanalysis with regard to contemporary literature"[8]).
The affinity with Beckett and Marguerite Duras immediatly comes
to mind. The opening pages of *Company*, the passages on the gaze,
the border line between seeing and not-seeing in Beckett's latest
texts, or the exploration of the indeterminate region of reversals
between life and death in Duras' *La Maladie de la Mort*, are cases
in point.[9]

In a less abstract-minimal form, Lacan's theory of *aphanisis* provides an insight into one of the major fictions of our times, Thomas
Pynchon's *Gravity's Rainbow*. Whatever else this novel is, it dramatizes on different levels the epistemological crisis of contemporary science and philosophy: the challenge to the hegemony of
causality in our modes of thinking, in the form of theories of "fundamental indeterminacy," undecidability, "acausal correlations,"
etc. As philosophical content, as *theme*, the subject is a fairly familiar
one by now. What is striking in *Gravity's Rainbow*, however, it that
it informs all levels of the writing and not only that of theme or
narrative. Characters have become molecules, accessible no longer
to psychology but as Pynchon says to "pharmacology." Things,
people, metaphors, are adrift or in orbit, oxymoronic, paradoxical
and non-deterministic modes of thought rule. The subject is no
longer a unit, a whole. Like Roger Mexico the statistician, he is
neither 1 not 0 but somewhere in between, in the passage, between
emergence and disappearance. His mode of being, like that of the
Lacanian subject, is precisely *aphanisic.* Just as the subject for Lacan
"appears only in that division," "manifests himself in this movement of disappearance that I have described as lethal" (*Four Concepts*, 228), Roger Mexico exists "in the domain of zero to one, not-
something to something.[10] This, on the level of fictional episte-

mology, is exactly of the same order of radical critique as Lacan is
to ego-psychology:

> But in the domain of zero to one, not-something to something,
> Pointsman can only possess the zero and the one. He cannot like
> Mexico, survive anyplace in between. Like his master I. P. Pavlov before
> him, he imagines the cortex of the brain as a mosaic of tiny on/off
> elements. Some are always in bright excitation, others inhibited. The
> contours bright and dark, keep changing. But each point is allowed
> only the two states: waking or sleep. One or zero. "Summation," "tran-
> sition," "irradiation," "concentration," "reciprocal induction"—all Pav-
> lovian brain-mechanics—assumes the presence of these bi-stable points.
> But to Mexico belongs the domain *between* zero and one—the middle
> Pointsman has excluded from his persuasion—the probabilities. (*id.*,
> 63-64)

The whole novel takes place "in a process of gap," the undefinable
suspension of the *Brennschluss*. No bi-stable referents here, no
"Pointsmanship," but a circular process, a circularity without reciprocity, "dissymetrical." The Lacanian topology of the subject
(the rim, the cut, the *vel*, etc.) opens up a whole new possibility of
apprehension of contemporary texts. How significantly new this
possibility is will be apparent if we set it against the remarks of
another analyst on contemporary literature. André Green, in the
article already cited, sees "modern writing" as becoming disjointed
between two poles, as tending to split between "a writing of the
body and a writing of the thought":

> On the body-writing side, representation no longer lays the foundation
> of a structured fantasy; it becomes fragmented into short-lived, eva-
> nescent bodily states, the writer failing repeatedly to communicate
> through the writing process this uncommunicable reality because nei-
> ther the spoken nor the written word can yield a rendering of it [. . . .]
> At the opposite pole we are witnessing the advent of a literature which
> I shall call that of the sublimated text—a text devoid of any represen-
> tation or meaning, a text which strives to say nothing beyond the mere
> statement of the writing process. (*op. cit.*, 31-32)

The distinction has all the force of bold simplification, and it
does show convincingly how writing today abolishes the "figurative
dimension." It also manifests (and here Green shows himself to be
the former student of Lacan) the importance of the concept of
drive (which Lacan elaborates in *Seminar XI*, precisely) as "a cross-
roads between the somatic and the psychic," "a go-between," a

structure of contradictions. But what Green loses in his clear-cut distinction is the *tension,* the operation which Lacan calls "subjectification," "a subjectification without subject, a bone, a structure, an outline" (*Four Concepts,* 184). Perhaps because he gives precedence to dichotomy and classification over tension and contradiction, Green largely misses the question of the contemporary text, another avatar in the complex dramaturgy of failed connections between psychoanalysis and narrative. If "on the body-writing side" Green mentions Artaud and Beckett (?), no particular text is mentioned on the other (one supposes he has Maurice Blanchot and Roger Laporte in mind), not to speak of the vast number of texts which would fall "in-between" (such as Pynchon, but of course many others). Green himself honestly acknowledges this and suggests that it is easier for the "psychoanalyst critic" (his phrase) to work on classic texts anyway because they are "doubly bound" and therefore lend themselves more readily to interpretation:

> the strict observance of the order of integration of the planes is conducive to the proposed deciphering process; scriptural characteristics point to preconscious representations which, in turn, make it possible, with the help of traces found in the written text, to deduce the unconscious fantasy" (*id.,* 28).[11]

Contemporary writing and its "unbinding" (as Green has shown), as well as Lacanian theory of the subject (as I have tried to show), play havoc with this type of analysis predicated on the "uncovering," the "deciphering" of truth, a dramaturgy of unveiling and resolution. Lacan's lesson (in the field of narrative analysis at any rate) is that not resolution but punctuation is what is required, and that a step toward it may be taken if texts are seen as existing "around the living moment of the *aphanisis* of the subject" (*Four Concepts,* 223).

III

This "living moment" is a far cry from the "dreary wasteland of *aphanisis*" refered to by Jameson. It has important implications for the study of contemporary texts, which I have barely suggested (and which will be the object of a further study). But I want to mention, as a coda, another version of it, a "post-modernistic" dramaturgy of subject, meaning and appearances. Systems, whatever their inertia or dynamism, are always caught in larger tectonics, they slide, they are shoved aside by others. In recent years, Jean Baudrillard has thus attempted to displace some of the major systems and assumptions of our time, and in the torrential post-apo-

calyptic rhetoric of his displacement, *aphanisis* appears indeed as
one of the names for the "desertification" of meaning. Relying in
turn on Paul Virilio's mystifying "aesthetics of disappearance," in
turn on post-Nietzschean nihilism, Baudrillard describes the advent of the "glaciation" of meaning and of the reign of simulacrae
and appearances. A new cast of actants appear: implosion, seduction, simulation. But all drama, all pathos has been drained from
the pageant. What remains is disappearance in its pure form:

> Disappearance, aphanisis, implosion, Furie des Verschwindens. In fact
> it is not so much nihilism any more: in disappearance, in the desert
> form, aleatory and indifferent, there is not even the pathos, the pa-
> thetics of nihilism—that mythic energy which is the force of nihilism,
> radicality, mythic denegation, dramatic anticipation. It is not even di-
> senchantment. It is disappearance purely and simply.[12]

End of a dramaturgy of the subject, of life, of "cruelty," of the
modernistic theatre of signs, a debacle of signs, a "semiorrhage."
Enter the object, enigmatic and fatal. If the object triumphs so
implacably, says Baudrillard, it is because it belongs to the order
of the accomplished, to that which cannot be escaped, whereas the
power of the subject, now receding, came from "the promise of its
accomplishment." Without going into Baudrillard's thesis in
greater detail, it seems fitting to end on this reversed view, this
veduta from another angle as it were. Seen like that, Lacan's efforts
appear as the (perhaps) last adventures of ironic subjectivity, of
the "insular economy" of the subject, doomed, because of his in-
sularity, to alienation and isolation. Most of our narratives (including the meta-narrative of psychoanalysis) rest on some sort of
conflict between the isolated subject and the outside world, the
subtle balance and imbalance of a world ruled by prohibition, law
and desire, but always the ever-renewing promise of accomplishment, the promise that there would never be an end to the story.
That is (was) the beauty of it, of the subject and his many stories
of which Lacan's may be the last baroque version. For if the subject
can no longer be whole and dominant, if his position has finally
been demonstrated to be untenable, then the beauty of his drama
may be passing from our world:

> The subject, the metaphysics of the subject, were beautiful only in its
> pride, its arbitrariness, its untiring drive to power, its transcendence as
> the subject of power, of history, or in the dramaturgy of its alienation.
> Outside of that, it is nothing but a miserable wreck, grappling with its
> own desire or its own image, unable to command a coherent represen-
> tation of the universe, and sacrificing itself to no avail on the dead
> corpse of history in order to try to resuscitate it.[13]

If the object now reigns supreme, the question may well be: will there still be narratives without a subject, narratives of the "pure, unreferential concatenation of things and events"?

Université de Lille III

NOTES

1 One of the best cultural magazines in Paris at the present time is *L'Ane, Le Magazine Freudien*, which comments on all aspects of culture and politics from a Lacanian point of view. Books based on Lacanian theory have recently been published on music, dance, political discourse, etc. . . .

2 Fredric Jameson, "Imaginary and Symbolic in Lacan: Marxism, Psychoanalytic Criticism, and the Problem of the Subject," *Yale French Studies* 55/56 (1977), 338-395; the passage quoted is on pp. 381-382, the italics are mine.

3 Independently of the quarrel one can have with what Jameson offers as a remedy, in this particular case, that "the notion of some relationship—still to be defined—between the subject and this or that individual character or 'point of view' should be replaced by the study of those character systems into which the subject is fitfully inserted" (*id.*,382).

4 In particular in "Subversion of the Subject and Dialectic of Desire," *Écrits*.

5 The phrase is from Moustapha Safouan, *La Sexualité Féminine dans la Doctrine Freudienne*, Paris: Editions du Seuil, 1976, p.69.

6 *The Four Fundamental Concepts of Psycho-Analysis*, ed. Jacques-Alain Miller, trans. Alan Sheridan (New York: W.W. Norton and Co., Inc., 1978), p.198. Further references to this work will be noted in the text.

7 J.Laplanche and J.-B. Pontalis, *The Language of Psycho-Analysis*, trans. Donald Nicholson-Smith (New York: W.W. Norton & Co., Inc., 1973), p.40.
Ernest Jones, "Early Developments in Female Sexuality," *Papers on Psychoanalysis* (Boston: The Beacon Hill Press, 1927).

8 André Green, "The Unbinding Process," *New Literary History* XII,1 (1980), 12.

9 "There is of course the eye. Filling the whole field. The hood slowly down. Or up if down to begin. The globe. All pupil. Staring up. Hooded. Bared. Hooded again. Bared again." (S. Beckett, *Company*, London: Calder, 1980, p. 27).

10 Thomas Pynchon, *Gravity's Rainbow*, (New York, Toronto, London: Bantam Books, 1973), p.63. I am indebted to Claude Richard for his illuminating comments on Pynchon and epistemology, some of which appear in his essay, "Le Graal du Référent," *Fabula* 2 (1983).

11 Green himself writes on *Hamlet* and Henry James. This is to say nothing of his remark that this literature "of which we are witnessing the advent" has its counterpart in nonfigurative painting and serial music. Surely, by 1971 when his article originally appeared, the cutting edge of innovation had already moved beyond "nonfiguration" and "seriality"? It may be worth observing also that when Safouan, after dismissing it, returns to *aphanisis* via the Lacanian version, he too turns to Henry James; in this case to *The Beast in the Jungle* of which he suggests a reading I would call, for all the Lacanian indirection, "modernistic" (in this case "psychological"). As for Lacan himself, he refers to Montaigne as the text in which the work of *aphanisis* is best to be observed.

12 Jean Baudrillard, *Simulacres et Simulation* (Paris: Galilée, 1981), pp.233-234.

13 Jean Baudrillard, *Les Stratégies Fatales* (Paris: Grasset, 1983), p.165. (transl. mine)

The Space and Dialogue of Desire: Lacan, Greimas, and Narrative Temporality

Ronald Schleifer

i. Lacan's Allegory: The Rhetoric of Temporality

The other moment in which the symbolic and the real come together is consequently revealed, and I have already marked it theoretically: that is to say, in the function of time.

—Lacan (*Écrits: a Selection,* p. 95)

Time is not a thing.

—Martin Heidegger

In "The Freudian Thing" Jacques Lacan attempts to narrative "the return to Freud in psychoanalysis." The form of his narration is a kind of polemical ventriloquism in which Lacan speaks for his adversaries, for Truth herself, and in a section entitled "the discourse of the other," for the desk behind which he stands as he talks. In this essay the narration of his discourse on and with *things* takes the forms of a colloquy with his audience, riveted "so respectfully in those seats to listen to me despite the ballet of calls to work" (E, p. 132), the plot of a murder mystery (E, p. 123), the frenzy of a tragic chorus (E, p. 124), the nonsense of a joke (E, p. 122), the allegory of Acteon's dismemberment (E, p. 124), a "game for four players" (E, p. 139), and, as I have said, the discourse—what Lacan calls the "fable" (E, p. 136)—of the desk.[1]

For Lacan, things are problematic: Truth herself says, speaking through Lacan, that "the trade route of truth no longer passes through thought: strange to say, it seems to pass through things. . . . Here, no doubt, things are my signs, but, I repeat, signs of my speech" (E, pp. 122-23). As opposed to this truth, Lacan defines the discourse of the desk as "piling pleonasm on to an antonomasis" (E, p. 136)—that is, multiplying language on a discourse which already misnames its object—and both this definition, and the discourse of "Truth," aptly describe two ways language brings together things and signs, two ways of understanding allegory. Antonomasis, Quintilian says, can be accomplished by the substitution of epithets or by the use of striking characteristics—that is, by either metaphoric or metonymic substitution. In "The Freudian Thing" Lacan gives voice to both forms of antonomasis. In the section entitled "the thing speaks for itself," the speaker—"the truth in Freud's mouth"—takes the form "of her who vanishes as soon as she appears," a "chthonian Diana in the damp shade," who says "I wander about in what you regard as being the least true in essence; in the dream, in the way the most far-fetched conceit, the most grotesque nonsense of the joke defies sense, in chance, not in its law, but in its contingence . . ." (E, p. 122). And in "the discourse of the other," we have the fabled discourse of the desk in which "the discourses concerning the ego and the desk . . . coincide point by point" (E, p. 132). Things signify speech, but speech itself signifies an Other speech—thus Joel Fineman has noted "a direct translation of the etymology of allegory: *allos*, other; *agoreuein*, to speak" designates the "discourse of the Other."[2] Thus allegory becomes, as Fineman says, "both theme and structuring principle" in psychoanalysis (p. 27). It is also, I am suggesting, a theme and structuring principle in Lacan's discourse in "The Freudian Thing" and elsewhere.

The central question for Fineman, following Lacan, is the central question of narrative theory: how does theme or structure manifest itself in time? how is the "reality" of time transformed into an "idea" of temporality? if the discourse of truth is "nonsense," how can it become the "fabled" narrative of the desk? how can the polyphony of ventriloquism—the split of discourses—summount its own tumult? "In order to appreciate the scope of this split," Lacan says in "The Freudian Thing,"

> we must hear the irrepressible cries that arise from the best as well as the worst, attempting to bring them back to the beginning of the chase, with the words that truth has given us as viaticum: 'I speak,' adding; 'There is no other speech but language.' The rest is drowned in their tumult.
>
> 'Logomachia!' goes the strophe on one side. 'What are you doing with the preverbal, gesture and mime, tone, and tune of a song . . . ?' To

which others no less animated give the antistrophe: 'Everything is language: language when my heart beats faster when I'm in a funk, and
if my patient flinches at the throbbing of an aeroplane at its zenith it is
a way of *saying* how she remembers the last bomb attack.'(E, p. 124)

This "way of *saying*" is the way of allegory in which truth comes to
inhabit time and things speak. But it is more than this, this dialogue: it is the way time comes to inhabit truth.

Several years ago Paul de Man, following Walter Benjamin and
others, redefined "allegory" in anti-romantic terms. Allegory, he
argued, eschewed the nostalgia enacted in Coleridge's "symbol" for
the more difficult pleasures of understanding and self-knowledge.
The knowledge of allegory is the knowledge of loss, and its rhetoric—as de Man entitled his essay—is "The Rhetoric of Temporality."[3] Geoffrey Hartman has recently raised again the question
of allegory in *Criticism in the Wilderness:* "A major problem of contemporary criticism is summed up by the question: can there be
nonallegorical kinds of reading?"[4] By "nonallegorical" readings
Hartman seems to mean something akin to Blake's visionary rather
than his allegorical poetry, the thinginess of truth's nonsense
rather than the desk's discourse. "The seduction of understanding
through fiction," Hartman continues, ". . . should provoke me to
break, however provisionally, the very frame of meaning I bring
to the text" (p. 274). Allegory, for Hartman then, "subdues" the
text to the synthesis of "one language" which "the textual surface
always in movement, always" betrays or exceeds: "allegorizing,
though driven by a desire for transcendence, remains skeletal, gri-
macing, schematic; . . . the no man's land between what can and
cannot be represented" (p. 90).

The function of allegory, then, like the function of the Father,
is repression: "the essential process behind the so-called paternal
metaphor," Régis Durand has written, "is a repressive gesture, the
constitutive repression: a passage from a world of pure difference
and meaningless oscillation to an anchoring, a stabilization through
some key symbols."[5] The father is not "himself the author of the
law," André Bleikasten has written; rather, he owes his authority
"to the specific *place* which he comes to occupy within the family
configuration in relation to the mother and child—a place . . .
'marked in life by that which belongs to another order than life,
that is to say, by tokens of recognition, by names.' "[6]

Here, then, we have that allegory of that other order than life,
the discourse of the Other, the discourse of the desk. Such an
allegorical narrative—linear, temporal, coherent—requires a kind

of repression. Yet as "The Freudian Thing" shows, Lacan's language is not—it cannot be—simply "one." This is why de Man's argument is important and clarifying: by contrasting the temporality of allegory to the illusory "stasis" of symbolism, he implies two discursive modes. The first, the temporality of rhetoric, recognizes time and the differences, the representations, temporality requires, while the second presents what Durand has called "empty time" (p. 63). This last is perhaps a contradiction in terms because time can never be "empty": it is defined, as de Man suggests, as minimally that in which relationships are enacted. What allegory does is mark meaningful relationships by time, and it makes them meaningful by creating gaps or the illusion of gaps in the continuity of the all-encompassing ecology of relationships. As Frank Kermode describes it in *The Genesis of Secrecy* following Propp and Greimas, a preliminary situation gives rise to a function which "develops into a proper name; so it becomes a character, whose life and death have a narrative; and then the function is lost in the character."[7] Kermode's "function"—it is really Propp's—is a relationship understood in ineluctably temporal terms: as Propp says, it is an action which "cannot be defined apart from its place in the course of action."[8] The functions of narrative are irreducibly temporal, which is why to seek them elsewhere—desiring transcendence, as structural achronological notation does and as Lacan asserts ego psychology does—is a form of "nostalgia" for what de Man calls the "illusory identification with the non-self" (p. 191).

Thus, de Man implies what Durand has described in Lacanian terms as the "two narrative modes" created by "two types of relation to the symbolic order" (p. 51)—Lacan's Imaginary and Symbolic modes of presentation and representation. The first of Durand's narrative modes—corresponding to Lacan's Symbolic—is "the successful achievement of the 'family romance,' a linear non-contradictory discursive and symbolic mode"; and the second—corresponding to the Imaginary—is "opposed to linear coherence, emphasizing discontinuity, oscillation, and non-differentiation" (p. 51). One is the mode of "fable," the other "nonsense." The narrative mode implied by the Symbolic and its "successful" repression and anchoring, recognizes time and the differences, the symbolic representations, temporality requires, and the mode implied by the Imaginary does not. The second narrates what Durand calls "the return of the narcissistic ego, its stasis, its empty time, and its suspension from the very knowledge of" the absent father (p. 63); it

enacts, in the "nostalgia" of Romantic notions of synecdochal symbols de Man describes, a form of "regression." What de Man calls
the "temporal difference" of allegory is a narrative mode created
by a "constitutive repression," while what he calls the "illusory identification with the non-self" of symbolism is another type of "relation to the symbolic order."

In a way, as I have suggested, these modes correspond to the
difference between the two discourses Lacan presents in "The
Freudian Thing," the metaphoric "nonsense" of truth and the metonymic "fable" of the desk. Yet in "The Freudian Thing" Lacan
represents truth in the allegory of Acteon as something, like a
signifier, which must be pursued and is never achieved; and his
"fable" of the desk enacts the Imaginary "identification with the
analyst's ego" (E, p. 135). The desk concludes: "it is in the disin-
tegration of the imaginary unity constituted by the ego that the
subject finds the signifying material of his symptoms. And it is
from the sort of interest aroused in him by the ego that the sig-
nifications that turn his discourse away from those symptoms proceed" (E, p. 137). Meaning, then, eschews time even as "truth"
engenders temporality. That is, the metaphor of Truth—a
chthonian Diana—becomes in narrative "a little metonymic," and
the metonymy of the desk behind which Lacan stands can be seen
to be metaphorically identified with the ego.

In this way, then, Lacan's allegory both enacts the subject's relationship to time as a kind of unconscious symptom, an Imaginary
identification, and it represents temporality as a condition of truth.
Fineman says,

> allegory initiates and continually revivifies its own desire, a desire born
> of its own structurality. Every metaphor is always a little metonymic
> because in order to have metaphor there must be a structure, and where
> there is a structure there is already piety and nostalgia for the lost origin
> through which structure is thought. Every metaphor is a metonymy
> of its own origin, its structure thrust into time by its very structural-
> ity. (p. 44)

Narration, then, is *temporizing* in both senses of the word: both
passing and *gaining* time so that the endless displacements and endless destructions of time can be deferred. As Fredric Jameson has
suggested, the danger of Lacanian analysis is "the temptation to
transform the notion of the two orders of functions [that is, the
Imaginary and the Symbolic] into a binary opposition, and to de-

fine each relationally in terms of the other. . . . We will however
come to learn that this process of definition by binary opposition
is itself profoundly characteristic of the Imaginary."[9] Its danger,
then, is the possibility of failing to recognize temporality in its
opposition: thus Jameson himself identifies the third term in Lacan's triad, the Real, with History. Its danger is to locate desire
only in its metonymic manifestation and, as Serge Leclaire says, as
simply "proper to the Imaginary . . . conceived of as *significative
mediation of fundamental antinomy.*"[10] It is the failure to situate desire, as A. J. Greimas does, as a spacing, a "punctuation," of discourse that is a little metaphoric, a little murderous.

Yet desire functions in Lacan as well as Greimas in the same way
de Man's eccentric definition of allegory does: it embeds the Imaginary in the Symbolic and "realizes" temporality. In *Le Discours
et le symbole* Edmond Ortigues describes

> Lacan's definition of the essence of the Imaginary as a "dual relation-
> ship," an ambiguous redoubling, a "mirror" reflection, an *immediate* re-
> lationship between subject and its other in which each term passes *im-
> mediately* into the other and is lost in a never-ending play of reflections.
> Imagination and desire are the realities of a finite being which can
> *emerge* from the contradiction between self and other only by the genesis
> of a third term, a *mediatory* "concept" which, by determining each term,
> orders them into *reversible and progressive* relations which can be *developed*
> in language.[11]

The crucial terms of this paragraph which I have italicized—"immediate," "emerge," "mediatory," "reversible and progressive,"
"develop"—are temporal terms, and the "emergence" Ortigues is
describing is the emergence of the subject and the Imaginary—the
emergence of desire—into time. And more than this: it is the
"emergence" of temporality itself as a concept, which emerges and
is recognized simultaneously with the emergence of the subject.
"Truth," "strophe and antistrophe," the desk, the Freudian
"thing," articulate temporality by recognizing, each in its Name
and structurality as allegory does, "temporal difference." "What
matters in the last resort," Bleikasten writes, "is not the living father
so much as the dead father, not the real rather so much as the
symbolic father or what Jacques Lacan calls the 'name-of-the-father,'
'the symbolic function which, since the dawn of historical time, has
identified his person with the figure of the Law' " (pp. 119-20).
Such an identification creates the difference between desire and
the law in which temporality itself, as well as narrative, "emerges."

Thus temporality is not a pole in a binary opposition, but arises out of such an opposition; it is *the condition of the Symbolic,* just as structurality is a condition of allegory, "a mediatory 'concept' which, by determining each term, orders them into reversible and progressive relations which can be developed in language."

This "development" is narrative: "desire has a history," Peter Brooks has written, "the story of its own past, unavailable to the conscious subject but persistently repeating itself in the transference, in the symptom."[12] Symptom, then, becomes the opposite of narrative as I have described it, the enactment of a confused sense of time: it is de Man's "symbol," the story not of the absent, but the phantom father, a ghostly "presence" that displaces the subject in the failure of repression: "the original repression," Durand writes, "is not so much rejected as grotesquely twisted, played with, and displaced" (p. 62).

Narrative, then, functions like allegory and *represents* temporality. Temporality is not a thing, something that can be presented, that can be present: thus Heidegger says "time is not a thing."[13] Rather, temporality is a "concept"—a "matter" in Heidegger's sense of a "concern"—that *must be represented.* It inhabits, then, Lacan's category of the Symbolic, its cause and product. The Real, the realm of "things," is, as Lacan says of perversion (and despite Jameson's assertion), "outside of time":

> The fantasy of perversion is namable. It is in space. It suspends an essential relationship. It is not atemporal but rather outside of time. In neurosis, on the contrary, the very basis of the relationships of subject to object on the fantasy level is the relationship of the subject to time.[14]

Lacan opposes a "thing" to an "object" here because "a real thing, one that has not yet been made a symbol, . . . has the potential of becoming one" (p. 46). The neurotic lives in a world of objects where time is confused—in "neurotic behavior," Lacan writes, ". . . the subject tries to find his sense of time in his object, and it is even in the object that he will learn to tell time" (p. 17)—while the psychotic, in a world of things, "disavows" time altogether.

Lacan's allegory, then, attempts to address both worlds, to bring together objects and things:

> Of all the undertakings that have been proposed in this century, [he writes,] that of the psychoanalyst is perhaps the loftiest, because the psychoanalyst acts in our time as the mediator between the man of care and the subject of absolute knowledge. (E, p. 105)

The psychoanalyst is the mediator of value, his medium is language, and his rhetoric an allegory of a marked temporality that transforms the reflection of desire into a spacious dialogue, the dyad of the analytical situation into a "game for four players." The analyst pretends he is dead, "cadaverizes his position," and, "under the respective effects of the symbolic and imaginary, he makes death present" (E, p. 140). He does so by articulating in his very silences the discourse of the Other to initiate a dialogue of desire.

ii. Knowledge and Power: The Genesis of Temporality

It is precisely because desire is articulated that it is not articulable.

—Lacan (E, p. 303)

The opposition of nonsense and fable that I have suggested governs Lacan's discourse is one that A. J. Greimas presents in *Structural Semantics* as corresponding to two modes of semantic analysis, qualificative analysis that analyzes the subjects of discourse as discrete units, the subjects of acts, and functional analysis that analyzes the subjects of discourse as constituted by their action, the subjects of knowledge (see VIII.1.d).[15] The first, like Freud's psychosis and Lacan's perversion, like speech-act theory—including Lacan's own radical speech-act theory which asserts "even if it communicates nothing, the discourse represents the existence of communication; even if it denies the evidence, it affirms that speech constitutes truth; even if it is intended to deceive, the discourse speculates on faith in testimony" (E, p. 43)—the first posits, as Freud says of psychosis, a conflict between an (Imaginary) ego and the outer world; while the second, like neurosis, like systematic structural analysis, constitutes the subject in relation to its functions by positing, as Freud says of neurosis, a conflict between the ego and the id.[16] "Paraphrasing Lacan," Greimas writes, "we can say two kinds of madness await mankind: on the one side, schizophrenia, the exaltation of total freedom in communication, ending in noncommunication; on the other side, a completely socialized and iterative speech, Queneau's 'You talk, you talk, that's all you know how to do,' which is also the negation of communication, discourse deprived of information" (III.4).

Greimas is describing the radically "bi-isotopic" nature of language inscribed in the distinction, of great importance to Lacan,[17] between "enunciation," whose subject selects the elements of discourse, performing an act which presupposes and "enacts" himself ("whatever . . . any enunciation speaks of," says Lacan, "belongs to desire" [FC, p. 141]), and "statement" (*énoncé*), whose subject is "determined retroactively" (FC, p. 139) by means of a functional analysis of discourse, an analysis of the subject that its combination of elements implies. "Linguistic activity," Greimas writes,

> creative of messages, appears first as the setting up of hypotactic relationships between a small number of sememes: functions, actants, contexts. It is essentially morphemic and presents a series of messages as algorithms. However, a systematic structure—the distribution of roles to the actants—is superimposed on this hypotaxis and establishes the messages as an objectivizing projection, the simulator of a world from which the sender and the received of a communication are excluded. (VII.3.d)

There is, then, the time of the enunciation—Lacan's famous variable sessions—which is a "thing" that, like all "things" in the Real, is a horizon only, with only the "potential" of becoming a symbol. More importantly, there is another kind of time, that of the statement represented in the tenses of discourse, which can only be symbolic. The time of enunciation is, as Lacan says, "outside of time," morphemic, and only becomes temporal when it is inscribed—that is, structured and "symbolized"—in discourse.

Such discourse is narrative and it is the intersection of nonsense and fable, qualities and functions, Real and Symbolic time. "Temporality (history)," Julia Kristeva writes, "is the *spacing* of this splitting negation, i.e., what is introduced between two isolated and nonalternating scansions (opposition-conciliation)."[18] That is, temporality arises in difference that cannot be categorized within the logical categories of opposition yet is more than pure accident, pure contiguity. Narrative, Greimas writes, creates a temporal succession "which is neither pure contiguity nor a logical implication" (XI.2.f), neither the contiguity of enunciation's "schizophrenic" morphemes (its algorithms) nor the necessary succession of the statement's systematic, socialized and iterative speech. This seemingly impossible difference is perhaps best visualized in the optical illusion, the outlined square, for instance, whose forward side can also be seen as its bottom, but never both at the same time. Such an optical illusion must "space" its double perception, and its doubleness—its opposition—is neither logical implication nor pure contiguity. The necessary non-simultaniety of its perceptions makes time itself

perceptible; it engenders temporality. In *The Confidence-Man* one
of Melville's characters tries to explain such a figure:

> "... if the bill is good, it must have in one corner, mixed in with the
> vignette, the figure of a goose, very small, indeed, all but microscopic;
> and, for added precaution, like the figure of Napoleon outlined by a
> tree, not observable, even if magnified, unless the attention is directed
> towards it. ..."[19]

Napoleon or Melville's goose is *there*, but it is figured by something
else. This figuring, however, is not of metaphoric substitution, but
of spacing: it is metomymic. Yet the metonym *functions* like substitution, like a metaphor: we cannot see both Napoleon and the
tree at the same time; it is one or the other.

This same "optical illusion" effect—this effected "spacing" of
temporality—is inscribed in what Greimas calls "linguistic activity."
Discourse, as I have said, is bi-isotopic—it is essentially split between what Greimas describes as the "power" of enunciation and
the "knowledge" of statement. To articulate this split Greimas dis-
tinguishes in his analysis between two actants, the Subject and the
Sender. The "semantic investment" in the relationship between the
Subject and the Object is "desire" (X.5); that between the Sender
and Receiver is "communication" (X.6), what he also calls "knowledge" (XI.2.e); and that between the Subject and the "circum-
stants" (the actants Helper and Opponent) is "power" (XI.2.e).
Thus Greimas posits the six actants of narrative and diagrams
them.

$$\text{Sender} — \boxed{\text{Object}} \rightarrow \quad \text{Receiver [knowledge]}$$
$$\uparrow \quad \text{[desire]}$$
$$\text{Helper} \rightarrow \boxed{\text{Subject}} \leftarrow \quad \text{Opponent} \quad \text{[power]}$$

Desire, as this diagram suggests, is both dependent on and situated
outside the Symbolic level of knowledge; it creates the space of
discourse, the possibility of dialogue. Here de Man's two discursive
modes, allegory and symbolism, inhabit the levels of knowledge
and power. As Greimas's arrows suggest, the former moves linearly
in time, while the latter refers everything, nostalgically, to the subject. Desire separates them, and in so doing engenders (or represents) the space of temporality.

Greimas himself suggests that psychoanalysis proposes "its own
model for semantic description" (X.13), itself, like his, an actantial

model, and in both models desire is central. As I noted in the introduction to *Structural Semantics,*

> without the diacritical separation created by desire discourse explodes into pure "affabulation," in which the plot of narrative is reduced . . . to its "moral," its "point"—the impossible extreme of a *non-figurative allegory;* and into the "nonsense" . . . of unconnected linguistic elements—the other extreme where language, lacking hypotactic connections, is elementally *literal.* Here the imaginary reduction of discourse, as Lacan might say, into the allegory of neurosis, where allegory's figures become literal symptoms, is absolutely severed from the dissociations of psychosis, where the elements of language remain unconnected. (p. lii)

Desire, then, makes discourse possible by marking the relationship between enunciation and statement, between allegory and things.

In Lacan the Sender is the Other, the level of knowledge that of the Discourse of the Other, and we can see why both he and Freud find the knowledge of the unconscious—and thus neurosis rather than psychosis—more amenable to analysis than the power of psychotic hallucination. For the Discourse of the Other creates the same effect of temporality as the optical illusion: "what this structure of the signifying chain discloses is the possibility I have, in so far as I have this language in common with other subjects, that is to say, in so far as it exists as a language, to use it to signify *something quite other* than what it says" (E, p. 155). The space between the messages of knowledge and power, like the optical illusion's double vision, is a metonym that functions like a metaphor: the articulation of the message creates the space between the levels inscribing temporality, so that the power of intersubjective communication, insofar as it is trans-subjective, presents knowledge from which the speaker is excluded.

In the space of this opposition the effect of temporality arises, that "sense" of time we have yet cannot "metaphorically" name: "What, then, is time?" Augustine asks. "If no one asks me I know; if I want to explain it to someone who does ask me, I do not know."[20] Time exists between the *power* of its illusory felt presence and our articulated *knowledge* of it which, apprehending its radical insusceptibility to articulation, erases its presence: to articulate time is to represent it by something else. Discourse "divides time," as Hartman says, "to make us aware of it" in what he calls "a ghostly, dimensional shift from action to observation,"[21] from power to knowledge, from the discourse of the self to the discourse of the other. To paraphrase Augustine, we are sensitive to the spacing, the differences, of time, yet that spacing cannot be named because it is the ground of naming and articulation altogether, the ground of the language into which (in another ineluctibly temporal passage) we are born.

Time is the ground of articulation and of language, and it is therefore—like language, like Lacan's subject—inscribed with death. "If the present were always present," Augustine reasons,

> and would not pass into the past, it would no longer be time but eternity. Therefore, if the present, so as to be time, must be so constituted that it passes into the past, how can we say that it is, since the cause of its being is the fact that it will cease to be? Does it not follow that we can say that it is time, only because it tends towards non-being? (p. 288)

Augustine is attempting the very explanation of time for "someone who does ask me" that he claimed earlier was impossible, and perhaps we can see now it is impossible because, as Lacan says, "the symbol manifests itself first of all as the murder of the thing, and this death constitutes in the subject the eternalization of his desire" (E, p. 104).

Desire manifests this temporality indirectly, as a kind of "resonance" of language (E, p. 102)[22]; this is why Lacan so insistently identifies desire and metonymy. In Augustine's answer to "what is time?" temporality inhabits the desire to explain engendered by the separate existence of an other who is neither a logical implication nor (because, as Lacan says, "I have this language in common" with her) pure contiguity. Desire cannot be fulfilled because, inscribed within the Imaginary, it erases its object—it "murders" the thing—in its articulation: in Greimas's narrative scheme, it does not recognize that the object of desire becomes an object of knowledge through which a message passes from Sender to Receiver, subject to subject. Thus desire becomes eternalized. Yet desire can inscribe itself within the Symbolic—it can become a little metaphoric—when it renounces its object altogether to recognize the mortal dialogue of subject to subject. "This is the only life that endures and is true," Lacan says,

> since it is transmitted without being lost in the perpetuated tradition of subject to subject. . . . nothing, except the experiments to which man associates it, distinguishes a rat from the rat, a horse from the horse, nothing except this inconsistent passage from life to death—whereas

Empedocles, by throwing himself into Mount Etna, leaves forever present in the memory of men this symbolic act of his being-for-death. (E, p. 104)

"Death destroys a man," E. M. Forster says: "the idea of Death saves him."[23] In the possibility of signification—the possibility in Greimas's terms of establishing the message as an "objectivizing projection"—the "idea" of temporality arises in the interplay of desire and humanity: "the moment at which desire becomes human is also that in which the child is born into language" (E, p. 103).

If the desire for death is a metaphor for the idea of temporality, it is a metaphor, like all the metaphors of the Symbolic, that also participates in metonymy. In fact, Lacan makes the desire for death a metaphor for metonymy precisely to inscribe desire's re-alization—not its fulfilment—within the Symbolic as opposed to desire's subsistence, as Leclaire suggests, in the Imaginary. The distinction I am making, then, is between the (Imaginary) desire for a particular object and a more global desire, the space of desire altogether which, inscribed within and inscribing temporality, is both the cause and the product of the discourse of narrative tem-porality: the mortal desire for death. In *The Discourse of Rome* Lacan offers three figures of man's freedom—the renunciation of desire imposed by the menace of death, the consented-to sacrifice of life for ideals, and "the suicidal renunciation of the vanquished partner." "Of these figures of death," Lacan writes, "the third is the supreme detour through which the immediate particularity of desire, reconquering its ineffable form, rediscovers in negation a final triumph. . . . This third figure is not in fact a perversion of the instinct, but rather the desperate affirmation of life that is the purest form in which we recognize the death instinct" (E, p. 104). It is the renunciation of power for "murderous" knowledge in which, after all, power and life and finally time itself are affirmed.

iii. "Strange Temporality": The Hesitations of Narrative

Impediment, failure, split. In a spoken or a written sen-tence something stumbles. Freud is attracted by these phe-nomena, and it is there that he seeks the unconscious. There, something other demands to be realized—which appears as intentional, of course, but of a strange tem-porality.

—Lacan (FC, p. 25)

Here, then, we have arrived at a kind of theory of discourse that
accounts for narrative temporality and situates it within the ecology
of human life. "The symbolic function," Lacan writes,

> presents itself as a double movement within the subject: man makes an
> object of his action, but only in order to restore to this action in due
> time its place as a grounding. In this equivocation, operating at every
> instant, lies the whole process of a function in which knowledge and
> action alternate. (E, p. 73)

This equivocation "operates" at every instant because in its operations "instants" are humanly realized: "the author of these lines,"
Lacan says, "has attempted to demonstrate in a logic of a sophism
the temporal source through which human action, in so far as it
orders itself according to the action of the other, finds in the scan-
sion of its hesitations the advent of its certainty" (E, p. 75).

This realization of temporality is the realization of desire oscil-
lating between the absurdity, the "nonsense," of our needs and the
plottedness, the "fable," of our demands, between the self and the
other: "the first object of desire is to be recognized by the other"
(E, p. 58). Thus Peter Brooks writes, "if Freud must unpack the
layered, substituted, metaphorical texts of . . . dream, screen
memory, obsessional symptoms, . . . and read them as metonymy,
metonymy itself speaks of desire, as Jacques Lacan has argued.
Desire is the motor of narrative. . . . Desire is also unarrestable,
always desire for something else, since it is constituted in the split
between need and demand, born from a lack, founded on fictional
scenarios of fulfilment" (p. 78).

That is, desire is *articulated* in the hesitations of narrative in
which the effect of temporality can be momentarily achieved in
the sense that Melville's goose is articulated and achieved in the
space created by other figures. Such hesitations are what Lacan
calls the "dialectical punctuation" of speech effected by the analyst
(E, p. 95): "the punctuation, once inserted, fixes the meaning;
changing the punctuation renews or upsets it; and a faulty punctuation amounts to a change for the worse" (E, p. 99). Greimas's
term for this punctuation is "the intrusion of history into perma-
nence" (XII.5.e) which "explodes" (XI.3.e) a "complex category"
(i.e. "discourse") into a "disjunctive category" (i.e. "statement" vs.
"enunciation"—or "knowledge" vs. "power"—or "unconscious" vs.
"conscious") and creates the "space" of temporality. Literary crit-

icism's term for this punctuation is "interpretation," and with this term we return to Lacan:

> Let us place ourselves at the two extremes of the analytical experience. The primal repressed is a signifier, and we can always regard what is built on this as constituting the symptom *qua* a scoffolding of signifiers. . . . Although their structure is built up step by step like any edifice, it is nevertheless, in the end, inscribable in synchronic terms.
>
> At the other extreme, there is interpretation. Interpretation concerns the factor of a special temporal structure I have tried to define in the term metonymy. As it draws to its end, interpretation is directed toward desire, with which, in a certain sense, it is identical. Desire, in fact, is interpretation itself. (FC, p. 176)

This special temporal structure Lacan speaks of can only be conceived in relationship to what it is not: like the catachresis of "table leg" or "mother tongue" Hillis Miller discusses,[24] it is a metonymic figure that is a little metaphoric.

Such figuration is both within and outside the temporality of discourse, which is why I am using the metaphor of "hesitation" to represent it. *Hesitation* is a complex figure, a confusion of the literal and the figurative. Literally, it is a pause, a stopping place, a "spot of time"; yet insofar as the time of discourse is relentless, it is only a figure for something else, the illusion of stopping, of meaning, of self. Hesitation, like representation—and, as I have argued, like temporality itself—is marked by difference, including the differences of discourse, the literal against the figurative, power against knowledge, time against meaning, the self against the other. It only exists, like the call slip in the library Lacan speaks of, in a system of differences that is a cultural artifact.[25] Such hesitation is like, Lacan says, "an indirect discourse, isolated in quotation marks within the thread of narration, and, if the discourse is played out, it is on a stage implying the presence not only of the chorus, but also of spectators" (E, p. 47); "the discourse in an analytic session," he says elsewhere, "is valuable only in so far as it stumbles or is interrupted" (E, p. 299). What it stumbles over, what it is interrupted by, is the space of desire, the dialogue of one discourse and another.

That is, the special temporal structure creates and fills gaps and responds to nothing—to Hamlet's ghost, to the uncanny doubleness of language that Lacan and Greimas describe, to the space of desire—the nothing that is not there and the nothing that is. Its language is Kierkegaard's irony, grinning at the devil with a language that willfully misunderstands, that turns the screw, the allegorical language of fiction. In "The Lady with a Dog" Anton Chekhov describes this action of imagination by narrating the development of the metonymic function of the lady with a dog into a fully named and characterized person, Anna. This is a story not of horror, but of love, yet it creates love against the relentlessness of time just as the gothic tale creates horror against nature's silence[26] and just as Oedipus attempts to create a future for himself against the crimes of the past. These two affects—Aristotle's pity and terror, Aeschylus's singing and tears—may well define the two most characteristic human responses to time.

Gurov, a middle-aged visitor to Yalta, accustomed to casual love affairs with various women, meets a young married lady with a dog and begins an adulterous affair with her. He is somewhat bored with the intensity of her feeling and guilt until the day they go to the mountains. Here is the only place in the story that the otherwise impersonal and omniscient narrator interrupts the continuity of the story with an explicit enunciation that betrays and exceeds the story's illusion of realism:

> Not a leaf stirred, the grasshoppers chirruped, and the monotonous hollow roar of the sea came up to them, speaking of peace, of the eternal sleep lying in wait for us all. The sea had roared like this long before there was any Yalta or Oreanda, it was roaring now, and it would go on roaring, just as indifferently and hollowly, when we have passed away. And it may be that in this continuity, this utter indifference to life and death, lies the secret of our ultimate salvation, of the stream of life on our planet, and of its never-ceasing movement toward perfection.
>
> Side by side with a young woman, who looked so exquisite in the early light, soothed and enchanted by the sight of all this magical beauty—sea, mountains, clouds and the vast expanse of sky—Gurov told himself that, when you came to think of it, everything in the world is beautiful, really. . . .[27]

Such a lyrical passage discovers in the incidental occurrence of an anecdote larger human significance even while it denies human significance in the face of inhuman time.

It does so by representing temporality in the allegory of the sea: the roar of the sea equals "continuity" equals the "never-ceasing movement" of time equals "salvation." This allegory is the irruption of enunciation into the story's statement, the mark of a chthonian underworld—a roar not unlike that which Wordsworth heard on Mount Snowden—that literally *marks* time. But by allegorizing temporality, Chekhov "immediately" erases the subject with the fable to achieve the impersonality of "salvation" and system. After the meditation on the indifferent sea, the realization of temporality, the whole world seems beautiful to Gurov, everything is somehow transformed.

At the end of the story Gurov repeats this narrative act. He sees himself in a mirror, his hair turning gray, and the momentary interruption of his vision of himself, the hesitation in his narrative, transforms his intention "to fondle her with light words" into the narration of his love-life culminating in the realization that "only now, when he was gray-haired, had he fallen in love properly, thoroughly, for the first time in his life" (pp. 43, 44). Here is a kind of "mirror stage" creating a hesitation in the time of narration. In Gurov's gaze, as Lacan would say,

> is this object lost and suddenly refound in the conflagration of shame, by the introduction of the other. Up to this point, what is the subject trying to see? What he is trying to see, make no mistake, is the object as absence. (FC, p. 182)

The object in absence is both Greimas's and Lacan's object of desire, and Gurov's "proper" love arises, not with the presence of this object, but with the recognition, marked by his gray hair, of temporality and death—with its absence that also carries the possibility of the dialogue, subject to subject, Lacan speaks of. That is, the discovery of beauty and love, of "ultimate salvation," is what the articulation of temporality—what Paul Ricoeur calls the "deeper experience of time"[28]—offers. Much as the ancient Athenians called the Furies the Eumenides (the benevolent ones), and prayed, in Aeschylus's play, that they might "Bless them, all here, with silence,"[29] so the narrative hesitation articulates—it falsely names—the horror of indifference as "salvation" and Gurov names the intimations of his own mortality he sees in the mirror as "love." Here is how functions gain names, allegories their meaning, in and against time.

Both passages—that of the story and that of the hero—turn the screw of experience to discover before death the ordinary, continuity, the concept of temporality itself. Such false namings, such as allegory, transformed the Greek Furies into benevolent deities; and in Chekhov's story the beauty discovered before the indifferent sea and the indifferent mirror makes the salvation of love possible. It makes salvation possible by discovering and humanizing—in a word, by punctuating—as the Greeks had done, and as Wordsworth does on Snowden, the chthonic origins of life, the relentlessness of time, inarticulately expressed in the roar of the sea, the silence of the analyst.

In "Narration in the Psychoanalytic Dialogue" Roy Schafer, following Lacan, defines the transference narrative as "new remembering of the past that unconsciously has never become the past" in which "the alleged past must be experienced consciously as a mutual interpenetration of the past and present."[30] This is precisely what Gurov discovers as he takes his gray hair as an allegorical figure for temporality. At the moment he sees himself in the mirror he intercalates the story of his life:

> Women had always believed him different from what he really was, had loved in him not himself but the man their imagination pictured him, a man they had sought for eagerly all their lives. And afterwards when they discovered their mistake, they went on loving him just the same. (p. 44)

Here, in the women loving him just the same, is the representation of experience, the transformation of the time of an indifferent world, in terror and in love, into a human image. It is Hartman's "subduing" the constantly moving, "becoming" experience with an allegory that betrays time by allegorizing it: by experiencing it, perhaps more "deeply" as Ricoeur says, as human. This takes place in and by means of discourse: Lacan has noted that in psychoanalysis the operative "cure" of hysterics is not memory but verbalization—the patient "has made it pass into the *verbe*, or, more precisely, into the *epos* by which he brings back into present time the origins of his own person" (E, pp. 46-47). Value is created and remains in the misdirected, mistaking language of allegory which points it out, horrible in the crime-ridden past of Oedipus, beautiful in the "salvation" that seems to speak out of that roaring, indifferent sea. It speaks from a hesitation in narrative, realizing in that hesitation's interpretation its own "global" desire, a desperate affirmation of life.

Thus love, in Chekhov's story, inhabits the Symbolic; like temporality, it is a shadow or unreal fiction without which we cannot live.[31] It appears in the hesitations in the narrative, where temporality reappears, not simply lived-in, but contemplated, allegorized, represented. Chekhov creates love before our eyes, while

death hovers underneath, a seeming benevolent Fury, the mother
of beauty, an under-roar for his whole story. At the end of "The
Lady with a Dog," instead of fondling, Gurov and Anna sit and
discuss their situation:

> And it seemed to them that they were within an inch of arriving at a
> decision, and that a new, beautiful life would begin. And they both
> realized that the end was still far, far away, and that the hardest, the
> most complicated part was only beginning. (p. 44)

Chekhov ends by having his characters talk, subject to subject,
thereby situating themselves in the complication of the time between beginning and end. At the end he—and they—like Lacan,
mark time in the story by creating the space of desire in which
time becomes human, speech dialogical and full, and the subject
achieves a little freedom. "I might as well be categorical," Lacan
says:

> in psychoanalytic anamnesis, it is not a question of reality, but of truth,
> because the effect of full speech is to reorder past contingences by
> conferring on them the sense of necessities to come, such as they are
> constituted by the little freedom through which the subject makes them
> present. (E, p. 48)

He makes them present, not in time, but in narrative temporality.

University of Oklahoma

NOTES

1 Jacques Lacan, *Écrits: A Selection,* trans. Alan Sheridan (New York, 1977). All
references to this book will appear in the text (E).

2 "The Structure of Allegorical Desire," in *Allegory and Representation,* ed. Stephen
J. Greenblatt (Baltimore, 1981), p. 46.

3 "The Rhetoric of Temporality," in *Interpretation: Theory and Practice,* ed. Charles
S. Singleton (Baltimore, 1969), pp. 173-210.

4 *Criticism in the Wilderness* (New Haven, 1980), pp. 88-90.

5 " 'The Captive King': The Absent Father in Melville's Text," in *The Fictional
Father: Lacanian Readings of the Text,* ed. Robert Con Davis (Amherst, 1981),
p. 50.

6 "Fathers in Faulkner," in *The Fictional Father,* p. 199. Bleikasten is quoting
Marie-Cècile and Edmond Ortigues, *Oedipe Africain.*

7 *The Genesis of Secrecy* (Cambridge, 1979), p. 94.

8 Vladimir Propp, *Morphology of the Folktale,* trans. Lawrence Scott (Austin, 1968),
p. 21.

9 "Imaginary and Symbolic in Lacan: Marxism, Psychoanalytic Criticism, and the
Problem of the Subject," *YFS,* 55/56 (1977), 350.

10 Cited by Anthony Wilden in *The Language of the Self* (New York: 1968), p. 143, n. 143.

11 Cited by Jameson, p. 378.

12 "Fiction of the Wolfman: Freud and Narrative Understanding," *diacritics*, 9 (1979), 78.

13 *On Time and Being*, trans. Joan Stambaugh (New York, 1972), p. 3.

14 Jacques Lacan, "Desire and the Interpretation of Desire in *Hamlet*," trans. James Hulbert, *YFS*, 55/56 (1977), 17.

15 *Structural Semantics*, trans. Daniele McDowell, Ronald Schleifer, Alan Velie (Lincoln, 1983). References are to chapters, sections and subsections. The "Introduction" is by Ronald Schleifer.

16 See Freud, "Neurosis and Psychosis" (1924), trans. Joan Riviere, in *General Psychoanalytical Theory*, ed. Philip Rieff (New York, 1963), p. 185.

17 See *The Four Fundamental Concepts of Psycho-Analysis*, trans. Alan Sheridan (Harmonsworth, 1977), chap. 11. All references to this book will appear in the text (FC).

18 "The Bounded Text," in *Desire in Language*, trans. Thomas Gora, Alice Jardine, Leon Roudiez (New York, 1980), p. 47.

19 *The Confidence-Man* (Indianapolis, 1967), p. 346.

20 *The Confessions of St. Augustine*, trans. John K. Ryan (New York, 1960), p. 287.

21 "Self, Time and History," in *The Fate of Reading* (Chicago, 1975), pp. 290, 287.

22 Lacan is following Indian poetics. See also Tzvetan Todorov, *Symbolism and Interpretation*, trans. Catherine Porter (Ithaca, 1982), for a discussion of symbolism, Indian poetics, and indirection.

23 *Howards End* (New York, 1921), p. 239.

24 See "Stevens' Rock and Criticism as Cure," *GaR*, 30 (1976), 28.

25 Jacques Lacan, "Seminar on 'The Purloined Letter,' " trans. Jeffrey Mehlman, *YFS*, 48 (1972), 55.

26 For such a reading of the gothic, see my "The Trap of the Imagination: The Gothic Tradition, Fiction, and 'The Turn of the Screw,' " *Crit.*, 22 (1980), 297-319.

27 "The Lady with a Dog," trans. Avrahm Yarmolinsky in *The Norton Introduction to Fiction*, ed. Jerome Beaty (New York, 1974), p. 42.

28 "Narrative Time," *CritI*, 7 (1980), 169.

29 *The Eumenides*, trans. Richard Lattimore in *Aeschylus* (Chicago, 1959), p. 171.

30 "Narration in the Psychoanalytic Dialogue," *CritI*, 7 (1980), 36.

31 I am paraphrasing Serge Leclaire: "That is Imaginary which, like shadows, has no existence of its own, and yet whose absence, in the light of life, cannot be conceived"; cited by Wilden, p. 92, n. 2.

FROM LA BOÉTIE TO MONTAIGNE: THE PLACE OF THE TEXT

ତୃ

Beryl Schlossman

le souvenir de ce mutuel amour

Lors entre aultres choses, il se print a me prier et reprier, avecques une extreme affection, de luy donner une place.

(Discours sur la mort de feu M. de la Boëtie)

As the LORD liveth, and *as* thy soul liveth, I will not leave thee.

(II Kings 2)

Biography, literary history, *petite histoire:* the particulars of the friendship between Michel de Montaigne and Etienne de la Boétie are well known.[1] Magistrate at the Bordeaux parliament, reader of the Classics, writer of verse in Greek, Latin and French and of the *Discours contre la servitude volontaire,* La Boétie became Montaigne's ideal and intimate friend: without exaggerating, one could call him Montaigne's great love. They met in 1557. In 1563 La Boétie took sick and, in the presence of Montaigne, died. After a string of love affairs, after his marriage and a second death, that of his father (Pierre Eyquem, Monseigneur de Montaigne), in 1571 Montaigne withdrew to his estate. The following inscription was found in Montaigne's library: "Privé de l'ami le plus doux, le plus cher et le plus intime, et tel que notre siècle n'en a vu de meilleur, de plus docte, de plus agréable et de plus parfait, Michel de Montaigne, voulant consacrer le souvenir de ce mutuel amour par un témoignage unique de sa reconnaissance, et ne pouvant le faire de manière qui l'exprimât mieux, a voué à cette mémoire ce studieux appareil dont il fait ses délices."[2] With this vow or dedication, Montaigne makes a reciprocal gift (and then some) to La Boétie, who had willed his library to Montaigne. So begin the melancholic delights of Montaigne's symbolic edifice, in and around reading and writing. With only a slight displacement in the text, the delights of memory declare themselves: Montaigne *a voué ce studieux appareil à cette mémoire dont il fait ses délices.* Thus Montaigne maps out the territory of his own version of *delectatio morosa,* his constant fever of love rendered as mourning. Thus he consecrates his labyrinthine workshop—another name for the *Essais.*

The relationship is complex, multiple, as full of subtle transformations as any work of baroque art. La Boétie seems to be by turns father, brother, friend and beloved for Montaigne. At the beginning of essay I,28, Montaigne underlines the symbolic tenor of his relationship to La Boétie; here at the center of Book I, he introduces La Boétie's *Contre Un,* and, in counterpoint, he introduces his own essay as a verbal attempt ("la mort entre les dents") to fulfill his symbolic inheritance from La Boétie: "Mais il n'est demeuré de luy que ce discours (. . .) et quelques mémoires (. . .) C'est tout ce que j'ay peu recouvrer de ces reliques, (c) moy qu'il laissa, d'une si amoureuse recommandation, la mort entre les dents, par son testament, héritier de sa bibliothèque et de ses papiers" (182). La Boétie's loving testament at the moment of death resonates in Montaigne's ears and thence in the *Essais* ever after. As proof of the richness and uniqueness of their relationship, Montaigne contrasts it with all others—between fathers and sons, brothers, husbands and wives, heterosexual lovers, homosexual lovers. The effect of this elaborate extended denegation is to leave Montaigne speechless, or so he says. Faced with the wholeness, perfection, uniqueness (182) and wholly spiritual quality (184) of the friendship—its infinite power, gathering together the strands of those possible relationships, simultaneously denied and implicated, knotted together, in the text of Montaigne's love—he remarks in the *a* layer of the essay: "Si on me presse de dire pourquoy je l'aymois, je sens que cela ne se peut exprimer. Il y a, au delà de tout mon discours, et de ce que j'en puis dire particulièrement, ne sçay quelle force inexplicable et fatale, mediatrice de cette union" (186-187). An overpowering affect pins Montaigne between the silence of infinite mourning and a feverish eroticism driven to commemmorate, invoke, dedicate—driven to spill over the margins of self-delineation, to construct a labyrinth of words. Mon-

taigne's friendship with La Boétie is a ceaseless awareness or repetition of its own loss—*d'en faire à tout jamais les obsèques* (376, ed.
de 1595)—suspended between love and death. Having accom-
panied his friend in his last passage, up to and into the transports
of death, Montaigne will never again be the same. Montaigne's
problematic of "alteration," anterior to the literary endeavor and
dramatically decisive as regards its focus and form, is emblematized
in Augustine's *Confessions:* "And ceaselessly Thou didst hit the
weakness of my sight with the violence of Thy light-rays upon me,
and I trembled with love and horror" (L.VII, C.X., 16).

Augustine's trembling with love and horror before the Father
indicates the meanings knotted in metaphor's rise and fall. According to Lacan, metaphor captures the essence of the paternal
function: the signifying term of procreation and the dimension of
negativity constitutive of death are indissociable. The symbolic
function of paternity is sustained by the Name-of-the-Father, iden-
tifying him as the figure of the Law and as the absolute Other.
While the other (*l'autre*) is, like the self, a source of knowledge, the
Other (*l'Autre*) opens a space or a theater of recognition rather
than knowing.[3] It seems that, given the unparalleled and spiritual
quality of the friendship with La Boétie, its acuteness and intensity
such that no other being could ever heal the wound caused by his
loss, Montaigne removes it from the realm of the dual relationship
(including agression, rivalry, etc.) and consecrates it within the
realm of the absolute Other. Montaigne thus raises the curtain on
the writing of the *Essais*.

The wound of paternal loss implicating the loss of a cherished
love object produces a prolonged and melancholic mourning.[4] The
mourner takes on the weight of the death of the beloved. Thus
Montaigne's interpretation of paternity and filiation leads him to
identify himself as "apprentif" of La Boétie's death (350) and to
identify the subject of his writing with those disquieting regions of
the self, its uncanny voyages and its "deslogement de l'ame" (351)
or passages—notably that of death. Montaigne establishes himself
in a filial, symbolic apprenticeship with respect to his friend; he
posits La Boétie's death as the site of an impossible *jouissance* that
ties them together even as it exiles La Boétie in death and Montaigne in solitude and absence ritualized as mourning: "En la vraye
amitié, de laquelle je suis expert, je me donne à mon amy plus que
je ne le tire à moy. (. . .) Et si l'absence luy est ou plaisante ou utile,
elle m'est bien plus douce que sa presence (. . .) Cette faim insati-

able de la presence corporelle accuse un peu la foiblesse en la
jouyssance des ames" (954). Montaigne describes his apprenticeship: "Je ne m'estrange pas tant de l'estre mort comme j'entre en
confidence avec le mourir" (949). This apprenticeship is rooted in
La Boétie's death, according to Montaigne's rhetorical terms in the
letter to his father: La Boétie's "deslogement" comes through to
Montaigne. The effect of the symbolic transmission of access to
the Other, coming from the mouth of the dying paternal figure,
calls forth in the self-proclaimed filial figure a new mastery of the
word. This *transmission* of the power of language takes place between Etienne de la Boétie and Michel de Montaigne, at the time
of La Boétie's death: and perhaps it is this transmission that operates the seemingly impossible erasure of the margins separating
two "souls": "En l'amitié dequoy je parle, elles [nos ames] se meslent et confondent l'une en l'autre, d'un melange si universel,
qu'elles effacent et ne retrouvent plus la couture qui les a jointes"
(186).

This mystical transmission ressembles the effusion of the prophetic spirit, which comes from God and cannot be passed on
through carnal inheritance. Montaigne's attachment to La Boétie
takes on the symbolic proportions of Elisha's relation to Elijah,
particularly at the moment of Elijah's ascension into heaven. Elisha[2]
is aware of his impending loss: he is asked: "Knowest thou that
the LORD will take away thy master from thy head to day? And
he said: Yea, I know *it;* hold ye your peace" (2 Kings 2:3). It seems
that this deep and secret knowledge is inherent in the transmission
of the prophetic power from Elijah to Elisha. Elisha asks expressly
for that transmission: "And Elisha said, I pray thee, let a double
portion of thy spirit be upon me" ("*Que me revienne une double part
de ton esprit!*") (2 Kings 2:9). It is in this sense, perhaps, that we
may reread Montaigne's remark: "Nous estions à moitié de tout;
il me semble que je luy desrobe sa part" (192). Elijah answers
Elisha's request: "Thou hast asked a hard thing: nevertheless, if
thou see me when I am taken from thee, it shall be so unto thee;
but if not, it shall not be *so*" (2,2:11). Elisha sees Elijah taken up in
the whirlwind and the prophetic transmission occurs. Elijah undergoes a Mallarméan "disparition élocutoire," counterpointed by
Elisha's passage into the prophetic voice. Montaigne's essay on
friendship and, especially, his letter to his father, indicate that La
Boétie's dying constitutes a "disparition élocutoire" for him: Montaigne takes on that disappearance, indeed, he absorbs it or takes

it up, as Elisha took up Elijah's mantle. Montaigne even *repeats* the "disparition élocutoire" by taking leave of the world and opening a passage into the *Essais*. Thus Montaigne enters the infinite spiral of writing: having loved La Boétie beyond all earthly boundaries, he reaps the whirlwind. And the obsessive and haunting *vision* of La Boétie's death, ceaselessly evoked in Montaigne's writing, sets off and consecrates the transmission: "si tu me vois pendant que je serai enlevé d'auprès de toi cela t'arrivera" (2 Kings 2:11).

De l'amitié

And so it does. He sees the beloved vanish into infinite heavenly space: he witnesses the leave-taking, the taking-away. The vastness into which the beloved disappears from sight is repeated in Montaigne's obsessive image of emptiness: "le vuide". And, as iconography, the consecrated empty space becomes a symbolic portrait in a painter's *tableau*. Montaigne begins essay I,28, by comparing himself to a painter: "Il choisit le plus bel endroit et milieu de chaque paroy, pour y loger un tableau élabouré de toute sa suffisance; et, le vuide tout au tour, il le remplit de crotesques, qui sont peintures fantasques, n'ayant grâce qu'en la variété et estrangeté. Que sont-ce icy aussi, à la vérité, que crotesques et corps monstrueux (. . .)" (181). The central image ("un tableau élabouré de toute sa suffisance"), at the exact center of Book I, was to be La Boétie's *Discours de la servitude volontaire*. But in fact Montaigne decided against publication of the *Discours* and that which is consecrated as the central core of Book I, as the portrait in its *suffisance,* is the contrary of *suffisance: "le vuide"*. The abyss opened by La Boétie's death is reified as Montaigne's permanent *insuffisance—* the outcry of bereavement, the impulse to give voice to that loss. The painter fills the emptiness around the central masterpiece with "crotesques," "which are fantastical paintings, lovely only in their variety and strangeness." This self-deprecating description of something ressembling the interlace of illuminated manuscript refers to the writing of the *Essais*. Montaigne immediately establishes a chiasmus, to figure that which he cannot unravel: the painter's central fullness (or presence) is the writer's emptiness (loss, or absence) and the painter's peripheral emptiness (or its substitute: decorative filler) is the writer's quintessential presence—the text, i.e. the arabesque of *essai(s)*.

Friendship, as opposed to love, is "la jouyssance comme estant

spirituelle, et l'ame s'affinant par l'usage (184). Montaigne's interpretation of the two kinds of love ("physical" and "ecstatic", according to the Scholastics[5]) is based on the impossibility of com-
bining friendship and sexual love in the same relationship. The
combination is desirable ("l'amitié en seroit plus pleine et plus
comble") but impossible, because of the Classical condemnation of
women ("par le commun consentement des escholes anciennes")
and the asymmetries of desire itself (185). The symbolic *jouissance*
Montaigne evokes seems to be predicated on an *ec-stasis,* a mystical
sublimation rather than a repression. It operates a mystical sewing-
together of their two souls, and an even more mystical erasure of
that seam, a dissolving of the limits and separations constituting
identity. Their souls "se meslent et confondent l'une en l'autre,
d'un mélange si universel, qu'elles effacent et ne retrouvent plus
la couture qui les a jointes" (186). It leads him to speak; it drives
him toward the prolonged arabesque of articulation in the *Essais,*
and yet the closer he gets to the knot of the *jouissance* itself, the
less he is able to answer to it. He does not know the source—or
rather, the *object*—of his *jouissance:* "Si on me presse de dire pourquoy je l'aymois, je sens que cela ne se peut exprimer, (c) qu'en
respondant: "Par ce que c'estoit luy; par ce que c'estoit moy" (186-
187). Faced with the inexpressible, unspeakable quality of his love
for La Boetie, Montaigne slips toward the use of personal pronouns, designated by Jakobson as shifters: rather than the message
itself, it is the proliferating potential of the system, or the code of
language that is emphasized here.[6] The deictic capacity of pronouns points toward the particular instance of enunciation. So it is
that the overflow of inexpressible emotion is channeled into the
creative function of language, resulting in the rare vocation of
Montaigne the writer of voluminous layers—always adding, rarely
crossing out. In this sense, Montaigne is comparable to Rousseau,
Balzac, Proust and Joyce, all writers of spectacular additions,
Proust's "paperolles."

The overflow of emotion is encoded as the logical impossibility
of the oxymoron, the figure of paradox.[7] The ordinary dual relationship, in which the other of aggression enters the realm of the
self and its desire, is characterized by Montaigne as "autres amitiez
communes" (188) liable to the reversal of love into hatred. But
Montaigne's relation to La Boétie implicates the Other in its paradoxical form—"un'ame en deux corps selon la tres-propre definition d'Aristote" (189). This oxymoron figures a double loss or

self-abandon as an overflow of boundaries; it will give rise to passion, agony, the inscription of a permanent dedication. Montaigne's metaphor is mystical and even alchemical: "C'est je ne scay quelle quinte essence de tout ce meslange, (c) qui, ayant saisi toute ma volonté, l'amena se plonger et se perdre dans la sienne; qui, ayant saisi toute sa volonté, l'amena se plonger et se perdre en la mienne, d'une faim, d'une concurrence pareille. (a) Je dis perdre, à la vérité, ne nous reservant rien qui nous fut propre, ny qui fut ou sien, ou mien" (187). The mystical tonality is neither precious nor decorative. Montaigne posits an "au delà de tout mon discours" (187) at the source of their "union", and therefore at the heart of the symbolic role taken on by Montaigne. The friendship is anticipated in an arabesque of hearsay, the circulation of language weighted with "quelque ordonnance du ciel" (187): the sublime desire of the two friends becomes imprinted with the circulation of language and is invested and concentrated in the proper name, the intensified codification of the subject's singularity, at the symbolic core of language: "nous nous embrassions par noz noms" (187). Situated somewhere between the seductive esthetic exchange of an operatic love-duet and the sacred ritual blessing (In the Name of) of the Church this description characterizes Montaigne's *dépense*—a conflation further complicated by the repressed Judaism of Montaigne's mother, Anthony de Louppes.

This *dépense* leads Montaigne back to "le vuide," "rien," "la faim," "la perte": the dimension of negativity, as Montaigne comes to know it through La Boétie's death, unfolds its mystical terms. The rest of his life, tainted by the loss of La Boétie and compared to the time spent with him "n'est que fumée, ce n'est qu'une nuit obscure et ennuyeuse" (192). The images of smoke and the dark night echo La Boétie's deathbed visions, crucial in the constitution of Montaigne's symbolic stance, and, as we shall see, his mystical experience of limits.

As if by coincidence, Montaigne alludes to the symbolic context of paternity by way of describing his own *passion*. A father seen playing with his children asks the observer not to judge him "jusques à ce qu'il fut pere luy-mesme, estimant que la passion qui luy naistroit lors en l'ame le rendroit juge equitable d'une telle action; je souhaiterois aussi parler à des gens qui eussent essayé ce que je dis" (191). Montaigne here maps out the form of the essay as a "trying out": *let them assay what I am saying.* He will take his own formulation and, out of passionate *dilection* or delight of love, turn

it around. For Montaigne's enterprise will be to assay the fraternity
of discourse: "C'est, à la verité, un beau nom et plein de dilection
que le nom de frere, et à cette cause en fismes nous, luy et moy,
nostre alliance" (183). Within this spectral framework we must read
Montaigne's *cheminement* through discourse—located in the mode
of "je" now that the "frere" has, in terms of dramatic representation (e.g. in the letter to Montaigne's father) vanished. Where? Into
the interstices of the Other: henceforth he will double the voice of
Montaigne who, in turn, out of the source of his passion founds
the essay as a process of winnowing—a gleaning evocative of the
Biblical gleaning of Ruth—and makes of it a labyrinth.

So that this passion, decisive as regards his vocation, also determines the *form* of that vocation—literally, in the terms of Montaigne's style, his slippery maintenance of voices and texts in the
wake or ruin of what gave rise to the narrative evocation of La
Boétie's death—i.e. the love that bound him to his friend, his "dilection." A confrontation of the textual grain of the *Essais* confirms
the reading of the latent context of their writing—the dialogical
background of the plurivocity embedded in what is presented as
a monologue. If monologue, then only with respect to the labyrinth
of spectral voices and *other* quotations it summons out of the smoky
night of Montaigne's solitude. His relationship to La Boétie is now
preserved within, or interiorized—there is no need for characterization or the "vraisemblable" (realistic semblance of imaginary
forms of dialogue). A reading of the *Essais* as text (and as a tex-
tualized collection or knot of texts, the individual *essais*) must take
this symbolic configuration into account. The gleaning of language, the winnowing of citation, multiplies Montaigne's inroads
into voice, indeed it reproduces a multiplicity of vocal passages in
an attempt to counter the silence of La Boétie's tomb and yet,
simultaneously, to consecrate it: "Where thou diest, will I die and
there will I be buried: the Lord do so to me,and more also, *if ought*
but death part thee and me" (Ruth 1:17). For Montaigne the space
answering to the Biblical "there" of Ruth exists on no map: it is a
textual site, the only possible answer to the parting imposed by
death and the only possible consecration and attribution of place
to the symbolic being displaced from its fleshly existence (the "deslogement de l'ame").

In the evocation of the "nuit obscure" caused by his friend's
death, Montaigne writes: "Il n'est action ou imagination ou je ne
le trouve à dire" (192). Pierre Villey glosses "à dire" as "man-

quant";[8] La Boétie, now lacking, now lost forever, must be recovered in words. The trajectory leading from La Boétie's death to the writing of the *Essais* is the passage, articulated by Montaigne between the lines of the epistolary account of La Boétie's death, from "manquant" to "à dire": *At certè semper amabo* . . .[9] At every turn, language brings love and loss face to face.

Quant à ses dernieres paroles

The *Discours sur la mort de feu M. de la Boëtie* was written in the form of a letter to Montaigne's father soon after La Boétie's death, in August 1563. With slight modifications, it appears in Montaigne's publication of La Boétie's writings (*Oeuvres*) in 1570. Clearly, it plays an important role for Montaigne, at the intersection of text and affect: as he writes it, Montaigne describes himself as torn between the "bon exemple" of La Boétie's discourse and the desire to give an account of it, and his own troubled ("desbauchée") memory which renders articulation impossible. By turns, this personal letter takes on the voices of testament, eulogy, biographical narrative and even autobiography.

La Boétie's deathbed becomes the stage for a mystical *jouissance*, shared (in part) with Montaigne, who will be the scriptor of its transmission. When Montaigne remarks in *De l'amitié* that life without La Boétie is evanescent smoke and emptiness, he underlines in mystical terms the irrevocable transmission, and perhaps the conversion, that has taken place, thereby anchoring his enunciation in the symbolic stance of his friend. For La Boétie states, in a preambula to his personalized farewell remarks, that he has learned "le peu d'asseurance qu'il y a à l'instabilité et inconstance des choses humaines, et mesme en nostre vie, que nous tenons si chere, qui n'est toutefois que fumée et chose de neant" (1351). The detachment from the realm of human activity is an integral part of the mystic's sublimation; and it is paradoxically inseparable from an intensity of passion that takes diverse forms. In La Boétie's case, the counter-balancing effect is due to his passionate confrontation of death and particularly insofar as the parting with Montaigne, above all others, lends a further dimension of significance to that experience.

Near the end, "n'ayant plus que l'image et que l'umbre d'un homme", writes Montaigne, pursuing the *visual* figures of evanescence initiated by La Boétie's figures of smoke and cloud, La

Boétie is subject to celestial *visions,* or "imaginations": " "Mon frere, mon amy, pleust à Dieu que je veisse les effects des imaginations que je viens d'avoir!" " (1358) Montaigne evokes the exchange of visionary communication which founds their enjoyment of friendship, but La Boétie can only describe his visions in a series of adjectives revealing their incommunicable quality: " "Quelles sont elles, mon frere?" luy dis-je. "Grandes, grandes", me respondit il. "Il ne feut jamais, suyvis je, que je n'eusse cet honneur que de communiquer à toutes celles qui vous venoient à l'entendement: voulez vous pas que j'en jouïsse encores?" "C'est mon dea, respondit il; mais, mon frere, je ne puis, elles sont admirables, infinies et indicibles" " (1358). La Boétie's visions led him to the *un*doing of speech, to the *dis*solution of the finite; his anaphoric discourse of the unspeakable, *l'indicible,* is located at the margins of language, where he himself is spoken by the dissolution or *défaillance* that afflicts him. As we see in this part of the text, Montaigne only partially comprehends the negative dimensions of *défaillance.*

But Montaigne does accompany La Boétie in his experience of death—a violent uprooting, a pain-filled intensity inhibiting language and giving language its stark passion, its truth. La Boétie's version of the negative dimensions of passage—*passio,* suffering, and *pesah,* the leap or passing over into another realm—symbolic, scriptural, ultimately eschatological—is consecrated by and through Montaigne. Thus, the swooning La Boétie takes leave of his wife: " "Je m'en vois dormir: bon soir, ma femme, allez vous en". Voylà le dernier congé qu'il print d'elle" (1359). But to Montaigne he says: *je m'en vois.* And so it is only Montaigne who witnesses this leave-taking: the partially shared enjoyment of mystical visibility—La Boétie's *imaginations*—echoes the prophetic transmission linking Elisha to Elijah: "if thou see me *when I am* taken from thee, it shall be so unto thee" (2 Kings 2:10). Montaigne will take up his pen to continue that infinitely extensive conversation, already formulated in terms of writing by La Boétie: "les discours que nous avions tenus . . . nous ne les portions pas seulement en la bouche, mais engravés bien avant au coeur et en l'ame" (1353). La Boétie's mystical *jouissance* affects his tongue—described by Montaigne as having new and visionary powers of eloquence— and Montaigne's pen. For La Boétie's powers ("A ce coup il sembloit que son esprit et sa langue s'efforceassent à l'envy, comme pour luy faire leur dernier service: car sans doubte je ne le veis jamais plein ny de tant et de si belles imaginations, ny de tant d'eloquence, comme il a esté le long de cette maladie" (1348)) lead him to the limits of language, the *indicible* of vision; and Montaigne, writing to his father, complains of the inadequacy of his own *style* to do justice to La Boétie's experience: "pour vous faire veoir ce courage invincible dans un corps atterré et assommé par les furieux efforts de la mort et de la douleur, je confesse qu'il y fauldroit un beaucoup meilleur style que le mien" (1347).

The privileged moment of transmission is located in the last scene of La Boétie's life, and it is countersigned by the call of Montaigne's name—La Boétie's final utterance. Montaigne describes what we are calling the moment of transmission in vivid, haunting terms; part of its symbolic, uncanny effect on the reader is the product of Montaigne's tripartite *resistance* directed against understanding the enormous weight of La Boétie's last articulation of desire and love.

Apparently, both of them realize that this is their last earthly conversation; La Boétie asks Montaigne to stay near him. He then asks him to make room for him, to create a space for him: "Lors, entre aultres choses, il se print à me prier et reprier, avecques une extreme affection, de luy donner une place" (1359). Montaigne's first rejection or denial of the potential meaning of La Boétie's request is on the grounds of reason or judgement: "De sorte que j'eus peur que son jugement feust esbranlé: mesme que luy ayant bien doulcement remontré qu'il se laissoit emporter au mal, et que ses mots n'estoient pas d'homme bien rassis" (1359). But the dying La Boétie holds his ground: "il ne se rendit point au premier coup, et redoubla encores plus fort: "Mon frere! mon frere! Me refusez-vous doncques une place?" " (1359) Montaigne continues to be obtuse in the name of reason. His second denial constitutes another refusal of the symbolic figuration of La Boétie's demand in the name of a literal interpretation of "place" as physical space: "puis-qu'il respiroit et parloit, et qu'il avoit corps, il avoit par conséquent son lieu" (1359). La Boétie corrects Montaigne's denegation: "Voire, voire, me respondit il lors, j'en ay: mais ce n'est pas celuy qu'il me fault" (1360). His third attempt emphasizes the symbolic dimensions of "une place"—not the corporeal space, but that of being itself. Montaigne must take up where the dialogue, the eloquence and the extreme affection shared with La Boétie leave off: "et puis, quand tout est dit, je n'ay plus d'estre" (1360). But Montaigne still does not seem to understand, for he answers: " "—Dieu vous en donnera un meilleur bientôt", luy feis je" (1360).

This third rejection is less a denial in physical terms of the symbolic aspect of "une place" than it is a displacement onto God of what La Boétie considers as Montaigne's role. As for Montaigne himself, we cannot know whether he was able to interpret his own denegations as such: all we know is what he writes in the *Essais*. But the style of those *Essais*, and the very project itself, demonstrate that Montaigne knew more than he was willing to let on about what was at stake in La Boétie's last request.

Thus at the end of his letter, Montaigne indicates the affective intensity of La Boétie's symbolic transmission: "Mais une heure aprez, ou environ, me nommant une fois ou deux, et puis tirant à soi un grand souspir, il rendit l'ame, sur les trois heures du mercredy matin dixhuitiesme d'aoust, l'an mil cinq cents soixante trois, aprez avoir vescu trente deux ans, neuf mois, et dix-sept jours" (1360). The transmission of singular voice has taken place and is sealed in the final *calling* (*l'appel*/*la vocation*) of Montaigne's name by La Boétie—his last word. But what of Montaigne's affective stance here? It seems to disappear or at least to break down, for the text ends on a note of impersonal precision. Just as Montaigne denied the significance of La Boétie's last wish, so he elides all mention of his own affect. Here again, however, the Freudian concept of repression allows for an interpretation of Montaigne's text. The painstaking numerical account of La Boétie's life and death resembles certain inexplicably petty and mathematically precise annotations in Leonardo's journal. Freud interprets them in the light of a list of small expenses for Caterina's burial; Caterina was, of course, Leonardo's mother, and it is his love for her which, become unconscious, found its representation in the symptomatic act of making obsessively detailed lists.[10] Thus Montaigne's love for La Boétie makes itself known in the apparently indifferent epitaph which marks his permanent plunge into mourning.

Feu de fiebvre

La Boétie's death constitutes a mystical *ecstasis* which is also Montaigne's experience; he responds to it with an ecstasy of mourning which, as will become clear, belongs to La Boétie—albeit *après coup*. This experience takes place at the cusp of significance which erases their limits or, as Montaigne would say, the seam joining their two souls together. So the boundary-less images of mystical experience—*fumée, néant, noche obscura*—take on an essential role in giving metaphorical and allegorical voice to an experience of the ineffable. One important visionary image, for others as well as for La Boétie, is the cloud or *nue:* "Mais le dimanche, il eust une grand' foiblesse; et comme il feut revenu à soy, il dict qu'il luy avoit semblé estre en une confusion de toutes choses, et n'avoir rien veu qu'une espesse neu, et brouillart obscur, dans lequel tout estoit pesle-mesle et sans ordre; toutesfois qu'il n'avoit eu nul desplaisir à tout cet accident" (1349). La Boétie's vision of the cloud continues the series of images and is itself exemplary of the terms of mystical experience: chaos (*tohu-bohu* in Genesis, here "une confusion de toutes choses"), the abyss (*le neant,* the vacuum from which the creation proceeds, *ex nihilo*), the limitless, indefinitely extensive or immeasurable dimensions (in this instance, of cloud and fog), and darkness (here, the "brouillart *obscur*", the "*espesse* nue": the focus of this term as well is in Genesis, and it is repeated elsewhere—"and the light shineth in darkness").

Montaigne's version of La Boétie's experience gives rise to a visionary vocabulary in which several elements cluster around the *nue:* separation, the abyss, the silence of the dying man, the ravishment of death and the sublime loss of the beloved for the mourner.[11] Perhaps Montaigne's constellation of terms can be read not only as an attempt to enter into the mystical apprenticeship of death but also, given Montaigne's passionate attachment to La Boétie, as an attempt to continue the reciprocity desired in friendship and love through *a sustained sharing of metaphorical language,* beyond the frontiers of silence (or the radical alteration of symbolic discourse) imposed by death. Thus when Montaigne evokes the "nuit obscure" endured since La Boétie's death, he seems to indicate the extent to which he has entered the mystical realm of that death— and, desiring it, made it his own.

Thus Montaigne writes with such authority about death, throughout the *Essais;* and, in the letter, he represents his dialogue with La Boétie within the terms of the experience of negativity. This experience takes on the dimensions of *tout ou rien:* after the vision of the "espesse nue, et brouillart obscur," Montaigne notes his remark to La Boétie: " "La mort n'a rien de pire que cela, luy dis je lors, mon frere.—Mais n'a rien de si mauvais", me respondit il" (1349). It should be clear that the urgent intensity of enunciation informing Montaigne's texts (as well as the texts of Ruth and The Book of Kings) has a common source in the enunciation of the Judaic God: "Le je qui dit *je suis celui qui suis,* ce *je,* absolument

seul, est celui qui soutient radicalement le *tu* dans son appel."[12]
The space opened up by Montaigne in the letter to his father, i.e.
the space created by his desire-laden entry into La Boetie's death,
is decisive with respect to his scriptural vocation. As such it constitutes a possible answer to the question asked with such passion
by La Boétie: *mon frere, me donneras-tu une place?*

On a conscious level, Montaigne is not quite able to assimilate
the symbolic consequences of this question, just as he is not quite
able to admit the "extreme affection" producing it as related to the
sexuality of amorous relationships. Of those with women, he
writes: "son feu, je le confesse, est plus actif, plus cuisant et plus
aspre. Mais c'est un feu temeraire et volage, ondoyant et divers,
feu de fiebvre, subject à accez et remises (. . .) La jouyssance le
perd, comme ayant la fin corporelle et sujecte à satiété" (184). And
yet the reader may sense that Montaigne is on shaky ground here,
for Montaigne describes La Boétie's parting in slightly displaced
terms of love—"moi qu'il laissa, d'une si amoureuse recommandation, la mort entre les dents" (182). The sublimation constitutes
a detour around the troubling domains of desire, since "l'amour"
is "volage": the Fall casts its shadow on love from within, for its
limitation is a structural one: "La jouyssance le perd". Montaigne
seems to say that the drives impose a finite dimension on love, and
he dismisses it—thereby safeguarding his own sublime love from
disquieting ambiguities.

But the continents of art, theology and psychoanalysis testify to
what Montaigne would judge to be a blurring of boundaries between different forms of love. That very blurring—or slippage,
or doubling—is at the core of the experience of the amorous subject. And, after all, Montaigne is as good an example as any that
love leads to words—a privileged form of what Georges Bataille
theorized as *dépense*. In *Fragments d'un discours amoureux*, Roland
Barthes evokes *dépense* or "la perte 'pour rien'," as integral to amorous discourse: "la Dépense est ouverte, à l'infini, la force dérive
sans but (l'objet aimé n'est pas un but: c'est un objet-chose, non un
objet-terme)."[13] Language becomes an infinite gift, an infinite *glis-
sade* circling around the beloved; the amorous subject never
reaches an end—the beloved is not the target, writes Barthes, but
then the beloved can never quite be possessed either. The only
possession is that which afflicts the subject in love—who gives what
he or she does not have, according to Lacan's parable of the egg,
the slice and the *hommelette*.[14] Who gives what cannot be given:

language. Perhaps the ultimate symptom of the *non-rapport amou-reux* lies here, for the infinite gift is impossible to give—it is always somewhere else; and its equally impossible reception would imply the (impossible) possession of the beloved as such.

And so it is no wonder that La Boétie could not quite make his last request understood; and no wonder that the unavowed emblem of Barthes' text, the indigestible fragment, is the silent telephone. But the impossible gift of language leads back to La Boétie's gift of his library ("d'une si amoureuse recommandation"), Montaigne's reinscription of it in his own library, and the amorous pleasure of the dedication. Thus, from one gift to another, the givers themselves are tied together. However, they are linked less by the material gifts than by the exchange of the *power* of language, in the case of La Boétie's transmission to Montaigne; and, under-lined in Montaigne's re-inscription of that gift in the commemmoration of his own library, that power takes the shape of a fragment of amorous discourse. Barthes writes: "On ne peut donner du langage mais on peut le dédier."[15] But he then qualifies even the dedication as ineffective, and notes that the only real possibility for an amorous gift of language lies in the *multiple inscription* of the beloved within the text.

Thus, despite his arguments to the contrary, Montaigne's predicament is an amorous one, as is his discourse. Infinite, and without aim; filled to overflowing with its own emptiness and offering what it does not possess; disseminating the fragmented presence of the beloved, and circling endlessly around the consecrated space of the beloved's absence—these formulations of love's discourse bear a striking resemblance to Montaigne's remarks, in the *Essais,* regarding his own writing.

L'escrivaillerie

The amorous solution is writing—the amorous subject dissolved, or suspended in solution. It would be only a slight exaggeration to see the *Essais,* particularly the third book, as an infinite love-letter.[16] Seventeen years after La Boétie's death, Montaigne writes in his *Journal de voyage:* "Ce mesme matin escrivant à M. Ossat, je tumbé en un pensément si pénible de M. de la Boetie, et y fus si longtamps, sans me raviser, que cela me fit grand mal" (1270). La Boétie's beloved presence and the solitude imposed on Montaigne by his death or absence are disseminated throughout the *Essais;*

indeed, the trial or assaying of different discourses—and, in book
III, of autobiography itself—is a form of textualization (an amorous solution?) of Montaigne's relationship with La Boétie and its
consummation in La Boétie's death as formulated in the letter to
Montaigne Père.

Montaigne is both melancholic and in perpetual mourning: he
finds his voice in the effects of the *épreuve/essai* of desire and death.
La Boétie's death leaves him at a loss—from without (as mourner,
he will retire from society) and from within (deprived of himself
by half, as melancholic): "In mourning it is the world which has
become poor and empty; in melancholia it is the ego itself."[17] The
défaillance—swoon and fall—of the melancholic mourner is formulated as emptiness (*rien, vide, faim, absence*—the recurring terms
of Montaigne's loss) and as hemorrhage, the wound's overflow:
"chacun se donne si entier à son amy, qu'il ne luy reste rien à
departir ailleurs", "les plaisirs mesmes qui s'offrent à moy, au lieu
de me consoler, me redoublent le regret de sa perte" (190, 192).
The term of loss—"sa perte"—articulates La Boétie's death as the
abrupt turn of infinite giving or overflow into total and over-
whelming emptiness: "the complex of melancholia behaves like an
open wound (. . .) emptying the ego until it is totally impover-
ished". "But the free libido (. . .) served to establish an *identification*
of the ego with the abandoned object. Thus the shadow of the
object fell upon the ego (. . .) The ego wants to incorporate this
object into itself".[18] The mourner must somehow reverse the loss
and turn the emptiness back into a form of overflow; the influx
of the object's shadowy presence leads from *privation* to *jouissance*
in the form of infinite mourning. Indeed, the *privation* itself becomes *jouissance:* "Est-ce pas un pieux et plaisant office de ma vie,
d'en faire à tout jamais les obsèques? Est-il jouyssance qui vaille
cette privation?" (376, éd. de 1595). The only possible recourse is
a visionary one: "La jouyssance et la possession appartiennent prin-
cipalement à l'imagination" (953). The infinite *dépense "pour rien"*
takes the form of an unending luxury of words: "Qui ne voit que
j'ay pris une route par laquelle, sans cesse et sans travail, j'iray
autant qu'il y aura d'ancre et de papier au monde?" (922) This
jouissance is a symbolic one. Montaigne's voyage leads him from
the love of La Boétie to its consecration and amorous solution in
writing, in an overflow of ink.

Montaigne's scriptural experience ceaselessly leads him back to
La Boétie's death, or rather, to its visionary dimensions meta-

phorically coded as *passage* and *voyage* by both La Boétie and Montaigne, according to the text of the letter to Montaigne's father. The evocation of these terms runs throughout the *Essais:* "je peins le passage", says Montaigne, "le voyage", "l'alongeail", "une route (. . .) d'ancre et de papier", forming a constellation of privileged terms referring to his scriptural and increasingly autobiographical activity. After La Boétie's vision, he mentions "le passage que j'ay desja franchy à demy" (1350); at the time of his second series of visions, Montaigne describes him as beginning "à tirer aux traicts de la mort" (defined as *s'engager dans le passage*). La Boétie takes communion ("feit ses pasques") and evokes the pascal transmission: "Je proteste que comme j'ay esté baptizé, ay vescu, ainsi veulx je mourir soubs la foy et religion que Moïse planta premierement en Ægypte" (1358). Even as La Boétie operates a symbolic transmission—of name and letter, of love's symbolic space—with respect to Montaigne, he awaits death ("elle": Montaigne's unavowed feminine rival, perhaps) with all the gallantry of a lover: " "Bien! bien! qu'elle vienne quand elle vouldra, je l'attends, gaillard et de pied coy": mots qu'il redict deux ou trois fois en sa maladie" (1358). One might well ask whether this declaration, from the writer of love sonnets, did not forever cristallize the disquieting image of femininity which Montaigne disavows and dismisses from the domain of love. After marriage, after a series of affairs . . . the writing of the *Essais.*

Montaigne himself notes that writing is symptomatic of emptiness and overflow, of disquiet and ruin; "L'escrivaillerie semble estre quelque simptome d'un siècle desbordé. Quand écrivismes nous tant que depuis que nous sommes en trouble? Quand les Romains tant, que lors de leur ruyne?" (923) Montaigne maintains both sets of affective figures—emptiness and overflow, preservation and ruin, within the paradoxical terms of his writing. His "simptome"—halfway between the medieval form, "sinthome", which, according to Lacan,[19] allows for the resonance of the name of Saint Thomas d'Aquin, and the modern form, "symptôme", which he says results from the injection of Greek into the French language—takes the form not of dialogue, but, rather, of *contradiction.* As in Freud's concept of the *Verneinung,* the yes and the no do not cancel each other out; they are maintained within the text. Montaigne's discovery, the symptom of his amorous solution, is the essay (or "assay", not to be confused with the modern notion of the essay) as a weave of contradictions, a *meandering* that preserves the self and the other—not unrelated to Joyce's notion of the text, in *Finnegans Wake:* a *meanderthalltale.*

Montaigne's *sinthome,* his "fleur du symbolique," is the essay as labyrinth, arabesque, textual interlace. The *Essais* constitute his response to La Boetie's final request, asked, in extreme affection, as a question. One might relay this question with another, unasked but pervasive: how is it possible to make of La Boétie's death an amorous *jouissance?*

The Johns Hopkins University

NOTES

1 Several critics have discussed the relationship between La Boétie and Montaigne in psychoanalytic terms; however, their interpretations and conclusions differ from my own (cf. A. Wilden, "Par divers moyens on arrive à pareille fin: A reading of Montaigne," *MLN* 83, (1968) pp. 577-97; J. Mehlman, "La Boétie's Montaigne", *Oxford Literary Review,* 4.1, (1979), pp. 45-61; F. Rigolot, "Montaigne's Purloined Letters", *YFS,* (1983), pp. 145-66.) Rigolot's article is particularly illuminating as regards Montaigne's literary models and textual revisions of the letter on La Boétie's death. Also of interest, although outside the scope of this paper, is the literary tradition of the *ars moriendi.* This immensely popular tradition of the early fifteenth century produced a wealth of devotional literature throughout the Renaissance, and located its own source in Jean de Gerson's *De arte moriendi.* (Cf. N. L. Beaty, *The Craft of Dying,* Yale Univ. Press, 1970.)

2 Quoted in the "Chronologie de Montaigne" in *Oeuvres complètes,* Gallimard, Bibl. de la Pléïade, 1962, p. xvi. Page references to Montaigne's text, including the letter to his father, refer to this edition, and will henceforth be found in parentheses following each quotation.

3 J. Lacan, *Ecrits,* Seuil, 1966, p. 278, 555 and *Séminaire III,* Seuil, 1981, p. 51.

4 Montaigne's condition evokes the context of *Hamlet* and the Shakespearean interpretation of paternity and filiation. Through Hamlet, Shakespeare articulates the dimensions of speech that he incarnates; scandal, thwarted act, lust and murder make Hamlet talk his way even into death. The act of murder designates the dead king as the agency of paternal power holding the keys to the other, i.e. the desired mother; and it is this very agency which consigns the holder of the keys to the symbolic region of the Other, and of the authentic King. So it is that the spectral King Hamlet, whose death has an unmistakeable aura of exile, makes himself heard by prince Hamlet. It is the effect of the symbolic transmission of access to the Other, coming from the dead King's mouth, that calls forth in *prince* Hamlet a new and subtle mastery of the word.

5 Cf. P. Rousselot, *Pour l'histoire du problème de l'amour an moyen âge,* Münster, 1909.

6 R. Jakobson, *Essais de linguistique générale,* Minuit, 1969, t.1, ch. 9.

7 Cf. E. Benveniste, *Problèmes de linguistique générale,* Gallimard, 1974, t. II, p. 256.

8 *Essais,* Librairie Felix Alcan, Paris, 1922, p. 249.

9 The mystical experience of limits which gives rise to poetic scripture centered on death and love is evoked by the same figure (*la noche obscura*) in the poetry of San Juan de la Cruz. For San Juan, the Song of Songs functions as the touchstone of metaphor, whereas for Montaigne, classical poetry fills this role.

10 S. Freud, "Leonardo da Vinci and a Memory of his Childhood", ch. 3, in *Standard Edition of the Complete Psychological Works*, The Hogarth Press and the Institute of Psychoanalysis, London, 1953-1974, vol. XI.

11 Montaigne's mystical terms reappear at the end of the nineteenth century in Mallarmé's late sonnet "A la nue accablante tu". It is a poem of loss, couched in the terms of mystical experience (*la nue, l'abîme*, the silence of *tu*, the sublime loss itself—*quelque perdition haute*) as absorbed and modulated by Mallarmé within the constellation of metaphors of his poetic language. The subject of the poem is death: its ravishment takes the form of a structural alternative. Who/ what has died assumes the sublime form of the "sépulcral naufrage", the shipwreck, or the meager form of "Le flanc enfant d'une sirène". *La nue* is *accablante*, crushing; an archaic meaning of *accabler* is *abattre, achever:* to kill, to bring down, to finish off. Mallarmé's cloud brings together the experience of death in its visionary dimensions, and that of the mourner's loss as well. The focus on the *"tu"*—a vocable that haunts this poem—thus opens out from the silence it posits as qualifying the "sépulcral naufrage": the silence takes on its singular "sépulcral" status in the wake of the *je/tu* relationship founding the act of enunciation (evoked in lines 5 and 6). Finally, as regards the mourner's vision or *accablement*, Mallarmé's "flanc enfant d'une sirène" confirms the context he shares with Montaigne. For the childish female flesh that makes of him another life-long mourner is that of his sister Maria, his "idéal dans la mort".

12 J. Lacan, *Ecrits, op.cit.*, p. 323.

13 Seuil, 1977, p. 99-100.

14 J. Lacan, *Séminaire* XI, Seuil, 1973, ch. XVI.

15 R. Barthes, *op.cit.*, p. 91.

16 Barthes writes: "Ce matin-là, je dois écrire de toute urgence une lettre "importante"—dont dépend le succès d'une certaine entreprise; mais j'écris à la place une lettre d'amour—que je n'envoie pas" (*Ibid.*, p. 30).

17 S. Freud, "On Mourning and Melancholia", *S.E., op.cit.*, vol. 14, p. 246.

18 *Ibid.*, p. 253, 249.

19 J. Lacan, "Le sinthome", Séminaire, 1975-76, in *Ornicar?*, Paris, vol. 5-11.

Oedipus Wrecks:
Lacan, Stendhal and the Narrative Form of the Real

❧

Juliet Flower MacCannell

La crystallisation de la maitresse d'un
homme, ou sa BEAUTÉ, n'est autre chose
que la collection de TOUTES LES SATIS-
FACTIONS de tous les désirs qu'il a pu
former à son égard.
Stendhal, *De l'Amour*, ch. xi

It is undoubtedly to semiolinguistics and structuralism that the enormous interest in narrative and narrative theory in the mid-twentieth century may be attributed. Using Vladimir Propp's *Morphology* and Claude Lévi-Strauss' *Mythologiques* in combination with certain of the Russian formalisms, the structuralists around Roland Barthes—Claude Brémond, A. J. Greimas, and Tzvetan Todorov—were, in French criticism at least, able to make major analytic strides in understanding the structure of narrative by formulating models for their deductive study. The very heart of narrative is laid bare in their work, which Barthes himself celebrated in his famous 1966 essay "Introduction to the Structural Study of Narrative" (translated into English in 1975).[1] Narrative, like a primitive myth, is seen by structural analysts as free from all mimetic constraints. It is that form which is not enslaved to reality. This freedom (of will; the arbitrary) is crucially important for structuralism. Narrative is, however, also the locus of a certain lack of freedom. In narrative one discovers the existence of certain bindings and constraints: to wit, the constraints of the linguistic code, or *grammar* itself (Saussure), and of the *social order* (Durkheim)—in short, the structures of that which Lacan has named "the Symbolic." But this particular set of constraints is not, for Barthes, a problem or a tragedy; the structural imperatives of narrative are for him a major cultural achievement. They overcome that very "first form" ever discovered by mankind—repetition, the mimetic imitation or reproduction of reality. The positioning of narrative vis-a-vis arbitrary cultural, rather than necessary natural limits, like Kant's cultural versus the natural order, sets us free by the very act of limitation itself: free from enslavement (via repetition) to the reality of the natural system (Barthes: 1966: 271-72). It is, therefore, with a tone of celebration that Barthes ends his essay with the correlation of the discovery of the grammatical structure of the sentence (and by extension of narrative) and the Oedipal narrative:

> Although we know little more about the origins of narrative than we know about the origins of language, it can reasonably be argued that narrative is contemporaneous with monologue, whose emergence seems to be posterior to that of dialogue. In any case, even without stretching the phylogenetic theory, it may be significant that man's offspring should have "invented" at the same time (around the age of three) both the sentence and Oedipus' narrative.
>
> (Barthes: 1966: p. 272)

The drama enacted or reenacted by narrative is the Oedipal myth in which culture, like ideal sexuality, is founded by an original absence of reality (of the Father), by a break with the I / thou relationship to the mother, and the disguised, guilty, and anxious desire for the death of the father, in all its anti-mimetic, fictive and narrative dimensions. Narratives as the burying of these primal wishes become in effect the triumph of civilization over the primal, the violent, the instinctual.

By the early 1970's one is no longer so sure of the positive qualities or aspects of the Oedipal, the narrative; the "three year old" one begins to write about is no longer a little boy, but a little girl, as in Lacoue-Labarthe and Nancy's interest in Schlegel's "little Wilhelmine" in *Lucinde*.[2] Oedipus has undergone the critique—feminist, Lacanian, deconstructionist—that psychoanalysis (both Freudian and Lacanian), in contrast to idealism and to the idealism of structuralism, had always already implied. In 1973 Barthes writes in *Le Plaisir du texte* about the passing, the overcoming both of Oedipus and of narrative:

> Death of the Father would deprive literature of many of its pleasures. If there is no longer a Father, why tell stories? Doesn't every narrative

lead back to Oedipus? Isn't storytelling always a way of searching for one's origin, speaking one's conflicts with the Law, entering into the dialectic of tenderness and hatred? Today, we dismiss Oedipus and narrative at one and the same time: we no longer love, we no longer fear, we no longer narrate. As fiction, Oedipus was at least good for something; to make good novels, to tell good stories. . . .

(Barthes, 1978, p.47).

And we hear the same tone of rueful defense of a declining Western culture in Thomas Hanzo's recent essay on Dickens' *Bleak House:*

The paternal metaphor has for so long served to designate the means whereby the individual enters culture that it seems to be necessary to human culture as Western thought understands it. Perhaps the metaphor will continue to serve and the familial source of individuality continue to be valued, though a critical awareness of the adoption of sexual roles will no doubt modify these judgments.

(1981, p. 192)

One of the founding myths, the foundational metaphors of our culture, has clearly come unglued; as the great Russian comparatist Bakhtin has taught us, once a value has to be voiced, it is no longer truly a value, but only a symbol of it, a topic of discourse, and it ceases to organize life (1973, p. 102).

Oedipus is waning: is narrative waning with it?

We can, with Barthes and Hanzo, mourn the passing of Oedipus or we can delight in it—as Deleuze and Guattari do, with their liberated return to the Imaginary and its schizophrenia. Still other roads can be taken: we can translate Oedipus into other cultures, non-Western ones, like Edmond Ortigues,[3] or we can, with Kristeva, try to explore structures that appear *before* the hegemony of the phallus over other signifiers occurs (in the castration complex), before the coercions of the symbolic (see her studies of the Renaissance madonnas,[4] for example). But whatever route is taken it is nevertheless clear that Oedipus, and narrative with him, will never be the same, will never again be the unquestioned and unconsciously accepted basis for our particular culture, our fictional structures.

Why not?

If there has been a loosening of Oedipus it has been due in no small measure to the writings of Jacques Lacan, to whom both pro- and anti-Oedipal stances have been attributed, but whose work clearly stands at the central point in the various directions that Oedipus has taken narrative theory. Of course, Freud discovered

Oedipus. He indeed made him the basis not merely of something like narrative, but all of civilization—and its discontents. But Freud's discovery hardly had the same kind of direct impact on literary theory that Lacan's has had, and for good reason. Freud's theory is so clearly derivative of literature that in fact literature seems to be devalued: the later, scientific theory unmasks structures covered over or only latent in the literary texts. This is not the case for Lacan's work, in which the concern for form and figure is at the heart of his theory, and it is literary form that brings insight to psychoanalysis.

Partly because Freud is introduced so belatedly into the French tradition—a tradition steeped since the 12th century at least in meditations on love and desire—the introduction is traumatic for French literature. In an "Eliotic" fashion Freud operates to reevaluate the canon, as the array of current reinterpretations of the tradition reveals: Foucault's history of sexuality as discourse (confessional), Derrida's rereading of Rousseau, Condillac, Genet, et al.; Deleuze on Kant and on Proust; Kristeva's recent very important work on 17th century quietism, the troubadours, and Celine among others; even Sarah Kofman's neo-Nietzschean reinterpretations of Kant and Rousseau or Lacoue-Labarthe's of Diderot[5]—can all be said to have been, if only topically, given impetus by the retarded entry of Freud into French life and letters.

But to say "Freud" means the Freud taught by Lacan, and Lacan's texts generate, like Rousseau's or Nietzsche's, opposing and contradictory interpretations of his rhetorical stance or attitude. It is not his political positions on the symbolic, the phallus, etc., that are the reason for his vast influence in disseminating Freud: who could or would say without hesitation just exactly what those positions are?* Rather, the fact that Lacan has, in the deepest way, *historicized* what in Freud is *universal* appears to be responsible for his enormous impact. Lacan has shown that the structures Freud revealed are just that—structures: he has shown that these structures are man-made, symbolic, institutions subject to change. But he has also shown that there are key, nameable historical turning points in which the elaboration of these symbolic structures deepens or weakens, expands or subsides. What Freud could do for individual psychic histories Lacan in fact does for the psychic history of his particular culture.

* The politics of feminism and its attitude toward Lacan make this abundantly clear: from Juliet Mitchell, Rosalind Coward and John Ellis to Jane Gallop and Jacques Derrida the range of interpretations is vast.

For Lacan has introduced what is, in effect, a two-tiered system into the structure of the *forms* utilized by the psyche in its dual states (the conscious and the unconscious). And once he makes the distinction between the Imaginary and the Symbolic, between processes and figures, between condensation and displacement, on the one side, and metaphor and metonymy on the other, then he gives us access to the *history* of these forms in the tension of their relationship to each other. For example, as a "primary process" condensation facilitates the freeflowing of psychic energy, it is a process of unbinding; at the conscious level, as the figure "metaphor," the same form is one of restriction of choices, a limitation of a paradigmatically defined set of options. The Imaginary and the Symbolic, even in the very same formal structure, carry opposite and contradictory meanings or imperatives. Such is the basic aporia of the dualized psyche, the crucial opposition that generates (its) history.

But Lacanian theory offers something more than this historical method—itself a valuable contribution—and it is to this something more that I wish to turn my attention here. Lacan, everyone knows, has a third element in his system, an element that exists beyond (or behind?) the opposition of the Imaginary and the Symbolic. It is an element that, for good or for ill, has resisted specification, discussion and exposition: the Real. (See below, p. 916.) And if it betokens something like an unOedipal situation then the lack of analysis and explication may be indeed significant. For if there were a possibility for a non-Oedipal situation that would not be a sidestep to another culture, nor yet a return to a paradisiac pre-Oedipal state (at least not in the naive sense), then such a possibility would have considerable impact on our attachment to Oedipus in a nostalgic and defensive mode. It is the dimly perceived possibility of what our culture—our literature, our ideal sexuality—would be if it were not dominated by the primacy of the phallus, the wound of castration, the Oedipal. The Real is the possibility of that which is always revolutionary.

And after all it is the desire for the Real* that exasperates both the artist and the child. Both artist and child must create metaphoric substitutes for the desire the Real incites in them, because the Symbolic, the Law, the *Non / nom du pere*, has already barred them from directly fulfilling that desire. It is thus that Oedipus has its positive, palliative effects: it frees us, at least, from the

---

* which may well turn out to be that signified which has slid under the domination of the (phallic) signifier: the *only* signified, the mother.

perpetual and painful knowledge of the object of our desire. Through Oedipus, through the fictional, we can look for our (guilty) origins, secure in the fact that we will never have to find them. Like God they will always, thanks to Oedipus, remain hidden by the protective veil of these fictions, these metaphors. The narrative quest for origins and for ends will and must always be frustrated by Oedipus: if desires are satisfied, the Father is dead, the Mother possessed and the story ends. (One might recall here *Rameau's Nephew* in which the philosopher says that without education the child would end by dashing in his father's brains and sleeping with his mother).

The question remains—and it is crucial for literature, as well as for the literary stance that sees itself necessarily dependent upon Oedipus for its glory—as to whether the loss of the (painful) privilege of the Oedipal metaphor is the end of the story, in both the literal and figurative senses. For Lacan, Oedipus is not only a fortunate misfortune, the pain and anxiety with which civilization must pay for its rewards: it is also a cruel trick. Lacan calls it *"un truchement"*[6]—a metaphor that does not have the honesty to be consciously rhetorical.

For what Lacan demonstrates, as Freud did not, is that the structural basis of Oedipus, the source of its symbolic potency, is a simple linguistic paradigm, in which a basic dialogic couple, I and thou (mother and child / peer and peer), becomes a grammatical structure capable of generating another participant: "I" and "you" generate, as Benveniste has so convincingly shown us, a third term, "he," "she," or most importantly "it," a third term that not only disrupts the initial dyad, not only comes to dominate it as hero or topic, but eventually legislates it. (Julia Kristeva's analysis of *Rameau's Nephew* suggests that "he" displaces and obliterates "you" in dialogue.)[7] The "he"—God, the father, It—becomes more than "he"; it expands to become the Symbolic, and it interrupts the direct exchange of the original dyad to such an extent that interhuman interaction *must* henceforth go through its particular circuit. (See Lacan, *Sem. II*, p. 94 ff.).

Grammar, the simple taking up of a position, becomes "metaphorized": and the complicity of metaphor and metaphysics, suspected from Bakhtin to Heidegger and Derrida, is not far off on the horizon. In moving to this rhetorical level from the grammatical, the very nature of the unconscious becomes denatured: the "it" or *id* is no longer the relatively simple container of unnamed, unspeakable desires for a *mother* who was both its displaced signi-

fier and its unnameable signified, it is now an entire network or
tangle of rules and regulations whose representative is the *father*.
This crucial displacement, cruelly ironic, is the great prank that
culture plays on the individual subject: Look for your mother and
you'll find your father.[8]

Thus the question of the Real naturally poses itself: now that we
have uncovered the trick, the mechanism of the division of the
subject into Imaginary and Symbolic, what do we do about it?
Clearly we cannot return to being positioned by ruses of rhetoric,
at least not naively; but what, if any, are the alternatives?

Without Oedipus are we condemned to the cultural sterility that
the Real and its mere repetition or imitation (*sans* the translation
of metaphor) gives us? Is the dyadic couple, the desiring couple,
after all, the Real?

In some ways, à la Hegel, Lacan has been thought to be a cele-
brant of the Symbolic, of the structural order, of the mediation
that the Symbolic—fortunately for civilization—makes in the overly
intimate I / thou relationship. If so, how could the Real have a *story*
that escapes the Symbolic? What kind of *form* could or would it
have? Clearly the traditional "love story" (see Erich Segal for the
stereotype), with its dying or cadaverous heroines, its melancholic,
dissatisfied heroes (Rene, Atala, Adolphe, etc.) who live on beyond
the women, is surely not the innovative form of story that a post-
Oedipal Real would require. Neither would the formlessness, the
symbolic absence that is the soap opera be a satisfactory alternative.

History has already moved us beyond Oedipus, and if there is
any possibility for constructing a post-Oedipal situation in life and
letters (and even in colleges of letters and science) it is plainly our
responsibility to discover it.

The basis for a post-Oedipal condition lies in the Real; but
finding the Real is no simple task, for on the one hand it demands
an impossible attempt to think form beyond Oedipal narrative con-
ventions, and on the other hand it squares off against the current
critical readings of the Real in Lacan: first, the assertion by Fredric
Jameson that the Real is "History itself," an open-ended narrative
that basically criticizes the closed, Oedipal form; second, a reading
that even the most lucid explicators of Lacan have difficulty escaping, the sense, as Malcolm Bowie writes, that the Real is impossible to distinguish from the Symbolic except in the fact that it
is "ineffable." (198, p. 135):[9]

> When we appear on the scene as subjects certain games have already
> been played, certain dice thrown. Things *are*. . . . The way beyond this

'laughable' Real is the uniquely human way offered by the Symbolic order: thanks to that order the dice may be thrown again. Secondly, however, the Real is that primordial chaos upon which language operates ... the Real is given its structure by the human power to name.

Neither of these conceptions is at all original, and the language of common sense plays a prominent role in the presentation of each. And their divergence is only apparent. They place a common stress on the limits of linguistic power; the Real is that which is radically extrinsic to the procession of signifiers. ... It is the irremediable and intractable 'outside' of language, the infinitely receding goal towards which the signifying chain tends; the vanishing point of the Symbolic and the Imaginary alike. ... The Real comes close to meaning 'the ineffable' or 'the impossible.'

Lacan's epigrammatical formulation of the Real as that "which resists symbolization absolutely,"[10] has, however, been completely overlooked for what it might contain as clues to the Real. In particular, a certain *literary* (and literary historical) way of reading that epigram. In our literary history, that is, there is more than one author who has "resisted symbolization absolutely" and a glance in that direction may indeed be revealing. I propose therefore to do a reading of an author whose writing seems often the very epitome of the Real, who indeed invents the Real narrative, and who yet shows neither signs of a sterile mimesis, nor of the sly detours of Oedipus and his metaphors. That author is none other than Stendhal.

My essay at this point necessarily moves in two directions at once: I will deal with the Real in Stendhal and with the Real as it has been construed by critics in the writing of Lacan.

I. Stendhal and the Question of the Real

Gérard Genette once remarked of Stendhal that he cannot be psychoanalyzed since he has himself already performed the task in his *Henry Brulard*, with its startling prefiguration of Freud: the auto-analysis of his physical desire for his mother, his rejection of the name of the father, the precise Oedipal paradigm which is quite clearly laid out in this curious autobiography. And the Stendhal text is in fact even somewhat closer to Lacan than to Freud on the Oedipal question: his is a quite lucid rejection of the original encounter with the *non / nom du père* in which, as an ideal male, he should have come to sacrifice his desire for his mother in order to

be constituted as a subject. Bowie describes the process in Lacan
thus:

> The original encounter with the legislating *nom-du-père* and the abiding
> lack and non-satisfaction to which the subject is thereby condemned,
> produce the complex pattern of intermingled aggression and subser-
> vience which is to mark the subject in his dealings with others. Lacan
> makes frequent use of Hegel's dialectic of master and slave as an easily
> reconstruable model for this process.
>
> ("Lacan," p. 135)

Condemned to this ambiguous condition, the Oedipally based
subjectivity must remain unsatisfied: it is the law of the *lack of
satisfaction of desire* that is by all accounts necessary for the newly
constituted subject to enter into mature, civil life. And yet this is
not so for Stendhal: he never gives up the hope for satisfaction.

Nevertheless, and at the same time, we have in Stendhal not only
an author of some of the greatest novels and narratives ever
written—some, like the *Italian Chronicles,* more than innovative in
form and structure—Oedipal in structure only to the extent that
Oedipus is critically treated therein. And Stendhal is an author
who meditated on the delights and the importance specifically of
a *civilized* love (see *Love,* ch. 6): there is no hint of "primitivism" in
his conception of a love that would not escape all form, only those
forms that would castrate it.

Stendhal is often seen as an anomaly, or rather an anachrony,
that is, as an eighteenth-century sensibility caught in the alternately
abject and over-florid world of the early nineteenth century. But
a real critical evaluation of his work from a post-structuralist stand-
point has yet to be done (J. MacCannell, forthcoming) and particularly a critical evaluation of his conception of *narrative,* which has,
as one might have suspected, never quite fitted comfortably into
our theories of narrative (with their Oedipal foundations). Stendhal has produced for us a compelling and important body of
narrative writing; and he has done so beyond certain of Oedipus's
strictures. The combination is potentially too intriguing not to war-
rant a second look, given the current Oedipal crisis. Bearing in
mind that Stendhal is also, in many ways, the author of the Real,
it would be well for us to reread him in tandem with Lacan. Or in
the older structuralist idiom, perhaps we should do a Stendhalian
reading of Lacan.

1. *Stendhal and the Death of the Father, the Absence of the Mother*

Stendhal, like Hegel, literally writes in the wake of a very concrete
"Death of the Father": the regicide that should have put an end
to ontotheological structures and delivered, at least for the bourgeoisie, men (and women) to each other again in a relation of
equality. The revolution, indeed, might have dealt the death blow
to the overvaluation of the symbolic system—to the oppression, the
domination, and positioning of its subjects.

Yet everywhere around him Stendhal sees not freedom, satisfaction, equality, but guilt, lack of satisfaction, and inequality. The
regicide of the French revolution has become, not a lifting of a
hated set of proscriptions for desire, but instead a new departure
for what Freud will later name as "Oedipus." The tyrant who mo-
nopolized love has been killed, and the love relations that now are
possible are nonetheless covered with a pervasive fictionality, a veil,
such that the knowledge of the guilt for the murder is evaded, to
be sure, but satisfaction is also thereby blunted. Such an (unconscious) guilt establishes morality on the basis of a fiction, especially
a fiction of innocent origins. And what Stendhal sees, indeed never
ceases to perceive, is the *difference* this moral foundation makes.
Whereas *before* the revolution one had at least the king's various
satisfactions to serve as the model for one's own libidinal development, *after* the revolution one continues to imitate the *principles*
that had underlain the monarchy, i.e., the dual principles of inequality and hierarchy. One moralistically, and willingly, submits
one's desires to being positioned by these principles—out of guilt—
and one is thereby more constrained than one had been under the
condition of real social difference in rank. This greater constraint
is ironically named "freedom" by the bourgeoisie; and what Stendhal sees is that a desire thus transformed metaphorically, transformed *in principle*, into "principle," is a desire that is lost. He terms
this newly created love-form *"l'amour vanité"*: love according to a
hierarchical *principle*[11] once the real hierarchy has been destroyed,
and re-created in fictional form, that of the Restoration. As Stendhal succinctly illustrates the new principle: after the revolution a
"duchess is never more than 30 in the eyes of a bourgeois." Stendhal is clearly narrating the "history" of desire, a history that has
political, social, economic, aesthetic and, above all, linguistic and
literary consequences. Under Louis XV, life, love and letters were,
in this history, otherwise.[12]

Well before the Revolution Diderot's Rameau remarks that "In the whole realm there is only one person who walks, and that is the king; the rest take up positions." And though his interlocutor hastens to add that there must be moments when even the king has to beg, what Rameau is saying here is that only the king has no need to "desire" in the modern sense, that is, he suffers no delay between wish and fulfillment; he need not contort or twist himself into "positions," the rhetorical positions of, in Lacanian terms, demanding, asking, begging, pleading, etc. The model for the fulfillment of desire is, for the 18th century at least, the model of the sovereign.

Stendhal carries this speculation on the structure of desire further, in that he sees the sovereign model for desire from the point of view of its demise; like Benjamin's storyteller, he narrates it from the moment just after its death. In his book on *Love* Stendhal delineates four types of love, three of which belong to the era of the king: the tasteful, the passionate and the physical. As the (perhaps unfortunate) result of regicide, a fourth type, "l'amour vanité," now exists. The king, the "standard" of good taste for choosing a romantic partner, is gone, as one no longer has an actual standard or model to imitate, one might have found oneself free to love *really* and not merely symbolically. But the death of the king has hardly put people face to face with elemental, less symbolic, unmediated forms of love: especially not the bourgeois, who clings above all to a fictional *principle*, the principle of imitation, imitation in the express absence of a real model to imitate.

Precisely parallel to Lacan's discovery that it is the *symbolic function* of the phallus, the *principles* of lack and non-satisfaction that it represents and therefore like all (guilty) symbols legislates, Stendhal uncovers the post-revolutionary, post-monarchical mode in which love (and the accession to maturity and civil life) occurs in the society around him. It is still resoundingly Oedipal [the denial and exclusion of the mother is so absolute for him that his novel *Le rouge et le noir* is structured to denote how necessary Mme. de Rênal's maternal "supplement" is for Julien, who has no mother] but its parameters have expanded, its personnel have changed, and its fictionality is all the more powerful for being all the more covert, all the less "real." No longer linked to specifically designated collective representations such as Kings and Queens Oedipus (re)appears under the rubric of "freedom." One now accepts the ideal, symbolic positioning of one's desire, one's sexuality as "natural"—a "nature" that can also always be redefined fictionally—

and one puts imitation of a (now unconscious) model between one-self and the other. Moreover it is a model formed by a series of prohibitions rather than prescriptions; the positive instruction on the choice of the love-object offered by the King is no longer available.

Kenneth Burke once remarked that a real hierarchy at least allows universal participation for all those whose lives it organizes, and also that it always allows for the potential of any of its partic-ipants to rise or fall within it—a cat may look at a king; a peasant can move a queen's heart (Burke: "Rameau's Nephew" in *A Rhetoric of Motives.*). But the fictitious "rational" bourgeois form of hier-archy—bureaucracy—is actually founded on an opposing idea, that of inequality of access and participation on the basis of *differences*—in characteristics, qualities or objects; in possessions of money, de-grees, in "interests" etc. It is in fact the differentiation of society, the plurality of systems that require bureaucratic, purely fictitious forms of organization, that makes its participants unable to know consciously the manner in which the "system" or "symbolic order" positions them. Small wonder that desire, without a central, sov-ereign will for its model (tasteful love); without the clear border lines that evince the desire to transgress fundamental divisions and opposition (passion), without the simple class division of lord and peasant that makes one the *object* of desire for the other (physical love)—small wonder that it loses all sense of clear-cut direction, that it can lose itself in the unending, multiple and criss-crossing corridors of differentiation. And it does so always with the fiction that it is free to "go beyond" those structures, which, in the long run, are after all fictions themselves.

Desire, since Rousseau and Kant at least, has not only lost its *aim*—satisfaction—it has also, with the advent of the bureaucratic organization of society (of which Stendhal makes an unending cri-tique) lost its *object*.*

Triangular desire now appears as the *form* of desire—only a simple Girardian triangle will not suffice here for it is literally a

---

* Isn't there a secret collusion between Kant's self-imposed blindness about aim in that throwing it to infinity makes the object abject?—it is a throwaway. Kant cannot admit the object-of-desire (sexuality) into his subjective system. (Rousseau's *Pygmalion*, a precursor of Kantian aesthetics, sexualizes the aesthetic object.) The object is affected by and infected with the deferral of the aim. Since Lacan criticizes Kant precisely for his infinite deferral of access—visual, verbal, sensual or sexual— to the object in "Kant avec Sade," [See J. MacCannell, forthcoming] it is unlikely that his Real would participate in the infinite receding of the object of desire that Bowie describes above.

political triangle positioning the aristocrat, peasant and bourgeois. Thus in a concrete sense, then, desire is lost in political terms as well. It is the bourgeois who is literally the "he," the third term that intervenes between the I and the thou: between peasant and aristocrat—and if, prior to the revolution the He was the King, now it is the bourgeois with his powerful symbolic device, the Law, at his disposal who will intervene between desiring couples. The bourgeois's entire existence is composed of *symbolically* (read: informationally), as opposed to the *"semiotically"* (read: sexually), conceived sign.

That this is Stendhal's vision is evident in Julien's speech to the jury, which merits him the death sentence from M. de Valenod, the bourgeois liberal who has become a "baron": for in this speech Julien points out the true nature of his crime, that of having been a peasant who

> ... born to a lower social order, and buried by poverty, [was] lucky enough to get a good education and bold enough to mingle with what the arrogant rich called good society.
>
> There is my crime, gentlemen, and it will be punished all the more severely because, in reality, I am not being judged by my peers. I do not see in the seats of the jury a single rich peasant, only outraged *bourgeois.* . . .
>
> *(Red and Black,* N.Y.: Norton, 1969; 388)

If Julien's desire for Mme. de Rênal and Mathilde has existed by dint of the earlier, pre-bourgeois, traditional mode (the desire between aristocrat and peasant), it is clear here that it is the bourgeoisie that have come to intervene, have truly made the revolution their own and canceled what perhaps ought to have been its goal— the lifting of peasantry out of poverty and ignorance. The aristocrat-as-father may be in fact destroyed, but his symbolic power now lies in the hands of the bourgeois, who now legally and permanently intervenes in the love of the dialogic couple, the I and thou.

2. *LE ROUGE ET LE NOIR, LA CHARTREUSE AND OEDIPUS*

A. The Paternal

Stendhal ironizes, in a fundamentally structural way, both men and women characters who are the dupes of the Oedipal *truchement.*

The de-naturalization, the breaking of the natural (real?) links that the Oedipal structure brings in the dawning of the nineteenth century takes fictional form not only in the realm of literature and of everyday life, but in the realm of the law: it is perhaps there that the most intense focus for Oedipus exists. For the revelation that the Enlightenment had made, that all links with origins are in ill-repute, that there are literally no legitimate genealogies, at the same time unleashed an enormous power for fiction; and especially the legal fiction of paternity.

Stendhal is, of course, aware of the fictional patriarchal power; in the post-Rousseauistic, post-revolutionary world the liberation of the child from its origins, from the name of the father has both begun and been simultaneously buried under the metaphysical cloak of the Law and of patriarchal power. In Stendhal's novels, origins (real paternity), which are so much a thematic feature of later nineteenth century texts are left explicitly blank in respect to his masculine heroes: is Julien the son of an aristocrat; is Fabrice really the child of Lieutenant Robert? Their real origins have only tangential importance for these men, children as they are rather of their society and the current stage of their civilization, more than they are the fruit of a passion between two lovers. But at the same time, neither is interested in seeing the fictional status and genealogies society will bestow on them as anything more than a convenience: Fabrice will become a man of the church, Julien a landed aristocrat via purely formal manipulations. Julien, indeed, has no clear genealogy, and pointedly resists the townspeople's suggestion that he may be the bastard son of an aristocrat—until such time as he has literally been made into a character in a fiction that is much more compelling than that promulgated by his society and culture at large: the narratives of their life "written" by Mathilde de la Mole—their love story, which is "un roman par lettres"; and his *Bildungsroman*, "the novel of my career" as Julien characterizes it.

But it is precisely this symbolization, this positioning in the most fundamental sense—which is structured basically by the barring of Julien's most real desire, his desire for the maternal Mme. de Rênal—that Julien, and finally Stendhal, too, resists. Julien fires the "pistol shot in the middle of the concert" and terminates the novel of his career just as it was about to have a conventional "happy ending."

The power of Oedipus, of Oedipal structures and forms is felt concretely by his characters as the central experience of their lives; both as victims and perpetrators of the structure. In *Le Rouge et le noir* Julien is the victim, and it is Mathilde who is the great Oedipal character. Recall the times Julien senses her hard, clear masculinity, and it is a masculinity acquired through her intense adoption

of the Oedipal structure. She becomes not a *mother* substitute for
Julien, but a (symbolic) *father:* she gives him education, a career
and a title; she supplies the fictional genealogical "history" necessary for their love story (the medieval legend of Marguerite de
Navarre and Boniface de la Mole), and finally she symbolically
castrates him, removing his head from his body, separating his
head from his heart, in punishment for his unsymbolic possession
of the only "mother" he has ever known, Mme. de Rênal. There
is no question in Julien's love for Mme. de Rênal of a desire for a
pre-Oedipal relation to the mother: in the current stage of civilization Stendhal feels (in correctly Rousseauistic fashion) that we
are always already motherless children. But the ability to wrest the
mother-like form from an altogether too-paternal world is a con-
quest, a gain of sorts, even if it is a satisfaction that is bought at a
certain price. What has happened in Julien's "return" to Mme.
de Rênal is that he has managed to (re)find—and for the first
time—the supplementary *situation* of the pre-Oedipal. He loves in
the mode Lacan interpreted Freud's transference to be, an original
repetition. He regains the discourse of desire without the Oedipal
story, and raises it to a higher power because it has already seen
its own death in the Oedipal narrative. He finds, giving up his
"freedom" in prison, the level of discourse, both of the I and the
I in relation to the thou, in the absence of and without the intervention of the *he*. He refuses any demand of the Symbolic Order—
theologic, theocratic, political, etc. And this refusal of the "possible" puts him in touch with the Real.[13]   In the final analysis
Stendhal believes that the goal of satisfaction of desire must remain
the object of consciousness, or consciousness ceases—as the 18th-
century *philosophes* knew—to exist. Yet he is realist enough also to
know that desire has been buried under the detours that the symbolic, the "Oedipal," the fictional has created to outwit the death
drive of the pleasure principle. Desire, once a term applicable to
any consciousness, has been reduced to one side of an equation, a
masculine form (whether assumed by women, like Mathilde, or by
men) a form determined only by its Oedipal, fictional structure,
in which its satisfaction must be forever deferred, and forever
ruled by the threat of death if its laws are not followed.

B. The Grammatical

But Stendhal does more resisting than this action-via-characters
we find here; before the letter he resists an even more primordial
form of the symbolic than the *fictional,* the *grammatical.*

In his highly laudatory 1840 review of *La Chartreuse* Balzac had only two criticisms of the novel. The first was that Stendhal had not turned his characters into ideal types, the kinds of ideal types that Society, in its menacing workings, was daily turning real people into, making them mere symbols of their epoch, their class, their nationality. If only, he writes, the *Chartreuse* had been subtitled "Fabrice, or The Italian of the Nineteenth Century." But it is the second criticism that is more interesting and more germane to our topic here: it concerns Stendhal's notoriously negligent style, which everyone knows relates to his hostility toward effusiveness, toward an overly metaphoric style, etc. Balzac asks, however, whether this can possibly excuse his *lapses of grammar?*

Stendhal is reputed[14] to have responded to this latter accusation, "Like a child I say I won't do it again." The grammatical lapses are to stand. Perhaps they are not accidental. And when one recalls that Mathilde weaves Julien into her fictional creation not by responding to the signification of his sensually expressed desire (Mme. de Rênal feeling the pressure of his hand and returning the pressure, etc.) but by using with him the "grammatical form of intimacy," *elle le tutoie,* (ch. 16) then we can no longer ignore the fact that Stendhal is alert to the very same equations between the grammatical, the symbolic and the loss of the real as Lacan is.

Condemned to death, Julien Sorel recalls the Count d'Altamira's remark that the verb to guillotine cannot be conjugated in all tenses: one cannot say "J'ai été guillotiné" (*Rouge,* ch. 42). One's own literal, real death cannot be narrated, cannot be forced into grammatical, merely symbolic form. The same holds true for literal, real desire.

What Julien is discovering here, in reestablishing his dyadic relationship to Mme. de Rênal, is the situation of the enunciation, in Benveniste's terms: he becomes the subject of the enunciation and reappropriates his discourse from his story. He is laying bare the construction, the device, by which all stories (Oedipal stories) are created: the grammatical creation of the third person, the use of the aorist which can only be spoken in the form of the third person. What Julien finds here is a level, the *semiotic* level[15] which lies below the level of grammar, and beyond its grasp.

C. The Feminine

Stendhal's reading of Lacan would also be a feminist reading, just as in some ways Balzac's would be as well, or Flaubert's: the only real topic of nineteenth-century French literature is the woman.

But there are crucial differences among these "realist" writers, French writers in the same tradition as Lacan. And there is a great distance between a Stendhal who can write of Mme. de Stael's *Delphine* "Je me suis senti presque entièrement dans le personnage de Delphine,"[16]—who can identify not only with all his narrators, male and female alike, but who can *sympathize,* in the technical sense, with his women—and a Flaubert who can say "Emma Bovary, c'est moi" and who can empathize but who cannot finally sympathize with her. Even the grammatical form of these utterances, the indirectness of the object, Emma, in Flaubert's famous quote as opposed to the equivalence of subject and predicate in that from Stendhal shows the critical differences.

One can also compare Stendhal to Balzac on this issue. Balzac treats with high irony the growing inequality of the sexes in his time (a growth based precisely on the process of metaphorization, the mechanism of idealization, of sexual identity) and the lucid position Stendhal takes on the same issue. Stendhal does not, as Balzac does, ironize his women ultimately: Madame de Rênal may be self-deceiving at times, Clelia has her silly vows; but his final sympathies are with these women who literally battle to make a place for the heart in the tangled network of Oedipal constructions that their civilization is. Recall that it is Rousseau's Saint-Preux who found in the differentiated urban society of his time that the entire locus of the heart had fled to the refuge of the woman in *La Nouvelle Heloise* in his letter from Paris (II, xxi; pp 254-56, Garnier, 1960): "Si Julie n'eut point existé . . ." he would love a Parisienne.

D. The Form of the Real in Stendhal's Narrative

As Julien moves from the small town of Verrières with its simple, visible symbolic structures and its equally simple forms of attack on those symbolic systems (it is really rather easy to criticize the town's status hierarchies, etc.) he moves to Paris, where, as Rousseau would have described it, civilization had "advanced" and "perfected" itself to such a degree that its entire mode of being is that of the sign, in the pejorative sense Rousseau was so adept at giving it. Julien is disgusted by the affectation of the doubled lettering, "the HOTEL DE LA MOLE," on the facade of the mansion; the Marquis's only real concern is with "which decoration confers the most distinction"; Julien's first major embarrassment is that he spells "cela" with two "l's."

Stendhal discovered the real flaw in the system of overdeter-
mination by signs—*boredom.* He also hints at how little its results,
for passion, differ from the traditional Christian repression. Stendhal's *narrative* demeanor suggests, in *Le rouge,* that neither reality,
nor desire, nor pleasure has disappeared, but rather that they
have simply been transformed into *principles,* the chief of which is
the aim of turning each of these elements into a symbolic form. It
is this move that the novel criticizes even more resoundingly than
the simpler crudely symbolic movements of the townsfolk of Verrières: because it is far more alluring, more compelling, it incites
every kind of desire—except the one, central, real desire: the desire for the "maternal" form of love.

Fredric Jameson's reading of Lacan suggests that the form the
Real would take is that of an open-ended as opposed to a closed,
circular structure. Stendhal's "reading" of the Real suggests instead
that its form would be dominated by circles: many more than a
truly "phallic" structure would like to see. As Peggy Kamuf,
Michèle Montrelay[17] and Derrida have all pointed out, circles and
enclosures partake of the feminine far more than of the masculine
in their unconscious imagery. And it is indeed the notion of an
open-ended structure, the slippage of the signifier, and the eternal
deferral of meaning that has the phallic properties.[18] Enclosures
and imprisonments abound in Stendhal[19]; never has freedom been
less a value than it is for this author, but they close almost exclusively around men. Women in Stendhal are what they are precisely
because they can accept the bondage that love brings, but at the
same time that particular bonding frees them from purely symbolic
enclosures (in a very technical sense; in Stendhal symbolism is finally linked to social forms, including the entire spectrum from
religion to public opinion[20]). Julien reads his fate in a newspaper's
torn fragment, and that fate closes around him at the end; Fabrice
fulfills the (Oedipal) prediction that he will end in jail; but what one
never knew or suspected was that that fatality could be outwitted;
that its central aim—lack of satisfaction of desire—could fail.

And some inhabitants of the circular form are equally freed
from its domination: Mme. de Rênal does not even have to be
faithful to her final promise to Julien (to survive, to raise his child),
just as Stendhal has left her free to be unfaithful to her husband. Considering how the fate of the adulterous woman in the
nineteenth century is to die unhappily (see Tony Tanner on the
transgression of the symbolic contract[21]), Stendhal's treatment of

the disentangling of the woman from the "symbolic," the contrac-
tual forms of social agreement via the love relation, should give us
pause.

The characters who are left with open-ended possibilities in
Stendhal's narratives, around whom circles do not close, are those
(generally women) who have consented wholeheartedly to the systematic Oedipal trick: there is not only Mathilde in *Le Rouge*, there
is Gina Sanseverina in *La Chartreuse*, who seems unable despite her
strongest efforts to relinquish the power that her place in the
system gives her, and that to the detriment of her heart. She
cannot, one should recall, even know her heart; it is Mosca who
must guess that she loves Fabrice, and it is an idea, he says, that
would horrify her were she conscious of it. Her desire for her
nephew must remain unconscious if she is to continue to function
as even a somewhat subversive element in the social order. The
open-endedness, the possible future of these characters is not,
however, "free" in the sense Mme de Rênal or Clelia are "free" at
the end of their stories; for these characters will always be simultaneously insatiable and dissatisfied; just as Oedipus demands of
his children.

It is women like Mme. de Rênal, or Clélia who have Stendhal's
vote for being the last vestige of consciousness-as-desire in a world
that since Kant, since de Sade, since the Revolution has become
ever more incapable of satisfying desire.

*   *   *

And could Lacan, who ends one of his seminars with a reference
to Stendhal's more than adequate understanding of love (that love
is the *only* concern of the psyche), to Stendhal's *De l'Amour*,[22] have
been fundamentally in disagreement with this reading of Stendhal's Real? Could Lacan, the author of the seminal essay, "Kant
avec Sade," in *Écrits* (765-792), have found this version of the Real
impossible or improbable? Read him on this point:

> "Experience shows us that Kant is more true [than Spinoza, who says
> that "desire is the essence of man"] and I have proved that his theory
> of consciousness, when he writes of practical reason, is sustained by
> giving a specification of the moral law, which, looked at more closely,
> is simply desire in its pure state, that very desire that culminates in the
> sacrifice, strictly speaking, of everything that is the object of love in
> one's human tenderness—I would say, not only in the rejection of the

pathological object, but also its sacrifice and murder. That is why I wrote
Kant avec Sade.

(1981: 275-76)

For if Lacan is not a "primitivist," if he, like Stendhal, is concerned
with the possibility of civilized love (see above p. 916), then the Real
for Lacan could very well be that which is not originary, but a
necessary supplement to the imaginary and the symbolic. These,
for the human language being, always precede all possibility of
access to the "real." Or to state in Lacanian terms what we have
depicted with Stendhal here, if desire is neither "primitive" need
with its forceful cries, nor is it the twisted, tropic petition for love
from the system (demand), then it occurs somewhere else than in
the Oedipal structure, with its infinite sliding of the signifier, the
infinite deferral both of meaning and satisfaction.

When Lacan writes that a signifier represents a subject—but only
to another signifier, and *not* to another subject (1981: 198–99), it
is tantamount to saying that one must give one's desire up to the
symbolic order.

But Lacan's very articulation of that structure (a structure he
explicitly critiques not only in "Kant avec Sade" but also in his essay
on "The Deconstruction of the Drive"—wherein internal conscience, the Law, and the drive itself are the painful origination of
the unconscious, etc.) can also be taken as a demurral, as an in-
citement to attempt a retrieval of desire from the system of signifiers, the "hieroglyphic" symbolic system of that structure. In this
respect, our Stendhalian reading of the Lacanian Real may not be
altogether out of place.

For if Lacan has drawn attention, in the psychoanalytic mode,
to form and figure in literature we can interpret this practice on
his part in two quite different ways, and we reach again the central
aporia of his work. On the one hand we can read this stress as it
is clearly possible to do as an *idealist formalism*, as the inevitable
development of fictional structures that human culture, based on
Oedipus, implies, and on which, at no matter what cost, human
culture depends. You do not have figures without that figure's
having been paid for with a repression, and that figure without
a history is a blind: the "wholeness" of shape of the classic epic totality, for example, is a wholeness bought at a certain price. Once
this is understood by Lacan, however, can we say that he (or at
least we) could begin to conceive of a *realist formalism*; figures

without blind spots, "tropes" that do not themselves blindly grav-
itate toward the Sun? Do we see the prospect of a tale, a "cunning"
tale Benjamin would have called it,[23] to counter our (white) mythology constructed of these tropes?

II. STENDHAL ON THE STORY, LACAN ON THE HISTORY OF DESIRE

1. Stendhal

Our most critical question now poses itself in a concrete manner
as a historical question. It concerns the change in consciousness
that occurs at the close of the Enlightenment, the installation of
legal, social, and cultural structures that operate to create, almost
literally, the unconscious as Freud described it. If one looks closely
at the literature of that epoch—and that literature's manner of
rewriting society's and culture's laws—one finds not only a massive
indication of the construction of the (unconscious) drive (look at
Balzac's "Etude de femme" or Kleist's stories), but one also
finds certain protests, certain attempts to discover alternatives to
the construction of the drive as that which powers culture and all
its forms, including the literary.

There are, for example, various formal speculations, such as
Friedrich von Schlegel's early concern with breaking up the
"wholeness" of the epic basis* of fictional form, of the Oedipally
based totality: he attempted to build his systematic totality from
fragments whose content was to deny the possibility of system and
totality. Such an ironic, self-contradictory mode is at least one of
the avenues taken in early romanticism, and it is the mode of choice
for those who decline absorption by the symbolic for the remainder
of the nineteenth and on into the twentieth century.[24] But such a
use of form against itself is not the most satisfactory mode available
for resistance to the Symbolic Order. Irony's self-consuming qualities, the gluttony of this mode, its infinitizing even within the
limited play of the (false) depth of a constant mirroring, worried
Schlegel not a little. (See his "On Incomprehensibility.")

Paul de Man has suggested the work of Stendhal is emblematic
of another possible mode of inhabiting of the house of culture, the
"prison-house of language," without either destroying its structure
or attempting to get out of it all together. There are no "primi-

---

* A gesture recently repeated by M. M. Bakhtin in his essay on "Epic and Novel"
in the *Dialogic Imagination,* and not repeated by Lukács.

tivist" assumptions from which one could retrieve a "before"—culture, language, history; rather more in the spirit of the "primitive" (or savage) mind, Stendhal stays within his own "world," the fictional world, and accepts its enclosure, its totality, its economy. He is certainly no engineer, in Lévi-Strauss's terms, striving to get beyond it. But his manner of dwelling is different; he wishes to live in that structure in an entirely conscious, rather than an unconscious mode.

One is to inhabit the structure with distance on it, by seeing through it. Its "reality" is a reality *in principle*, not the Real itself. The Real, that is, does not exist either inside or outside of the "prison-house of language": it exists where sexuality exists for Lacan, in the interstices, the gaps in the structure, what Lacan calls the "rim."

To inhabit the house of culture in this way is to run the very real risk of death. For if one inhabits the modern cultural household (and economy) of the world after the political revolution in power and after the "Copernican" revolution in morality (both of which owe so much to the freedom to make fictions) one ought, by rights, agree to relegate one's desires to the unconscious: if one does not, if one keeps the object (*l'objet petit a?*) in view, one returns to the Real, "returns" to the impossible. Stendhal attempts to retrieve the object of/for desire from metaphoric distortions, from being merely figurative.[25] His method will vary with circumstance, epoch, personalities and political situations: in the contemporary scene, for example, dominated by speech (especially in the form of remembered quotations as in "Vanini Vanini") he will imagine it as unvoiced or more successfully expressed by *signs* other than the verbal. (Speech was given to man to hide his thoughts—the epigraph of a chapter in *Le Rouge*.) In other scenes he locates desire there where it has not (yet?) become distorted into the unsatisfiable (masculine) mold of the libido[26]: i.e. in certain women, in certain men after they have met these women, in the ellipses, in the famous, etc., etc.

Desire, then, will be that which will have had no "reality principle" and no "pleasure principle" either: but it is also not without a form. The maternal model will exist for Stendhal, will regulate the form of the fiction in as binding a fashion as the death of the father ever did. Yet it is not a maternal model as it has existed in Western culture, itself legislated into the unconscious: with the mother consciously existing only in idealized form (the virgin, the non-sexuality of the virgin birth) and unconsciously as the unnameable object of unspeakable desires. It is those women who are real mothers, women completely conscious of sexual reality, that attract Stendhal; fictions of innocence have no allure for him: he remarked once that the most desirable room (in the house of culture?) would be for him "a salon in which all the women have had lovers."

The retrieval of such a Real in no wise negates History, Culture, Civilization—to the contrary; it is only through their collective and individual experience that the Real can even be conceived. And if this reminds us not so much of Freud and Marx as it does of Hegel there is certainly a reason for it. For the Real that Stendhal's narrative strives for and indeed achieves is a conscious reality that nonetheless exists in the mode of the sign: that is, it has no pretensions to "primitivism" or "naturalism" that still hovers around Rousseau's sign-consciousness and which opens the way for the construction of the unconscious as a necessary but unhappy accompaniment to the construction of the freedom of fiction.

2. Lacan

There is reason to believe that, as Jameson writes, Lacan does identify the Real with History itself. But far more than the Real, it is historical Realities that Lacan demonstrates in his *Seminars*, and these Realities are not the Real. They consist of signs that "man is not completely in man" (Freud), that our history is our fiction. We have exited from the simple interhuman circuit and our being has become the discourse of the Other (we might borrow Bakhtin's term and call it "the dialogic"). Lacan demonstrates these historical realities as what they are, histories of figures—Huyghen's clock as it figures the clockwork Cartesian subject; Hegel's failure to comprehend the correct figure for his understanding of power relations, the steam machine (Lacan asks, did we ever concern ourselves about masters and slaves until we had a powerful machine to compare human labor with, to compute it against? And a machine more powerful than the master[27]). Our history, figuratively,[28] shows only the widening arena of the play of forces, the inequalities and differentials, that form and inform the psyche-as-subject. Lacan notes, for example, the difference between implements such as tables and chairs, in which we see our "symbolic" unperceived portrait, and the "machine" which is, he writes, "autre chose" (*Séminaire II*, p. 94).

What Lacan tries to tell us is that we have gone beyond anthropology: although it is certainly clear that of late we witness a certain
desire for a return to anthropology.[29] He writes that Hegel discovered that "the reality of each human being is in the being of
the other" (*Séminaire II*, 91 ff.): that Man's desire finds its meaning
in the desire of the other, not so much because the other holds
the key to the object desired, as because the first object of
desire is to be recognized by the other. But what Freud discovered
is that "man is not completely in man," he lives in another, fictive,
Oedipally based dimension. The internalized *non/nom du père* acts
as this otherness within the self.

Which amounts to saying that for Lacan the Real does not escape
the Symbolic, does not overthrow it or pre-date it, or go back
behind it. The Real lurks in it, in the very signifiers out of which
the Symbolic is constructed. It is a construction whose method
consists in separating signifiers not from their *referent* (their referents are already symbols) but from the aim of satisfaction, from
conscious desire—and a desire for the Real as opposed to the Symbolic other. Lacan only hints at alternatives, but we should know
that it is in the silences that significance may lie. And what is suggested by the terms (albeit not the logic) of his exposition; is it that
one retrieves the Real not by overthrowing the symbolic, culture,
language, civilization, but by resisting its formative *principles*? Can
we not call it, as he does, "deconstructing the drive"? For if in the
essay by that title Lacan's central effect is to demonstrate that the
law of the Law, the drive of the drive, is to deflect the psyche from
the aim (satisfaction):

> Between these two terms—drive and satisfaction—there is set up an
> extreme antinomy that reminds us that the use of the function of the
> drive has for me no other function than to put in question what is meant
> by satisfaction. . . . Satisfaction is paradoxical. When we look at it more
> closely, we see that something new comes into play—the category of the
> impossible. In the foundations of Freudian conceptions, this category
> is an absolutely radical one . . . . the path of the subject passes between
> two walls of the impossible. . . . [But] impossible is not necessarily the
> contrary of the possible, or since the opposite of the possible is certainly
> the real, we would be lead [sic] to define the real as the impossible.
> Personally I see nothing against this especially as in Freud it is in this
> form that the real, namely, the obstacle to the pleasure principle, ap-
> pears. The real is the impact with the obstacle; it is the fact that things
> do not turn out all right straight away . . . . But I think this is a quite
> illusory and limited view of Freud's thought on this point. The real is

934   JULIET FLOWER MAC CANNELL

distinguished ... by its separation from the pleasure principle, by its
desexualization, by the fact that its economy, later, admits something
new which is precisely the impossible.... no object of any *Not*, need,
can satisfy the drive.

(166-67)

By default, *Lacan's* goal would be a retrieval not of instinct, but
of the aim as Freud named it—satisfaction.

Lacan once remarked, in the *Discours de Rome*, that only desire
can counter the symbolic order which defines and positions us
absolutely from before our birth—our figural, linguistic, literary
and cultural history. But we must be extremely cautious about the
nature of desire in Lacan if we are not to resort either to the
instinctual, animal or the metaphysical variants of desire[30] one
might suppose as its essence. For a Lacanian desire that would not
be only a libido (marked with a male sign) one would have to go
neither to need nor to the symbolic order but to the fact of a real
heterogeneity: it exists *between* two signifying beings. As such, if
the desire is to make any sense at all, it would have to be taken as
the eighteenth century took it, as the *cardinal*, the only *real* feature
of *consciousness*. But it is a consciousness attainable, for us, now
only in the modality, the temporality of the psyche, the *nachträg-
lich*—in declining, after the fact, the idealization of sexuality, the
idealization of fiction, the idealization of the lack of finality (called
"freedom") that exists under Oedipus.

But any subtraction from the symbolic order is neither a permanent condition achievable by the revolutionary overthrow of the
Symbolic—Stendhal at least saw the failure of that particular gesture all too well—nor is it a return to some hypothetical pre-sym-
bolic, re-representational condition (like Kristeva's *chora*). Rather
it is a matter, in one's loves, of significant deletion, the deletion of
the symbolic factor.

*   *   *

Lacan once wrote that Hegel saw the advent of Napoleon as the
corrective to an original imbalance, an imbalance that had fueled
the very machinery of culture itself: the unequal distribution of
power between the sexes. Napoleon embodied the "other pole,
more carnal, more feminine" of the Spirit that History had, until
then, repressed (*Séminaire II;* 94). And yet, for Lacan, and despite
Hegel's assertion, the restorative did not come; the basic social
contract between the sexes, the one that is more primordial than
the Oedipal one, is not returned to its original foundational term,

desire. The advent of the (bourgeois) political form of the "he" or the third party to intimate relations is the interloping, grammatical term that literally legislates the relation of the other two. Instead, a new kind of machine is elaborated, one that does not play off the all-too simple forces of the older opposition, male/female. The machine is elaborated in the figure of the French revolution: the machine of freedom, the fiction-making machine. This machine, we could call it the law (of thermodynamics, of grammar, of the "steam machine"[31]) which has the capacity to translate simple oppositions into powers out of all proportion to their simple source. It is driven by an elaborate system of repressions and expansions, drives that outstrip the elementary structures of culture (e.g. the logic of the Greek sentence, for example, that, stylistically [no parataxis] forms the basis of Greek epic: Auerbach: *Mimesis* 1959:7 ff.) The combination of "freedom"—the fictional freedom that Oedipus brings—with the power of its machine is deadly for desire.

Stendhal spent his particular fictional capital analyzing the machinery of the symbolic order: its economy (the opening pages of the *Rouge*), its bureaucracy (*Lucien Leuwen, le Rouge*), its secular and sacred politics (*la Chartreuse,* even "Vanina Vanini," with its portrait of the craven functionaires of Metternich), its philosophy (*Le Rose et le vert* with its depiction of the "Kantian" Mina in Koenigsberg), etc., from within. He discovers its power to lie in the *principle,* Oedipus's, of the lack of satisfaction of desire.[32] Stendhal also dispensed his fictional capital by demonstrating brief episodes in which the adherence to the principle is broken, devising schemes for getting around it (recall the ingenuity of those characters who can manage to satisfy desire). At the simplest level this occurs in Stendhal via the simple tactic of substituting one code for another, substituting, for example, gestures for words, the form of the chronicle for the form of the tale, music for art, even one language for another,* e.g. German for French, or English, etc. For Stendhal consciousness simply does not exist outside of the mode of the sign, but that does not, for him, imply enslavement to the codes, the Symbolic orders, by which those signs have already organized themselves. One must reappropriate language for one's own purposes; and innovation of this sort consists in the "bricolage" of using one set of tools for a job for which they were not intended— especially for the "job" of deconstructing desire.

Extricating desire from the distortions and biases, the intermin-

---

* Recall Stendhal's wish for *"la mentula,* as hard and as moveable as the index finger whenever I wish," ("Les Privilèges") with its language change.

able relays, the eternal deferral of satisfaction of the *drive*—this appears to be the central task of Stendhal's *oeuvre*. Lacan, it will be remembered, rewrites Freud's "Instincts and their Vicissitudes" precisely in order to demonstrate how radically the drive in Freud is the antinomy of satisfaction. And if Lacan's is a suggestive reading of Freud's text (which bears a great deal of resemblance to Rousseau's depiction of the obstacles to desire[33]) is it any wonder that his "re-Reading" follows patterns that recall Stendhal?

Stendhal's "happy few" significantly enough rarely fit any of Freud's "libidinous types"[34]; they are in touch with their "erotic" instincts, like the erotic obsessional, etc., and they often do ritual obeisance to guilt for transgressing institutional rules (Clélia puts out the light during love-making to keep her vow to the Madonna not to see Fabrice again if her father is saved, etc.); but the central, the main *guilt*, the Oedipal guilt for the origins of one's sexuality, is entirely deleted from the story of the "happy few": they die, yes, but only *after* they have obtained that from which Oedipus ought to have barred them—satisfaction. If, as we have stressed, the most fundamental law of the symbolic order is the lack of satisfaction of desire,* if the machine of culture is literally *driven* by the excess of desire over satisfaction,[35] then obtaining satisfaction from that system is tantamount to halting the drive, the source of (symbolic) power.

The brief, momentary halting of the machine that occurs in Stendhal (the sabotage of its grammar; unbinding the rhetoric that flowers on top of that grammar; the supplementary "return" to the "mother"; the analysis of the political and sexual order of the bourgeoisie) is not *per se* productive of narrative. But these do produce the gaps; they are the *tmesis*, as Barthes called it, which produce the "bliss" of reading and writing. And the story that narrates the act both of stopping the fiction-making machine—the machine of the possible, the potential, the powerful—by examining both the impossibility of satisfaction, and ironically, simultaneously, its *reality*, makes a good narrative against narratives.

University of California, Irvine

---

* The analyst's desire is not a pure desire. It is a desire to obtain absolute difference, a desire which intervenes when, confronted with the primary signifier, the subject is, for the first time, in a position to subject himself to it. There only may the signification of a limitless love emerge, because it is outside the limits of the law, where alone it may live. (Lacan, *Four Concepts*, 1981:276)

NOTES

1 Roland Barthes, "Introduction to the Structural Study of Narrative," *New Literary History*, 6:2, 1975 (Winter), 237–71. A recent book edited by Robert Con Davis, *The Fictional Father: Lacanian Readings of the Text* (Amherst: U. of Massachusetts, 1981) provides a clear paradigm for studying narrative from a post-Lacanian Oedipal perspective. Included in the collection is Thomas Hanzo's "Paternity and the Subject in *Bleak House*," cited below.

2 Philippe Lacoue-Labarthe and Jean-Luc Nancy read *Lucinde* in their study of romanticism, *L'Absolu littéraire*. In another article, "L'Imprésentable," *Poétique*, 1975, they discuss how the female figure has always been one that Western thought has attempted to "overcome"—philosophically, aesthetically and physically.

3 Marie-Cécile and Edmond Ortigues, *L'Oedipe africain* (Paris:Plon, 1966), 301–03.

4 Julia Kristeva, "Motherhood According to Bellini," in *Desire in Language*, (N.Y.: Columbia, 1980), pp. 237–270.

5 Julia Kristeva, "L'Abjet d'amour," "Ne dis rien," *Tel Quel*, 1982, pp. 17–44, as well as an unpublished paper entitled "Woes of Love" (private communication). Jacques Derrida's *Grammatology* (1967) is a study of Rousseau, and his *Archeologie du frivole* studies the final madness of desire for the 18th century, the desire to desire; Sarah Kofman's book, *Le Respect des femmes* (Paris: Galilée, 1982) has much to say on the subject of Kant and women; Lacoue-Labarthe's study of Diderot's *Paradoxe* in *Poétique*, "Diderot et le paradoxe de la mimesis," 1971, is marked by the Freudian "logic" as is his "Theatrum analyticum" in *Glyph* 2; and of course, he and Jean-Luc Nancy have written a book on Lacan, *Le Titre de la lettre*, (Paris: Galilée, 1973).

6 Lacan, *Ecrits* (Paris: Seuil, 1966), p. 98.

7 Julia Kristeva, "La musique parlée, ou remarques sur la subjectivité dans la fiction, à propos du 'Neveu de Rameau' " in Michèle Duchet and Michèle Jalley, eds., *Langue et langages de Leibniz à l'Encyclopedie* (Paris: 10/18, Union Générale d'Editions, 1977), pp. 153–224; see esp. 162 ff.

8 Although they do not state this explicitly, such would appear to be the message of those recent feminist texts that concentrate on the *daughter* as opposed to the *son* from the point of view of psychoanalysis: Jane Gallop, *The Daughter's Seduction* (Ithaca: Cornell, 1982) and Peggy Kamuf's *Fictions of Feminine Desire* (Lincoln and London: U. of Nebraska, 1982), with its very fine chapter on the daughter in *La Princesse de Cleves*. Of course it is Jacques Derrida who has made the radical reinterpretation of Freud and the daughter in his essay, "Coming into One's Own," in Geoffrey Hartman, ed., *Psychoanalysis and the Question of the Text: Selected Papers of the English Institute, 1976–77* (Baltimore: Johns Hopkins, 1978), pp. 114–48. Here Derrida demonstrates how the subject of the utterance *fort/da* is for Freud not the absence of the child's *mother*, but the death of Freud's *daughter*, and his favorite daughter, Sophie, by whom the "descent of the community [is] insured"—but only as a "nameless name, a figureless figure," p. 144.

9 Fredric Jameson, in the early article on Lacan, writes that the only form that the real could take would be that of "History itself": ". . . the diachronic evolution of History itself, the realm of time and death both of which radically transcend individual experience in their very structure" ("Imaginary and Symbolic in Lacan" in *Literature and Psychoanalysis [Yale French Studies]*, 1977, p. 394), a statment which suggests an open-endedness to the form, and would forego any possible closure. In the later *The Political Unconscious* (Cornell, 1980), Jameson makes a different move and tries to discover fantasy or "protonarrative structure as the vehicle for our experience of the Real," p. 48. He cites A. J.

Greimas' "semiotic rectangles" as furnishing the "graphic embodiment" of the libidinal content of ideological systems. The move between the more existential stance of the first piece and this relatively strong formalism should give us pause. For Bowie's "Lacan," see John Sturrock, ed., *Structuralism and Since* (N.Y.: Oxford, 1979), pp. 116–153.

10 Lacan, *Séminaire I: Les Ecrits techniques de Freud* (Paris: Seuil, 1975), p. 80.

11 Stendhal, *Love* (London: Penguin, 1975), pp. 44–45. The French original is more explicit:

> "Une duchesse n'a jamais que trente ans pour un bourgeois, disait la duchesse de Chaulnes; et les habitués de la cour de cet homme juste, le roi Louis de Hollande, se rappellent encore avec gaieté une jolie femme de la Haye, qui ne pouvait se resoudre à ne pas trouver charmant un homme qui était duc ou prince. Mais, fidèle au principe monarchique, des qu'un prince arrivait a la cour, on renvoyait le duc: elle etait comme la decoratiion du corps diplomatique." (Paris: Garnier-Flammarion, 195, p. 32)

12 Stendhal, *Love*, p. 35. Even though Jameson objects to writing history from the point of view of the story of desire, his thesis of the creation of a political unconscious, ideological in structure, depends heavily on his contention that psychic fragmentation occurs in the early 19th century with the advent of capitalism and bureaucracy (*Polit. Ucs.*, pp. 62–3; 66–67); but if we agree in any measure with first Lacan's and now Kristeva's assertions that Love is the *only* question for analysis of the psyche, then how can Jameson really avoid this particular history (indeed he does not, as his chapter on "Realism and Desire" shows). For Kristeva, see the essay on "Woes of Love" cited above; for Lacan, see "A Love Letter": "Speaking of love, in analytic discourse, one does nothing else," in Juliet Mitchell and Jacqueline Rose, eds., *Feminine Sexuality* (New York and London; W. W. Norton & Company, 1982), p. 154.

13 Lacan, "The Deconstruction of the Drive" (*Sem.*, May 6, 1964), writes:

> The real is distinguished, as I said last time, by its separation from the field of the pleasure principle, by its desexualization, by the fact that its economy, later, admits something new, which is precisely the impossible.
> (cited in *The Four Fundamental Concepts of Psycho-Analysis*, ed. J. A. Miller [New York and London: W. W. Norton & Company, 1981], p. 167).

14 Cited in Georg Lukács, *Studies in European Realism* (New York: Grosset and Dunlap, 1965, p. 76). Lukács takes the remark as a virtual apology for a hastily written text. Yet Stendhal is painfully conscious of rules of grammar, takes them ultimately very seriously (see the opening passage of *Love* where he twists the "first and third persons" into ironic inversion—pp. 25-6, "First Attempt at a Preface.") The entirety of Balzac's review is reprinted in Emile Talbot, *La Critique stendhalienne de Balzac à Zola*, (York, So. Carolina: French Literature Publications Company, 1979).

15 I take this in Kristeva's and Barthes's sense of the level below that of grammatical logic; what Kristeva calls the "chora" or the non-expressive arrangement of forces in the pre-representational.

16 Cited in Jacques Félix-Faure, *Stendhal, lecteur de Mme. de Stael: Marginalia inédits* (Aran, Switzerland: Editions du Gand Chene, 1974), p. 13-14; *Journal*, 3 fevrier, 1805.

17 See Peggy Kamuf, *Fictions*, pp. xiv-xvii; and Michele Montrelay, *L'Ombre et le nom*, (Paris; Minuit, 1977). Jane Gallop, *q.v.* pp. 28-32, does an exposition of Montrelay's recentering of feminine sexuality.

18 Jane Gallop argues along these lines in *The Daughter's Seduction*, p. 20ff.

19 Victor Brombert's many studies have noted this, including the recent publication in Geoffrey Hartman, ed., *Romanticism*.

20 See my article, "Stendhal's Woman," forthcoming in *Semiotica*.

21 Tony Tanner, *Adultery in the Novel: Contract and Transgression* (Baltimore and London: Johns Hopkins, 1979).

22 Lacan, "A Love Letter," in Mitchell and Rose, *op. cit.*, p. 170.

23 Walter Benjamin, "The Storyteller," *Illuminations*, p. 102; Benjamin sees the fairy tale as a tale of cunning as opposed to the myth, which imposes its structure on those who participate in it. It is interesting to note that the Romantic interest in the short story as a form that is similar to yet different from the novel appears in the same epoch of which we are writing here: with Goethe's desire to see the "impossible" in the short story; Kleist's improbable truths; and Schlegel's keen interest in the form as one that is more "real" than the "Kantian arabesque" of the purely novel form. The short story, with its erotic genealogy (Boccaccio, Chaucer, etc.) may indeed be considered as having an alternate genealogy to the novel, with its supposed "descent" from epic, and may have more to do with the kind of satiric and romantic tradition Bakhtin discusses in his "Epic and Novel" in *The Dialogic Imagination* (Austin: U. of Texas, 1980).

24 See Paul de Man, "The Rhetoric of Temporality," in C. S. Singleton, ed. *Interpretation: Theory and Practice*, (Baltimore: Johns Hopkins, 1969). This by now classic essay deals with the problem of language as instrument that one encounters in writers after the Romantic movement that we discuss here, and cites Stendhal's writing as offering possible alternatives.

25 My paper (forthcoming *Semiotica*) discusses this as do Lacoue-Labarthe and Nancy in *L'Absolu littéraire*.

26 This phrase from Lacan was made infamous by Derrida's use of it in his 1975 essay "The Purveyor of Truth" *Yale French Studies* 52, p. 98, as the prime indication of "phallogocentrism." Yet of course, Lacan is right, too, since the (Freudian) libido has little to do with feminine sexuality.

27 Lacan, *Séminaire II: Le moi dans la theorie de Freud et dans la technique de la psychanalyse*, (Paris: Seuil, 1978), p. 95.

28 See my "Speaking of Love: Rhetoric, Politics and self in Rousseau and Stendhal" in *Gradiva*.

29 Certain indications of a turn from larger systems of signification toward the simpler forms of interhuman circulation are evident in recent films like *Night of the Shooting Stars,* where there is a 'Virgilian' perspective on the significance of war for those whose lives are subjected by it but who simply decline to buy into its symbolization. V. N. Volosinov's (Bakhtin's) essay "Discourse in Life, Discourse in Art" in *Freudianism: A Marxist Critique* (New York: Academic Press, 1973) is a brilliant exposition of the balance maintained between, on the one hand, the tendency to "metaphor" (personification) and "metonymy" (sheer contiguity) in the exchange of the sign; and he is careful to make it a verbal sign ("well") that carries no signification or referent in itself.

30 See Jonathan Culler, *On Deconstruction* (Ithaca: Cornell, 1982).

31 *Séminaire II*, p. 95.

32 Consider Freud's remarks on "reality" in *Beyond the Pleasure Principle* to see how Lacan may be opposing the Real to "principle":

> Under the influence of the ego's instincts of self-preservation, the pleasure principle is replaced by the *reality principle*. This latter principle does not abandon the intention of ultimately obtaining pleasure, but it nevertheless demands and carries into effect the postponement of satisfaction, the abandonment of a number of possibilities of gaining satisfaction and the temporary toleration of unpleasure as a step on the long indirect road to pleasure. The pleasure principle . . . often succeeds in overcoming the reality principle to the detriment of the organism as a whole. (New York: Bantam, 1959, p. 26)

Stendhal once wrote of a certain English garden (in Milan) where the twisting and unfamiliar roads led one, suddenly, to a familiar shrub or statue; likewise, he writes, Borges-like, of a man running after his abducted wife and away from the police only to find two hours later that he was farther from his wife and closer to the police. Michael Wood (*Stendhal* London: Elek, 1971, pp. 9-12), who cites this passage from the *Pensées: Filosofia Nova*, shows how aware Stendhal is of the Oedipal structure of narrative—certainly his heroes are fated enough in the Oedipal mode. But in Stendhal that is the point: as in Lacan, Oedipus is "un truchement culturel."

33 See my essay, "Nature and Self-Love: A Reinterpretation of Rousseau's 'passion primitive' " *PMLA*, 92 (1978), 890-902.

34 Freud, "Libidinous Types," in *Character and Culture* (New York: Collier, 1963), pp. 210-14.

35 Derrida writes of imagination as the excess of desire over the power of satisfaction, *De la Grammatologie* (Paris: Minuit, 1967), p. 263.

The Purloined Punchline: Joke as Textual Paradigm

☙

Jerry Aline Flieger

"Freud, the very name's a laugh . . . the most
hilarious leap in the holy farce of history."
Jacques Lacan, "A Love Letter"[1]

The Clue in Full View

Freud clearly loved nothing more than a good story, except perhaps a good laugh. From Dora to Moses, from Oedipus to the
Jewish marriage broker, Freud's cast of characters plays out the
human drama in suspenseful narratives spiced with anecdote and
warmed with wit. Little wonder, then, that some of Freud's most
provocative insights concern the twin esthetic mysteries dear to his
heart: the writer's magic (which he calls "the poet's secret") and
the joker's art.

In his own "return to Freud," Lacan has followed the master
story-teller's example. For Lacan's own artful use of pun, allusion,
and narrative technique creates a performative theoretical discourse which reenacts the plot of intersubjective desire which it
analyzes. Lacan's work thus tends to speak to questions of narrative
and textuality in an oblique manner, by example. In order to elaborate a Lacanian theory of narrative, one needs to decipher the
clues in Lacan's own sometimes turgid and hermetic text.

In one of the best examples of Lacan's narrative craft—the much
discussed "Seminar on 'The Purloined Letter' "[2]—Lacan passes on
a useful lesson learned from Poe's arch-sleuth, Dupin: the best
clues, he tells us, are always at once marginal and obvious ("Perhaps a little *too* self-evident," S.P.L., p. 53). Once such marginal
yet obvious clue to Lacan's own difficult work, it seems to me, may

be found in the first volume of *Écrits* (Paris: Editions du Seuil,
1966), in which Lacan alludes in passing to Freud's seminal text
on joke theory:

> For, however neglected by our interest—and for good reason—*Jokes
> and their Relation to the Unconscious*[3] remains the most unchallengeable
> of Freud's works because it is the most transparent, in which the effect
> of the Unconscious is revealed to us in its most subtle confines. (*Écrits
> I*, p. 148, my translation)

What are we to make of this puzzling statement of simultaneous
homage and disparagement? Why does Lacan *marginalize* Freud's
text ("however neglected by our interest—and for good reason—")
at the same time that he insists on its "transparency" and its
centrality as "the most unchallengeable of Freud's works?" Perhaps
like the purloined letter of Poe's detective tale, which has been
hidden in plain sight, Freud's work may be a *somewhat too evident*
clue to understanding Lacan's own version of the Freudian master
narrative. For if Freud's transparent text is clearly about what it
promises to be—"Jokes and their Relation to the Unconscious"—
it is also about the transmission of sexual desire in a socio-linguistic
circuit. In addition, it may be read as a model story, a paradigm
tracing the possibilities of narrative itself. Indeed, such a reading
of Freud's "transparent" essay on the joking process as an "evident"
clue to the functioning of textual processes seems to suggest that
Lacan's own punchline—the discovery that everything human is
textual, caught in an intersubjective narrative web—has been purloined from Freud. Yet in returning this punchline or message to
its initiator, we find that it has been transcribed in Lacan's hand,
and that this transcription will in turn permit us to rethink the
joking process itself, so that it no longer appears as a guarantor of
identity or as a cementer of the social bond, but rather as a
symptom motivated by the same pre-text of desire which gives rise
to the literary text.

In order to reread the Freudian paradigm in Lacanian terms,
with an eye to formulating a Lacanian theory of literary narrative,
I want to trace the following chain of metonymic equivalences:
subjectivity as intersubjectivity; intersubjectivity as narrative/text;
text as "feminine" symptom; femininity as (form of) subjectivity.
This chain may be described as *metonymic* because in Lacan's view
of intersubjectivity as a kind of text, each of these processes or
phenomena is an overlapping link which leads inevitably to the
next. And this metonymic chain in turn describes a circular itin-

erary or plot, in which the final point—which visits that question, perplexing to Freud and to Lacan alike, of the nature of femininity—returns to the point of departure, a questioning of the role of the subject not only in the creation of the literary text, but in the forming of the larger human plot or text. For the question of feminine subjectivity—and of whether "she," as subject, can speak or write—is a central one in Lacan's work, and it is a question which must be addressed in reading that work as (at one and the same time) a narrative, a theory *of* narrative, and a theory of human intersubjectivity and sexuality *as* narrative.

I

Subjectivity as Intersubjectivity

> Generally speaking, a tendentious joke calls for three people: in addition to the one who makes the joke, there must be a second who is taken as the object of the hostile or sexual aggressiveness, and a third in whom the joke's aim of producing pleasure is fulfilled.
> Freud, *Jokes and their Relation to the Unconscious,* p. 100

A Classic Plot

In the third section of the essay on jokes ("The Purposes of Jokes"), Freud tells the story of the origin of joking itself: the joker-protagonist overcomes a series of adverse circumstances and enjoys a happy ending of sorts ("Jokes make possible the satisfaction of an instinct—whether lustful or hostile—in the face of an obstacle which stands in its way," p. 101). Thus the happy ending, the satisfaction of a lustful or hostile instinct, is achieved only by the circumlocution afforded by the joking process ("Jokes circumvent the obstacle and in that way draw pleasure from a source which the obstacle had made inaccessible," p. 101). The scenario of the development of the obscene joke, which Freud uses as the paradigm for all tendentious joking, unfolds like a classic boy-meets-girl narrative, complicated by an equally classic love triangle.

PART I: BOY MEETS GIRL. "The one who makes the joke" (p. 100) encounters a desirable "object," gets ideas, and makes

them known in "wooing talk" which he hopes "will yield at once
to sexual action" (pp. 98-99). The first in a series of detours from
direct satisfaction of "a lustful instinct" is thus necessitated by the
obstacle of social convention: wooing must precede action. Now if
the wooing proves unsuccessful—if the object resists because she
is offended or inhibited—the frustrated wooer "turns positively
hostile and cruel" and begins to express himself in "smut" or "sexually explicit speech" (pp. 98-100). A second detour from direct
satisfaction is thus experienced, since the sexually exciting speech
becomes an aim in itself ("sexual aggressiveness . . . pauses at the
evocation of excitement and derives pleasure from the signs of it
in the woman," p. 99). PART II: BOY LOSES GIRL. As if the
woman's inhibition did not pose problems enough for the wooer's
design, enter a second male—a potential rival and a decidedly im-
portune third party ("The ideal case of resistance of this kind on
the woman's part occurs if another man is present at the same
time—a third person—for in that case an immediate surrender is
as good as out of the question," p. 99). Alas, even if girl wants
boy, the implicit rivalry—a kind of shorthand for the whole
corpus of societal laws and prohibitions governing sexuality—interrupts the natural course of events. PART III: JOKE CON-
QUERS ALL. But, never fear, boy does get girl, by "exposing her
in the obscene joke" and enjoying the spectacle of her embarass-
ment ("By making our enemy small, inferior, despicable, or comic,
we achieve in a roundabout way the enjoyment of overcoming
him," p.103). Thus "boy" gets satisfaction only in the sense that
one "gets" a joke, by effecting an imaginary exposure, humiliation
or put-down which is clearly both voyeuristic and exhibitionist in
character: the hapless woman, Freud tells us, has now been exposed
before a listener who has "been bribed by the effortless satisfaction
of his own libido" (p. 100). The pleasure game is played out between poles one and three, joker and listener, at the expense of
pole two (who is often so offended as to leave the room, Freud
tells us, "feeling ashamed"). In the Freudian scenario, the locker
room joys of male bonding have replaced the original aim of seduction, since the joker actually "calls on the originally interfering
third party as his ally" (p. 100). EPILOGUE: BOY GETS BOY?
Indeed, "boy" wins the attention and complicity of his rival-turned-
accomplice in this plot, and the complicit listener in turn receives
a free entertainment, the "effortless satisfaction of his own libido."
Pole three, the listener-voyeur, seems to enjoy the happiest ending
of anyone in this narrative of obstructed and deflected desire.

But the freeloading listener does not escape unscathed. Elsewhere, Freud points out the aggressive nature of the capture of the listener's attention by the device of ideational mimetics (pp. 192-193). If the listener gets pleasure from the joke process, it is only because he is taken in by the joke itself, caught unawares by the punchline. Boy must capture boy by an expert delivery, or the joking transaction will fail. Indeed, in a later elaboration on the technique of nonsense humor, Freud points out the pleasure which the joker takes in "misleading and annoying his hearer" who "damps down his annoyance" by resolving "to tell the joke himself later on" (p. 139, n.) to the next victim in the joking chain. Thus the joking triangle is always a quadrilateral of sorts, a social chain in which the imaginary capture of both the joke's object (pole two) and its listener (pole three) is perpetuated with a changing cast of players. Even though the joke *seems* to function as a tool for establishing community (between one and three) and for allowing the ego of the victorious joker to triumph over adversity by circumventing obstacles to satisfaction, the joking process nonetheless turns out to be as double-edged as its punchline. For the joking process is a circuit in which no one's identity remains uncontaminated by exposure to the Other's desire. In the case of the joker himself, the joke betrays an incapacity to fulfil the original design, except in imagination (boy never really gets girl, after all); while in the case of the butt of the joke, the process signifies vulnerability to humiliation or exposure. As for the listener of the joke, the transaction entails being taken in by the joker's bribe of pleasure, and being "used" to arouse the joker's pleasure (Freud: "I am making use of him to arouse my own laughter," p. 156); the listener, moreover, is subsequently *compelled* to pass this stigma of pleasure along to the next unsuspecting victim in the chain. As Freud insists, "a joke *must* be told to someone else . . . something *remains over* which seeks, by communicating the idea, to bring the unknown process of constructing a joke to a conclusion" (p. 143, my emphasis).

More Love Stories

Freud of course wrote *Jokes* early in his career (the first edition was published in 1905), but he returned to it again and again, both by allusion to the original theory and by repetition of the master-plot in a number of other avatars. Version number two is another shady story of love, aggressivity, and renunciation, even more classic than the first.

The subject of Freud's second love story is Oedipus; the desired object his mother.[4] In the classic myth, of course, boy does indeed get girl, by simply eliminating the paternal rival. The bad joke is thus pulled on the subject by the Father/Fate, who reveals the punchline—"your girl is your mother"—too late to allow Oedipus to avert the tragic short-circuit, the incestuous bond. Significantly, Freud points out the importance of the dramatic device of surprise in this revelation.[5] We might say, then, that the sudden revelation of the mystery, after the subject's prolonged and circuitous voyage towards a veiled truth, functions like a punchline of sorts, depending on the same sort of "bewilderment and illumination" (*J.R.U.*, pp. 11-14) which produces the impact of the joke. (It is also an instance of "the rediscovery of something familiar"—all too familiar in the case of Oedipus—discussed in the fourth section of *Jokes*.) The shock of the revealed truth does of course finally obstruct the "wooing talk," undoing the incestuous bond which should never have been consummated in the first place, and reestablishing paternal legitimacy. But once the incest has been committed, it is too late to establish the comic bond (the understanding and complicity between male rivals, poles one and three of the joking paradigm), for the happy ending relies on a series of deflections and a play of "almosts."

Freud's own retelling of the Oedipal myth, however—the postulation of a normal outcome to the Oedipal phase in human development—[6]reinstates the happy ending of the joke paradigm: the subject identifies with the rival father, renounces the impossible love, and chooses a substitute love object to ensure the long-circuiting of his desire. Similarly, in the joking scenario, the illumination at joke's end is no longer the exposure of a tragic crime, but the unveiling of some other forbidden (but less menacing) "truth." (Freud repeatedly reminds us that the joke always has something forbidden to say, and that the primary function of the joke-work is thus to disguise the joke's point—until its revelation in the punchline—and to soften its punch by "wrapping" it in acceptable form [p. 132]). The comic long-circuit is thus necessarily a theatrical one, a drama of disguise and facade, which requires at least three layers of layering. First, it must veil its own point, in order to surprise the listener at joke's end. Second, it wraps the point in taste and good humor, in order not to offend the listener at the (always partial) unveiling. Finally, as the superimposition of the Oedipal triangle on the joking process suggests, the joke cloaks the primal urges of love and aggressivity which found all human creativity (does not Freud insist that all non-innocent jokes are "hostile or obscene"? p. 97). Indeed, Freud's own comic retelling of the Oedipal myth is already a creative textual process: Freud effects a weaving of motive and action in which the fundamental impulse (towards the short-circuit of incest, a death-like quiescence of desire) always remains disguised, perhaps even to the master story-teller himself.

Story as Creative Play

To the reader acquainted with Freud's own account of the creation of narrative (in the 1908 essay "Creative Writers and Day-dreaming," *S.E.*, 9, 143), all of this talk of disguise and facade will seem uncannily familiar. For Freud's own *Poetics* insists on the role of veiling (*Verkleidung*) in the creative process: the writer softens his own daydreams—themselves already "veiled" versions of the selfsame hostile and erotic impulses which motivate the joking process—by "changes and disguises" (*S.E.*, 9, 153). In other words, in order for the writer to satisfy his own wish, he must display his "object" to a voyeur (the reader), but only after an appropriate veiling has taken place. Like the joker, who says something forbidden in an acceptable way, the writer stages a tasteful strip tease, consummating his own pleasure by establishing a bond with the reader. The writing triangle, when superimposed on the first two, emerges as yet another circuitous retelling of the masterplot of human desire, in which the final union is one of social complicity rather than a short-circuit of illicit libido. The joking triangle may be overdetermined thus:

2
desired female-butt of joke
Jocasta-Mother
Writer's "daydream" object-character

1	3
desiring subject-joker	intruder-accomplice-joke hearer
Oedipus-Child	Laius-Father
writer-dreamer	reader

Interestingly, both of Freud's major esthetic treatises—the essay on writers and writing, and the work on jokes—insist on the relation of creative activity to child's play, first as a source of pleasure entailing the rebellion against logic and propriety, and second as the initial social process by which the child gains mastery over reality, replaying unpleasant experiences to his own liking. In *Beyond the Pleasure Principle* (1920), a third work which holds clues crucial to an understanding of the Freudian esthetic (*S.E.*, 18, 3), child's play is described as two different manifestations of the compulsion to repeat.

In the first of the scenes described by Freud, the often-discussed *"Fort-Da"* game of Freud's grandchild, the child compensates for the absence of the real object (the Mother, who presumably has been "taken out" by the Father) by casting away and retrieving the substitute objects, his toys, in a kind of yo-yo repetition which *he* controls absolutely. Like the writer or the joker, the desiring child comes to terms with privation or frustration with a creative solution which affords him a compensation for the satisfaction denied by the interference of the third party (the Father who initiates him into social contract or comic bond to which all human beings are subject).

In Freud's second version of the play situation, the social interaction is not implied (with other actors in the wings) but explicit: the child repeats an unpleasant experience (a visit to the family doctor, for instance) by playing at it later on with a playmate (*S.E.*, 18, 11). Only in the repeat performance, the usually younger or smaller playmate is forced to be the patient, the *object* of the experiment. The mechanism by which the child moves from a passive to an active role, mastering reality, is thus strikingly similar to that by which the joke's hearer gains vengeance on the teller by repeating the joke to the next victim (see above, p.000). Freud's own repetition of the original boy meets girl anecdote, then—replayed as "boy meets adversary/doctor"—reveals that desire may be experienced not only as an impulse to possession of a libidinal object but also as an impulse to domination or mastery. Frustration of either aspect of desire, the hostile or the erotic, seems to inflict a stigma of sorts, activating a compelling urge to pass the experience along, by sharing (or inflicting?) the pleasure.

Enter Lacan, who hears the joke of human intersubjectivity from Freud, and captivated in his turn, resolves to retell it with his own inflection, insisting on the "Imaginary" nature of all happy endings.

II

Intersubjectivity as Text

> This is precisely where the Oedipus com-
> plex[. . .] may be said to mark the limits that
> our discipline assigns to subjectivity[. . . .]
> The primordial Law is revealed clearly
> enough as identical to an order of Language.
> Lacan, *Écrits I*, p. 156

Joke as "Imaginary" Capture

In his very useful translation and study of Lacan's "The Function
of Language in Psychoanalysis,"[7] Anthony Wilden emphasizes two
vectors of Lacan's Imaginary order (pp. 155-177), as that enthrall-
ment with a fellow being which is first manifest in the mirror stage
of human development (the vector of aggressivity or capture,
aiming at the incorporation of the image of the other); and the
vector of identification with the other as a fellow being, an alter
ego or like self (pp. 166-168). Laplanche and Pontalis have pointed
out (in *Le vocabulaire de la psychanalyse* [Paris: P.U.F., 1967]) that
Lacan also uses the term Imaginary to designate a type of understanding or logic which is "essentially predisposed to delusion" and
in which resemblance and identification play a major role, enabling
the subject to maintain certain illusions about his *own* identity or
"image." (Lacan concedes that some such "delusions" are necessary
to the maintenance of mental health.)

Now according to Freud's explanation of the joking process as
a kind of defense mechanism against the obstacles to desire posed
by reality, the joking reaction would seem to qualify as one of those
patterns of Imaginary behavior which function as a support of the
subject's self-image. For, as we have seen, the mirage of the joker's
identity as victor in the joking transaction is a Lacanian *méconnaissance* of sorts, supported by mechanisms of mimetic capture and
identification (see above, p. 000) Similarly, Freud's view of the
writer's activity seems to suggest that the creation of a literary text
is a related Imaginary transaction, since it depends both on the
writer's identification with his object (the hero of his narrative) and
the reader's identification with the writer's desire, "misrecognized"
as that of the novel's protagonist, thanks to the technique of dis-
quise or veiling.

But of course Lacan's insistence on the illusory nature of all Imaginary triumphs suggests that the transparency of Freud's masterplot masks a more complicated story. For it is equally possible to argue that the joking process functions in the Symbolic register, both because of it Oedipal sub-plot, emphasizing the third term, and because of its reliance on the Symbolic order of language to effect a resolution of the Oedipal rivalry.[8] In other words, one could argue that the Symbolic register, identified by Lacan with paternal Law, designates the domination of the pleasure principle by the reality principle[9]: the human subject's encounter with "real" obstacles, ensured by the very existence of an Oedipal third term, initiates all creative response. This is the punchline of Freud's master anecdote, as retold by Lacan (and relaying, as the old joke says, "some good news and some bad news"): the Symbolic reign of Law both deprives and enables, frustrating the subject's desire and offering the possibility of creative recompense.

"The Unconscious Is Structured Like a Language"

Lacan's purloined punchline then, concerns the inevitability of the encounter of every human subject with an excessive circuit of desire, and declares the primacy of the Symbolic order in this *Unconscious* intersubjective system. In an important essay on Lacan and Lévi-Strauss, Jeffrey Mehlman defines this intersubjective linguistic Unconscious as "a third domain, neither self nor other, but the system of communicative relations by which both are necessarily constituted and in which they are alienated" ("The Floating Signifier: from Lévi-Strauss to Lacan," in *Yale French Studies*, 48[1972], p. 17). In other words, if the "Unconscious is structured like a language," to cite Lacan's celebrated formula, it is because as the locus of intersubjective involvement, the Unconscious is the very condition of language.

Once again, we may look to Freud's "transparent" text of joking for an "evident" clue to understanding Lacan's doctrine. For the main point of *Jokes* is that the joke-work (condensation and displacement) is grounded in primary process. The paradigm of desiring intersubjectivity is written in the very language of the Unconscious itself.

Now for Lacan, condensation and displacement, the fundamental modes of primary process, are associated with metaphor and metonymy, the fundamental modes of language. Borrowing from Roman Jakobson, Lacan defines these functions as the two intersecting axes of language: metaphor corresponds with the vertical axis of selection (the "paradigmatic" axis in Jakobson's system), while metonymy corresponds with the horizontal axis of combination (Jakobson's "syntagmatic" axis).[10] Metaphor, moreover, as the substitution of one word *for* another, is associated in Lacan's system with the process of repression, which excludes the original term from the spoken or conscious discourse; while metonymy, as the linking of one word *to* another, is associated with the excessive chain of desire which acts like the motor of language, driving the signifying chain forward into meaningful combinations.[11]

Thus for Lacan the metaphoric and metonymic structures are themselves metaphors for intersubjectivity (the trope of metaphor representing the function of repression in which the conscious/unconscious split ["*Spaltung*"] occurs; the trope of metonymy representing the social community of interrelated subjects). Or it might be more accurate to say that both figures function as synecdoches for the system of language to which they belong; for in Lacan's theory, metaphor and metonymy seem to function as "parts which represent the whole," moments in language which illustrate and reenact the functioning of the whole system as a desiring circuit of interrelated subjects.

The Art of Procrastination

In a fascinating essay on *Beyond the Pleasure Principle* ("Freud's Masterplot," *Yale French Studies*, 55/56 [1977]) Peter Brooks has described the interworkings of metaphor and metonymy as the motor of narrative plot. Brooks argues that an oscillation between a kind of horizontal drive toward the ending of the story and a vertical blockage achieved by all the repetitions or doubling back in the text provides a kind of "grammar of plot, where repetition, taking us back again over the same ground, could have to do with the choice of ends" (p. 286). In other words, the rhythm of narrative plot is a comic rhythm, a movement of starts and stops which defers the final imaginary solution. When one views the narrative process through the transparent theory of the joking process—as a play of blockage (metaphor) and forward movement (metonymy)—one perceives that the work of fiction, like the living subject who creates it, is motivated by energies which must be bound or contained by metaphoric repetition so that the narrative (to borrow a phrase from Freud) may "die in its own way."

In "Desire and the Interpretation of Desire in *Hamlet*," (translated in Yale French Studies 55/56 [1977], p. 11), Lacan describes the circuitous nature of the plot of Shakespeare's famous tale in similar terms, emphasizing the role of the hero as a procrastinator, an idler who is forced to feign madness "in order to follow the winding paths that lead him to the completion of his act" (p. 13). In this story of detours and deliberately missed opportunities, Hamlet's desire seems to be engendered by a privation: the absence of the slain father. Lacan points out that the plot is prolonged by a series of missed appointments (pp. 41-44) which are emblematic of the failure of the desiring subject to attain his goal or to possess the object of his desire. But what, exactly, *is* Hamlet's "objective"? If one reads *Hamlet* in terms of the Freudian masterplot (the Oedipal-joking-writing triangular circuit), it becomes clear that the missing and desired object is not the dead father, but the guilty mother (and her alter-ego Ophelia, the sister-figure who is tainted by Hamlet's desire). The missed appointment to which Lacan refers, then, could be read as Hamlet's failure to consummate the incestuous union, that infantile short-circuit which is also the original temptation in the joking circuit. The forbidden incest, furthermore, may itself be read as a metaphoric stand-in, "veiling" the final satisfaction of death (return to the womb = return to the tomb).

One might say, then, that the missed appointment upon which Lacan focuses functions as a kind of comic obstacle, allowing the play to go on in a prolonged detour from its fatal and tragic conclusion. Yet Hamlet's procrastination has its own double meaning: if, on the one hand, it is an avoidance of the incestuous "Imaginary" solution, the short-circuit of desire, it is at the same time an avoidance of compliance with the Symbolic Law. In other words, Hamlet's postponement is a hesitation between complicity with the maternal incest (which as a guilty onlooker, the son "enjoys" vicariously) and compliance with the paternal demand for vengeance. Of course, just as in the case of Oedipus, it is already too late for Hamlet to establish a comic bond with the interfering third party: the father who could save him is dead, and Hamlet is in effect a co-conspirator in the crime of incest, because of his guilty silence. The choice for Hamlet, then, is not "to be or not to be," but how long to prolong being, whether to opt for the pleasure-death of incest or the punishment-death to which he is sentenced by the Father's Law, whether to go to death by the long or the short route. Hamlet's final act, of course, is a sacrifice to the Symbolic, a coming to terms with the Law. The play ends in that fatal duel scene, wherein Hamlet "demands satisfaction," and finds it, in death. When the comic possibility is finally relinquished, so is the fiction itself: the play comes to its timely end, after its dalliance with impossible comic detours. From Lacan's reading of *Hamlet*, then, we may perceive that the destiny of plot parallels and repeats that of the human subject, caught in a text of sexual and linguistic intersubjectivity. Narrative or plot thus replays the human comedy itself: in a perverse gesture of deflection from goal, each of us plays a comic role of dalliance en route to the final scene of the intersubjective play in which we are cast.

III

Text as (Feminine) Symptom

> "The symptom *is* a metaphor . . . just as de-
> sire *is* a metonymy."
> > Jacues Lacan, "The Instance of the
> > Letter in the Unconscious"

> "For this sign is indeed that of the woman."
> Lacan, "Seminar on
> > 'The Purloined Letter' "

Narrative as Perversion

In Freud's *Three Essays on the Theory of Sexuality* (*S.E.*, 7, 125), a clear distinction is drawn between two types of sexual aberration. Writing that perversion is the *negative* of neurosis, Freud insists that any perversion—including the specific perversion of fetishism which denies the observed fact of the castration of the desired female object—both displaces and satisfies sexual desire with an object which has been substituted for the original unattainable one. (Or, as Lacan would have it, the new object takes the place of what the subject is deprived of.) In neurosis, on the other hand, the desire is not displaced but is repressed into the Unconscious, leaving the neurotic symptom to signify what it has replaced. Trans-

coding Freud's theory into linguistic terms, Lacan has maintained
that the neurotic symptom is metaphoric in nature, because it replaces the original repressed sexual meaning with a non-sexual
term. (Both hysteria—which is the result of unsatisfied desire—
and obsession—the result of impossible desire—are thus metaphoric functions for Lacan.)[12] In the essay on *Hamlet,* moreover,
Lacan differentiates between the metaphoric neurosis and the metonymic perversion in terms of the presence or absence of the
subject in the symptomatic behavior: whereas the subject experiences a gratification of sorts in the perverse solution to desire, in
the neurotic or hysteric solution the "real" subject is barred or
silenced, repressed into the unconscious chain. (This is perhaps
another way of framing Freud's assertion that the hysteric is not
capable of recounting her own history, without the intervention of
the analyst.) In any case, Lacan's theory emphasizes the symptomatic nature of both metaphor and metonymy as responses to ob-
structions of desire.

In addition to defining perversion as the negative of neurosis
(in the *Three Essays* cited above), Freud emphasizes that perversion
is a derailment of sorts, a sidetracking by which desire is deflected
from its original biological aim.[13] (Similarly, Lacan refers to metonymy as a "derailment of instinct," insisting on the fetishistic
nature of the metonymic displacement [*Écrits I,* pp. 277-278]). In
the introduction to his work on jokes, written at the same time as
the *Three Essays on a Theory of Sexuality,* Freud defines the term
esthetic as an "attitude towards an object . . . characterized by the
condition that we do not ask anything of the object, *especially no
satisfaction of our vital needs*" (*J.R.U.,* p. 10-11, my emphasis).
Readers like Peter Brooks and Jeffrey Mehlman[14] have not failed
to point out the implication in Freud's companion definitions of
the *perverse* and the *esthetic:* by Freud's own logic, esthetic processes—including joking and textual/literary activity—may be considered "perverse," since they depend on deflection and deferral
of desire, which is sidetracked from its original goal in order to
produce a pleasure clearly dissociated from "the satisfaction of vital
needs." Yet in a Lacanian reading, this view of esthetic processes
as both perverse and excessive need not imply a divorce from the
mundanities of real life (as does, for instance, the Kantian view of
the esthetic as that which is unsullied by utilitarian concerns or
goals), since for Lacan the literary work must be understood as a
function of the subject's involvement in a social web of Others.

Now insofar as metaphoric "repression" results from an encounter with the restraining and censoring agent of Law, it might be associated with the Symbolic register. Metonymy, on the other hand, might be associated with the Imaginary register, both because it seems to offer a satisfactory ending with a substitute object (happy endings are always suspect for Lacan) and because it is associated with a denial or misrecognition of the obstacles or privations to which the human subject is exposed (as in the denial of castration by the fetishist, for example). The interworking of these two orders or registers—in the joking process as in the literary text—stands as evidence that the Imaginary and the Symbolic modes are not successive stages of human development so much as coextensive principles of intersubjective experience.

The emphasis on one or the other of these functions in the literary process, however, will inevitably be reflected in one's critical perspective.[15] For depending upon which register is perceived as the dominant one in the esthetic act of writing, the reader will either see the literary process as an exercise of identification with a poet of superior vision (the artist as seer or Legislator of Mankind); or s/he will view the literary process as an intersubjective (Symbolic) circuit which traps both author and reader in an ongoing "end-game" played according to the rules of farce. In the second perspective, the Imaginary confidence in the literary process as a cure for desire is considered to be illusory, for the text is read as a symptom of the inexhaustibility of the desire which generates it.

The Gender of Symptom

> A man man enough to defy to the point of
> scorn a lady's fearsome ire undergoes the
> curse of the sign he has dispossessed her of.
> Lacan, "Seminar on
> 'The Purloined Letter' "

If Lacan himself may be considered to have written a "transparent" text—containing an "evident" clue concerning the intersubjective nature of the textual process—it is doubtless the "Seminar on 'The Purloined Letter,' " which comments on desire as a metonymic process, a transmissible symptom in a social chain. In

the Seminar, the desire of each of the players results not merely
from privation, the absence of the object of satisfaction (the purloined letter): it also results from contact with other desiring
agents, and as such, functions as a contractable social contagion.
Even to enter the game is to function as an object oneself, in a
curious kind of relay where the letter is passed from hand to hand.
In a dazzling display of wit, Lacan describes this game as a play of
a group of ostriches ("*l'autricherie*"), each of whom imagines himself secure, head in the sand, even as he is plucked bare from
behind.[16] This circuit of desire obeys the inexorable logic of farce,
summed up in the pithy (and somewhat untranslatable) French
aphorism "*à trompeur, trompeur et demie.*" For in this game of rogues
and dupes, each Dupin is duped in turn; each rogue is assured of
his comeuppance at the hands of a more clever scoundrel, "a rogue
and a half."

Now the notion of the *gender* of the symptom of desire is central
to Lacan's Seminar on Poe. Indeed, for Lacan as for Freud, femininity seems to be a stigma (of castration? or passivity?), a symptom
signifying a vulnerability or privation which may be passed from
player to player. Throughout Freud's work, the question of the
relation between symptom and gender—a question which under-
lies not only the "boy meets girl" formulation of the joking scenario, but also the classification of the disorder of paranoia as
"male" and the disorder of hysteria as "female"—is complicated by
Freud's own hesitation between two views of sexuality. In some of
his works, Freud seems to argue for a natural and gender-specific
sexuality—as in his early formulation of symmetrical Oedipal
phases for boys and girls, with each sex attracted to the opposite
sex—while in other works (primarily in the *Three Essays* on sexuality
discussed above), he seems to assume a natural bisexuality,
whereby both sexes, as possessors of a "male" libido, are initially
attracted to the maternal love object. According to this view, femininity is an acquired trait which the girl child learns to accept
reluctantly, after the discovery of her anatomical "deficiency."[17] In
any case, Freud consistently associates the gender "male" with an
active and armed state, and "female" with a passive and disarmed
condition.

The notion of femininity as transmissible stigma and the corollary
notion of the feminizing effect of entry into the desiring circuit
are both crucial considerations for that "frame" of discussions on
Poe's celebrated story (Johnson on Derrida on Lacan on Poe)[18] to

which I wish to return in concluding this essay. The gender-related facts of the case *appear* "evident" (perhaps too evident?): the original victim in the desiring circuit (the Queen) is archetypically female; and she is clearly "violated" by the theft of the incriminating letter. Like pole two in the original joking circuit, her (guilty) sexuality is "exposed" to (and by) the Minister's male gaze. But once again, the "evidence" may be misleading: even this initial act of violation, apparently perpetrated by male on female, is marked by ambiguity of gender, owing to the phallic nature of the letter which the Queen-as-Ruler initially possesses. (Derrida, of course, has argued that Lacan's reading is phallocentric, agreeing with Marie Bonaparte that the purloined letter signifies the clitoris rather than the phallus, based on its anatomical position in the Minister's room.) In Lacan's reading, the Queen seems to begin in the "male" position of power and possession, and is only subsequently feminized as a result of the castrating act of the Minister. And as the plot thickens, so does the ambiguity: the male ravisher, now holding the phallic sign of power, has moved to an exposed position where he is vulnerable to attack by the next "duper," Dupin. This explains Lacan's characterization of the letter as a curse, a kind of "hot potato" destined to be passed on, and which inevitably causes its holder to get burned, as the next object of the next trick. In this curious game of tag, the player is never so feminine as when it is "his" turn to be "it," when s/he is *possessed* of the phallic object (and not when "she" is castrated or deprived of the phallus, as psychoanalytic convention would have it). As Barbara Johnson points out, the curious message of the purloined letter is that "femininity" seems to be a position or locus: anyone may be on the spot, the butt of the joke. (Indeed, we have seen that in the joking paradigm one is feminine if "she" has something the other wants—attention, love, maternal breast—and thus the feminine "object" is the holder of a certain ambiguous power over the desiring subject.) The ambiguity of the "on the spot" position of the letter's holder may be described as follows: one is stigmatized and objectified by the very power that defines her/him as agent. (The person who is "it," after all, is galvanized to action by this stigma, compelled to act.) This is the paradoxical gist of farcical logic: *à trompeur, trompeur et demie.*

The logic of farce also seems to inform the Lacanian concept of desire as excess (the surplus of demand over need),[19] since Lacan insists that the pur-loined letter is not only stolen but "pro-longed"

in its "excessive" journey. In Lacan's reading, the purloined letter
is above all else a chain letter whose accruing returns are assured
(à trompeur, trompeur *et demie*), and which thus provides a punchline of sorts to the archetypal nonsense joke. Why does the chicken
cross the road, if not to come home to roost?

Literary Trickery

Thus Lacan's retelling of Freud's masterplot clears up several
points in the too transparent "boy meets girl" scenario. In Lacan's
version, for instance, it becomes obvious that the supposedly distinct and gender-identified roles of the joking triangle are not only
often exchangeable but are actually coincidental or superimposed:
each player is active *and* passive, desiring *and* desired, giver *and*
receiver, not only successively but simultaneously. Since one only
receives the punch line (like the purloined letter) in order to give
it away, the notions of "active" and "passive" lose their specificity,
as do the corollary notions of "male" and "female" gender.

Lacan's version of Freud's masterplot also clearly reveals the
fetishistic nature of the desiring circuit. In Lacan's narrative, each
successive theft is concealed in the replacement of the missing object by something similar which veils its absence, a simulacrum of
the original letter. The sleight of hand is all important: the ravisher
must put something in the place of the stolen letter, so that the
victim will remain unaware of the trick, for a time at least. In this
case, then, the feminine position (of dupe) is that of a fetishist
whose attention is fixed on a substitute for the missing object of
desire.[20] In this way, Poe's theft reproduces the technique of the
joking exchange, which also depends on a sleight of hand, a displacement of the listener's attention until the final unveiling of the
punch line. Of course the listener is a willing victim in this entertainment, since he voluntarily lends his attention to the joker-
trickster who has lured his "victim" with the promise of pleasure.

Similarly, the literary text "passifies" its reader-receiver by a
bribe of pleasure, enlisting the reader's cooperation in a pleasure-
circuit which would otherwise remain incomplete. But just as in
the joking transaction, which depends on the art of the joker's
technique (or delivery) in order to produce its effect, the textual
transaction depends on the writer's art, and thus places the artist
himself "on the spot." For if his art fails, if we fail to enjoy his text

(like a joke fallen flat), the writer's very identity as poet—craftsman is shattered. His "image" is always constituted by an Imaginary bargain—the willing suspension of disbelief—which entails the reader-spectator's acceptance of a literary code different from that governing everyday communication. The completed pleasure circuit of the text, whether narrative or poetic, relies on a tenuous agreement to grant the writer a certain poser of enchantment, and to accept the "bribe of forepleasure" which veils and softens egotistical material. The textual exchange, like the joking exchange, is a power-play on the part of the subject, initiated (paradoxically) by privation or impotence. It is thus an Imaginary satisfaction enabled by the Symbolic Law (the "truth" of the renunciation which the substitute satisfaction "veils"). The joking/literary transaction is, then, the *negative* of the analytic transaction—yet another triangular drama, but one in which the analyst plays two of the three roles ("object" and listener). And in this particular triangle, the analyst must *refuse* the "bribe" of pleasure, adopting a posture of scepticism vis-a-vis the truth of the subject's discourse, in order to break the Imaginary bond between subject and object (the transference). If the analyst *fails* to refuse to get involved, he will of course prejudice the result of the therapy, as is evinced, for instance, by Freud's celebrated failure with Dora.[21] (This recalls Freud's assertion that if the hearer becomes emotionally involved with the topic of the joke, his sympathetic reaction will jeopardize the joke's effect or impact.)

What each of these instances of the desiring circuit finally underscores is that the Imaginary and the Symbolic are not distinct developmental phases in human life, but interacting registers of a continuing intersubjective discourse. Indeed, the joking paradigm demonstrates how an interplay of recognition and misrecognition, bewilderment and illumination, passivity and activity, establishes the essential plot or rhythm of all creative endeavor. This recognition (of the interworking of Imaginary and Symbolic registers) is accentuated in many contemporary texts, which—rather than insisting on writing as a triumph of "activity," a display of masculine mastery—have opted to emphasize the desire which motivates the textplay. This is perhaps the sense of the poststructuralist emphasis on the *écriture féminine,* and on *écriture as* "féminine": the stigma of femininity as symptom becomes the privileged metaphor for the writer's own situation in desire.

IV

Femininity as Subjectivity (Can "she" write?)

> And what does this experience, precisely,
> teach us about the phallus, if not that it
> makes a joke of phallicism?
> Moustafa Safouan, "Feminine
> Sexuality in Psychoanalytic Doctrine"[22]

Our circular itinerary has visited several questions—the comic nature of intersubjectivity, intersubjectivity as text, text as play of metaphoric and metonymic symptom, symptom as "femininity"— and has arrived at a puzzling punchline. In Lacan's version of Freud's transparent master narrative, the closing line seems to read (comically) neither BOY GETS GIRL nor even BOY GETS BOY but BOY *IS* GIRL. For Lacan, the role of "second"—the objective locus in the master paradigm—is a role which we all play in turn.

But if Lacan's lesson for the subject (pole one, the joker/writer) is that he too may be "female," it still remains unclear whether the obverse is also true: can "she" assume subjectivity? Can the "shifter" "I" shift genders?[23] Can "she" become the agent of desire, the active pole, the joker? What happens if "she" refuses to mediate the (male) comic bond?[24] In terms of Freud's original scenario, what happens if "she," however offended by the male conspirators, refuses to leave the room, feeling ashamed?[25] In other words, what does a woman want? The question, first posed by Freud, reverberates throughout Lacan's work, and leads inevitably to a second inquiry: What is Woman? Can "she" want anything at all?[26]

Indeed, in his later work, Lacan not only speculates about the femininity of metaphoric symptom (as veiling or masquerade) and of metonymic desire (as a perverse circuit which castrates its participants), but he also comes to posit "Woman" herself as symptom of the male system which her myth sustains ("the Woman does not exist").[27] As Jacqueline Rose and Juliet Mitchell have pointed out in their introductory notes to Lacan's essays in *Feminine Sexuality* (New York and London: W. W. Norton, 1982), there has been a lively debate as to whether Lacan's position may be considered to be a *feminist* critique of the structures of patriarchy, refuting an Imaginary notion of "The Woman," or merely the latest patriarchal strategy for relegating femininity to the idealist and absolute category of "Otherness," in which Woman is destined to function as a predicate to the male subject.

For while Lacan appears to espouse the Freudian notion of bi-sexuality, refuting the notion of pre-given gender, he nonetheless insists on defining femininity as a linguistically determined locus (Rose: "Woman is excluded by the nature of words, meaning that the definition poses her as exclusion. . . . Within the phallic defi-nition, the woman is constituted as 'not all' in so far as the phallic function rests on an exception—the 'not'—which is assigned to her" [*Feminine Sexuality*, p. 49]). Thus Lacan insists on assigning woman to an objective role—the role of the excluded term—even while he insists that that exclusion is linguistically rather than biologically determined. Indeed, Lacan's exile of the feminine subject from language is reminiscent of Freud's theory of the feminine hysteric as a "blocked" speaker whose symptoms include lying (the misuse of language) and pantomime (the non-use of language). Freud refers to the hysteric's discourse as "an unnaviagable river whose stream is choked by masses of rock," and thus suggests that it is the analyst's function to steer a course through the shoals of "her" obstructed discourse.[28]

Lacan is again following Freud's lead by insisting on woman's position as object—or even as absence—in the linguistic system. Even though he insists that this position is not inherent, but is rather a position *conferred* by language ("woman is not inferior, she is subjugated" [Lacan] *F.S.*, p. 45), Lacan nonetheless insists on the insoluble character of the feminine linguistic dilemma (Rose: "All speaking beings must line themselves up on one side or other of this division of gender, but anyone can cross over and inscribe themselves on the opposite side from that to which they are ana-tomically destined," *F.S.*, p. 49). One could argue that by placing the phallus at the center of the signifying system, Lacan has as-sured the predicative status of woman, and has also effectively canceled the possibility of finding an answer to the question which persists throughout his later work ("what does a woman want?"). For as long as woman cannot speak, as long as she is excluded from the subjective roles in the desiring triangle (poles one and three, joker and future joker), she is condemned to her role as "wanted woman," the *object* in the hunt for the feminine subject.

Other Voices

Feminist theorists have not failed to point out the ideological problems inherent in Lacan's definition of femininity as acquired (or required?) linguistic trait, persisting in a critique of phallo-

centrism by pointing out the hidden agenda which informs the
grounding of libido (or speech itself) in the male body. Luce Irigaray, for example, argues that the metaphorization of female sexuality (by which the clitoris is represented in terms of the phallus)
represses the feminine term in its specificity, replacing it by the male
term (of which it becomes a deficient copy).[29]

Similarly, Gayatri Spivak has emphasized the ideological functions of this repression of feminine sexuality. In a recent essay, she
has pointed out that the threatening aspect of feminine sexuality,
the "scandal" that must be repressed, is the biological fact that
woman's pleasure is excessive, insofar as it functions "perversely"
in its independence from reproductive process ("French Feminism
in an International Frame," *YFS*, 62 [1981], pp. 154-184). In the
same volume of *Yale French Studies*, Naomi Schor raises the related
issue of the gender of theory. (For Freud, of course, the paranoid-
theorist is essentially male; the female paranoid is considered an
aberration.)[30] Schor points out that female theorizing seems to be
grounded in the body, even in Freud's account, and that this is the
source of its "feminine" specificity. This argument is reminiscent
of Kristéva's characterization of feminine writing as a kind of *jouissance*, a pleasure grounded in the heterogeneity of a pre-Oedipal
semiotic mode.[31] But as Schor herself argues, any such emphasis
on the grounding of theory in the female body is in fact "a risky
enterprise" (p. 215), since any valorization of the essential and
biologically unique aspects of feminity may reinforce the conclusion that biology is destiny.[32]

Of course, Lacanian theory represents the antithesis of this essentialist view, because it maintains that gender is a linguistic rather
than a biological distinction. Even more importantly, the notion of
subjectivity itself is problematized by Lacan in a way which has
profound consequences for his theory of femininity and feminine
sexuality. In her introduction to the essays in *Feminine Sexuality*,
Jacqueline Rose sums up Lacan's rebuttal to feminist objections
concerning the male orientation of psychoanalytic theory:

> He [argues] that failure to recognize the interdependency of these two
> concerns in Freud's work—the theory of subjectivity and femininity
> together—has led psychoanalysts into an ideologically loaded mistake,
> that is, an attempt to resolve the difficulties of Freud's account of fem-
> ininity by aiming to resolve the difficulty of femininity itself. For by
> restoring the woman to her place and identity (which, they argue, Freud
> out of "prejudice" failed to see), they have missed Freud's corre-

sponding stress on the division and precariousness of human subjectivity itself. . . . Re-opening the debate on feminine sexuality must start,
therefore, with the link between sexuality and the unconscious. . . . For
Lacan, the unconscious undermines the subject from any position of
certainty . . . and *simultaneously* reveals the fictional nature of the sexual
category to which every human subject is nonetheless assigned. (*Feminine Sexuality*, p. 29)

In other words, Lacanian theory exposes the privilege of the
(male) primary signifier as an Imaginary construct: the phallus is
precisely what no one "himself" ever has. Yet the effect of this
theory, as we have seen, is to lead "woman" back to her place (Rose:
"The question is what a woman is in this account always stalls on
the crucial acknowledgment that there is absolutely no guarantee
that she *is* at all. But if she takes up her place according to the
process described, then her sexuality will betray, necessarily, the
impasses of its history," *F.S.*, p. 43.). Thus if she agrees to exist at
all, "woman" must take up her impossible place on the Other side
of the divide.

There are of course many feminist theorists—among them Kristéva, Schor, Spivak, Alice Jardine—who have taken a position on
feminine sexuality which lies somewhere between the extremes of
the essentialist biological view and the non-essentialist linguistic
view espoused by Lacan (a view which threatens to do away with
"woman" altogether). These theorists generally do posit an essential difference between male and female sexuality/subjectivity, and
they tend to concur that this difference is grounded in the body,
rather than in a purely linguistic or symbolic determination.[33] For
Naomi Schor, however, a theory of feminine subjectivity must re-
consider the givens of linguistic theory. Schor proposes supple-
menting the Lacanian theory on metaphor and metonymy—which
she sees as reflections of a masculinist perspective on sexuality and
subjectivity—with a theory of synechdoche, which she considers to
be a uniquely feminine trope.[34] Gayatri Spivak and Alice Jardine
both insist that the search for an authentic feminine subjectivity
must be grounded in the "Real" (to use Lacan's term for the third
register of human experience), that is, in a critique of the assumptions and attitudes of partriarchy. Their studies attempt to retain
the radical thrust of Lacan's reevaluation of subjectivity without
reentering that impasse by which woman becomes only locus or
socio-linguistic construct.

"Return to Freud"

Now it is ironic that Lacan's later work, which continually poses the question of the nature of femininity, seems to have lost sight of that important clue to the enigma hidden in Freud's "transparent" essay on the joking process. Before describing the "boy meets girl" scenario which enacts the fundamental narrative of desire, Freud makes a few seemingly marginal, and deceptively obvious, remarks about the nature of sexuality in general:

> It can only help to clarify things if at this point we go back to the fundamental facts. A desire to see the organs peculiar to each sex exposed is one of the original components of our libido. It may itself be a substitute for something earlier and go back to a hypothetical primary desire to touch the sexual parts. . . . The libido for looking and touching is present in every one in two forms, active and passive, male and female; and, according to the preponderance of the sexual character, one form or the other predominates. (*J.R.U.*, p. 98)

Now this characterization of sexuality clearly manifests the bias which persists throughout Freud's work: the identification of active with male and passive with female. But Freud's own joking scenario reveals that the terms active and passive are ambiguous at best, and are coextensive with all three loci of the joking triangle. In this "pre-text" to the joking discussion, moreover, it is the common nature of human sexual experience, be it male or female, which is emphasized: *all* sexuality is first manifest as an active voyeurism or corollary exhibitionism. Freud goes on to suggest that the differences may be culturally determined, maintaining that the female's urge to exhibitionism is "buried under the imposing *reactive* function of sexual modesty" (p. 98). The final sentence of this passage further reinforces the emphasis on cultural variables as determinants of female sexual expression: "I need only hint at the elasticity and variability in the amount of exhibitionism which women are permitted to retain in accordance with differing convention and circumstances" (p. 98). "Convention" permitting, women seem as likely as men to engage in active exhibitionism, the primal expression of libido.

The essential point, furthermore, of Freud's allusion to the commonality of human sexual experience seems to be that it is entirely possible to regard the masculine and the feminine as *different* sexualities without entering into the Lacanian impasse, using that perception of difference to authorize an exclusion of either gender from the creative role of "subject." It would seem, ironically, that Freud's own most "transparent" formulation of the origins of human sexuality is ultimately more compatible with the feminist view—of the *specificity* but not the *essentiality* of "Femininity"—than is that of Lacan. For Freud at least seems to imply, perhaps unwittingly, that even if the female experience of subjectivity is not *identical* to the male experience, owing to sexual difference, there is nevertheless enough common ground on the subjective side of the linguistic divide to accommodate male and female subjects alike. This is perhaps the most important lesson to be gleaned from the "evident" clues in the joking paradigm (with the help of Freud's "Minister" Lacan): if man and woman do exist on opposite sides of a linguistic divide, as Lacan would have it, neither side necessarily initiates the creative activity by which we may attempt to scale the wall.

Lacan has placed a telling epigraph at the head of the third section of "The Function of Language in Psychoanalysis," the same essay in which he alludes to Freud's essay on jokes:

> Between man and love,
>   There is woman.
> Between man and woman,
>   There is a world.
> Between man and the world,
>   There is a Wall.
>
> Antoine TUDAL, in *Paris in the Year 2000*
> (*Écrits I*, p. 170, my translation)

Like the aphorism which describes the farcical circuit of the joking paradigm as well as the intersubjective workings of the literary text (*à trompeur, trompeur et demie*), Lacan's cryptic epigraph contains some good news and some bad news. For if the Wall of desire as emblem of Law is an unavoidable part of our intersubjective experience, Lacan's "return to Freud" suggests that the graffitti which will inevitably appear on the Wall may be read as a comic response to the Symbolic barrier of Law. And as the work of feminist writers and theorists attests, "she" writes on the Wall as well.

Rutgers University

NOTES

1 *Seminar XX* (1972-3), in *Feminine Sexuality*, eds. Juliet Mitchell and Jacqueline Rose (New York and London: W. W. Norton, 1982), p. 157.

2 Translated in *Yale French Studies*, No. 48 (1976), pp. 39-72. (Hereafter referred to as *S.P.L.*)

3 James Strachey, trans., *Standard Edition of the Complete Works of Sigmund Freud* (hereafter referred to as *S.E.*), 8 (New York and London: W. W. Norton).

4 For Freud's treatment of *Oedipus Rex*, and his account of the Oedipal complex, see *The Interpretation of Dreams* (1900), *S.E.*, 4-5; and the *Introductory Lectures on Psycho-analysis* (1916-17), *S.E.*, 15-16.

5 See Section V of the *Interpretation of Dreams* for Freud's discussion of the dramatic technique of *Oedipus Rex*.

6 See "The Dissolution of the Oedipus Complex" (1924), *S.E.*, 19, 173.

7 Anthony Wilden, *The Language of the Self* (New York: Dell Publishing Co., Inc., 1975).

8 For a discussion of Lacan's Symbolic register, see Wilden, *Ibid.*, pp. 249-270.

9 Freud, "Two Principles of Mental Functioning," *S.E.*, 12, 215.

10 Roman Jakobson, "Two Aspects of Language and Two Types of Aphasic Disturbances," in *Fundamentals of Language* (The Hague: Mouton, 1956), pp. 55-82.

11 In "L'Instance de la lettre dans l'inconscient," *Écrits I*, p. 274, Lacan elaborates on Saussure's linguistic theory, recasting the formula S/s to represent the figures of metaphor and metonymy.

12 Lacan on *Hamlet*, *op. cit.*, p. 17.

13 In "L'Instance de la lettre dans l'inconscient" (*Écrits I*, p. 278), Lacan calls metonymy the "derailing of instinct . . . eternally extended towards *the desire of something else*" ("*le désir d'autre chose*").

14 See Jeffrey Mehlman, "How to Read Freud on Jokes: the Critic as *Schadchen*," *New Literary History*, 6, No. 2 (Winter 1975), pp. 439-61.

15 See, for instance, Fredric Jameson's "Imaginary and Symbolic in Lacan: Marxism, Psychoanalytic Criticism, and the Problem of the Subject," *Yale French Studies* 55/56 (1977), pp. 338-95.

16 *S.P.L.*, *Écrits I*, p. 24.

17 "Some Psychological Consequences of the Anatomical Distinction Between the Sexes" (1925), *S.E.*, 19, 243.

18 See Barbara Johnson's "The Frame of Reference: Poe, Lacan, Derrida," *Yale French Studies* 55/56 (1977), p. 457.

19 For Lacan's distinction between need, demand, and desire, see Wilden's discussion on pp. 185-92 in *The Language of the Self*.

20 See Freud's "Fetishism" (1927), *S.E.*, 21, 149.

21 For a series of essays on Freud's "Fragment of an Analysis of a Case of Hysteria" (1905), *S.E.* 7,3 see *Diacritics* 13, No. 1 (Spring 1983), *A Fine Romance: Freud and Dora*.

22 In *Feminine Sexuality*, p. 134.

23 For a discussion of pronouns as "shifters," see Wilden, *op. cit.*, pp. 179-185.

24 René Girard's concept of mediated desire, for instance, centers on the relation between the two male terms in the Oedipal triangle. For a critique of this perspective, see Toril Moi's "The Missing Mother: the Oedipal Rivalries of René Girard," *Diacritics* 12, No. 2 (Summer 1982), pp. 21-31.

25 In this context, see Jane Gallop's "Why Does Freud Giggle When the Women Leave the Room?"—paper read at the *Women and Humor* section of the NEMLA Conference, Hartford, Conn., March 1979.

26 For a discussion of Lacan's definition of Woman, see Monstafa Safouan's "Feminine Sexuality in Psychoanalytic Doctrine," in *Feminine Sexuality* (cited above), pp. 132-36.

27 For Lacan on The Woman, see Rose's Introduction to *Feminine Sexuality*, p. 48.

28 Cited from Sharon Willis, "A symptomatic Narrative," *Diacritics* 13, No. 1 (Spring 1983), p. 48.

29 *Ibid.*, p. 51.

30 Freud's theory of paranoia is the subject of Naomi Schor's "Female Paranoia: The Case for Psychoanlytic Feminist Criticism," *Yale French Studies* 62 (1981), pp. 204-219.

31 Julia Kristéva, *Desire in Language*, ed. Leon S. Roudiez, (New York: Columbia University Press, 1980).

32 In the same issue of *Yale French Studies*, Gayatri Spivak voices similar reservation about the "essentialist" view of radical feminists (p. 181).

33 See, for example, Spivak's aforementioned piece in *Feminist Readings: French Texts/American Contexts, Yale French Studies* 62 (1981), pp. 154-84, and Alice Jardine's "Pre-Texts for the Transatlantic Feminist," in the same issue of *YFS*, pp. 220-236.

34 For Schor, synechdoche "represents" clitoral sexuality, as a "part for the whole" feminine sexual process (*YFS* 62, p. 219).

Literature and Collaboration:
Benoist-Méchin's Return to Proust

❦

Jeffrey Mehlman

> I always think of Swann's story as Proust's
> equivalent of Wagner's Prize Song from *Die
> Meistersinger.*
> —M. Hindus, *A Reader's Guide
> to Marcel Proust*

Might psychoanalysis itself, it has recently been asked, be *une histoire juive*—a fragment of Jewish history or, even more, an elaborate Jewish anecdote?[1] In the course of the colloquium—in Montpellier—which pondered that question, D. Sibony chose to accord
one Jewish joke emblematic status: Katzmann, intent on Gallicizing
his name, translates *Katz* (= *chat*) and *mann* (= *l'homme*), and ends
up as Monsieur Chalom.[2] The onomastic malaise, the interlin-
guistic inventiveness mediating a blind and self-defeating aggression against the (name of the) father invite one to conclude that if
indeed psychoanalysis may be construed as *une histoire juive,* it is in
the sense of the anecdote just related. Call it the case of the Cat
Man.

Sibony's joke may be found, in a curious transformation, toward
the end of *A la recherche du temps perdu.* The narrator encounters
Bloch, Proust's prototypal assimilated Jew, in the Guermantes
salon: "J'eus de la peine à reconnaître mon camarade Bloch, lequel
d'ailleurs maintenant avait pris non seulement le pseudonyme,
mais le nom de Jacques du Rozier, sous lequel il eût fallu le flair
de mon grand-père pour reconnaître la 'douce vallée' de l'Hébron
et les 'chaînes d'Israël' que mon ami semblait avoir définitivement
rompues."[3] The attentive reader realizes that in his flight from
Jewishness, Bloch has inadvertently taken on the name of the *Ju-*

dengasse—la rue des Rosiers—which Charlus, a thousand pages earlier, had deemed the only address fit for him.[4] Here, then, is an
exemplary version of the vacuity of snobbery in Proust: even as
Madame Verdurin is recognized in the Princess de Guermantes,
so does one detect the Jewish ghetto in the pseudonymous French
aristocrat. Jacques du Rozier is the butt of the same joke as Monsieur Chalom. We may call the episode for short Proust's *S/Z*.

In a first approximation, the much vexed question of "psychoanalysis and literature" (or "psychoanalysis and narration") might
be transcribed as (Freud's) *Cat Man* vs. (Proust's) *S/Z*—with the
psychoanalytic traditionalist affirming Monsieur Chalom's (sympathetic) understanding of Jacques du Rozier's plight and his
(more advanced?) adversary contending that on the contrary, *S/Z*
is a far more insightful rendering of matters than the *Cat Man*.
And yet it is precisely the refusal of that mirror-like stand-off (between snobs), the intuition that new understanding can emerge
only in a rigorous disruption of such symmetry, that constitutes a
principal contribution of Lacan to textual interpretation. It is the
effects of such a disruption which structure the remarks on
Proust—and one of his readers—that follow.

Our social existence, Proustian orthodoxy has it, is a long lesson
in the vanity and illusions of snobbery. We are all ultimately
Jacques du Rozier, and can evade his fate only if genius and good
fortune allow us to abandon social life entirely for the realm of
art. Here, then, is an evocation of Proust—forsaking social inter-
course for esthetic contemplation—on the path to that realization:

'Le jour de mon arrivée,' raconte Reynaldo Hahn, en évoquant le souvenir d'un séjour qu'il fit chez des amis avec l'auteur des *Jeunes Filles en
fleurs*, 'nous allâmes ensemble nous promener dans le jardin. Nous pas-
sâmes devant une bordure de rosiers du Bengale, quand, soudain, il se
tut et s'arrêta. Je m'arrêtai aussi, mais il se remit alors à marcher et je
fis de même. Bientôt il m'arrêta et me dit avec cette douceur enfantine
et un peu triste qu'il conserva toujours dans le ton et dans la voix: "Est-
ce que cela vous fâcherait que je reste un peu en arrière? Je voudrais
revoir les petits rosiers." Je le quittai. Au tournant de l'allée, je regardai
derrière moi. Proust avait rebroussé chemin jusqu'aux rosiers. Ayant
fait le tour du château, je le retrouvai à la même place, regardant fixe-
ment les roses. . . .

In this anecdote, quoted from Jacques Benoist-Méchin's *Avec
Marcel Proust*, we find our author pondering in isolation the hidden
essence of a rosebush, speculating on the mystery of which the

bush formed but a "lid (*couvercle*)."[5] That development, in fact, serves as Benoist-Méchin's introduction to the esthetically crucial episode of the *madeleine,* an "experience of the same order."[6] Consider, then, in the fragments of Proust we have assembled, that in order to evade the disillusionment attendant on perceiving the rue des Rosiers in du Rozier, one flees society for art—and the hidden essence of a *rosier.* What is striking, that is, is not so much the street name behind the pseudonym, which is but a witty exemplification of Proust's orthodoxy about Society, but the recurrence of the same term (*rosier*) at the core of a fantasy of Art. For that repetition constitutes an implicit violation of his philosophy. As though the opposition between Art and Society, thematized in Proust under the rubric *contre Sainte-Beuve,* in this case would not hold. In Proust? It should be acknowledged at this point that the link between the *madeleine* episode and Hahn's anecdote about the rosebush is established not by Proust, but by Benoist-Méchin. It is to his reading, then, that we shall turn.

*   *   *

Jacques Benoist-Méchin is a name rarely quoted in Proust scholarship. In literary history, he perhaps merits a footnote as the musician-friend of Joyce who transcribed into music for him (and his printer in Dijon) the ballad—of the Jew's daughter—in the "Ithaca" section of *Ulysses.*[7] It is not as a footnote to English literature, however, but as an appendix to French history that he is no doubt best known. For he is the principal protagonist of the appendix—on "The War Question of January 1942"—to R. O. Paxton's *Vichy France: Old Guard and New Order, 1940-1944.*[8] And if indeed collaboration with the Nazis "was not a German demand to which some Frenchmen acceded," but "a French proposal that Hitler ultimately rejected," then Benoist-Méchin was without doubt France's exemplary collaborator.[9] For it was he, as Darlan's roving negotiator with the Germans and Secrétaire-général à la vice-présidence du conseil, who attempted to negotiate with Hitler's ambassador Abetz a more favorable peace settlement in exchange for a French declaration of war against Britain and the United States. That venture failed and Benoist-Méchin was soon to lose his power in Vichy, but it was precisely the nature of his project which branded him a collaborator *par excellence* and resulted in a death sentence—from which he was eventually pardoned—after the Liberation.[10] Benoist-Méchin would live out the rest of his years—

until 1983—as a historian, and it is within that context that his anomalous volume *Avec Marcel Proust* was to appear: first in 1957, then in 1977.[11]

The book is in part an early essay (1922) on music in Proust, the author's "first completed text," and in part a memoir (from 1957) of his brief but decisive encounter with Proust in 1922. One wonders what it meant for the would-be architect of collaboration with Hitler to imagine his life in terms of the legacy of a Jewish (or half-Jewish) novelist. One suspects that *Avec Marcel Proust* was written out of a profound sympathy with the Proustian thesis of the ultimate incommensurability of art and life—as though, if indeed there were a "Proustian" dimension to his existence, it would be permanently secure from contamination by, say, his book of 1939, *Eclaircissements sur 'Mein Kampf'* and all that ensued thereafter.[12] In Benoist-Méchin's words: "Quel rapport y a-t-il, me demandais-je, entre mes préoccupations d'aujourd'hui, entre *la Musique du Temps perdu* et les *Soixante Jours qui ébranlèrent l'Occident?* Se peut-il que je sois l'auteur de l'un et de l'autre? ... Je leur trouvais si peu de traits communs qu'ils me paraissent appartenir moins à deux époques d'une même vie qu'à deux vies différentes, n'ayant aucun rapport entre elles. . . ."[13]

According to his memoir, reading Proust was for Benoist-Méchin an illumination: "il projetait un faisceau de lumière sur la zone d'ombres où je me débattais encore. D'où l'impression que certaines de ses analyses venaient à ma rencontre pour me tendre la main."[14] Retain the *faisceau,* but even more the quality of the light. Here is the scenario of the encounter. Benoist-Méchin, stationed in the Rhineland in 1922, dreams of Franco-German friendship, visits the Francophile scholar E. R. Curtius, and persuades him to allow him to intervene in securing Proust's permission for a German edition of excerpts from *La Recherche.* Benoist-Méchin writes to Proust, who agrees to the project in a courtly letter to which we shall return. The novelist even agrees to receive his young admirer several weeks later (during his leave) at 1 A. M. in the Ritz, as was his wont. Benoist-Méchin arrives, is struck first by the pink taffeta shade of the lamp in Proust's room, the sole source of light in an otherwise dark chamber, then by the long-suffering "Assyrian" physiognomy of Proust in what was to be the last year of his life. They talk, mostly about music, for two hours before Proust pleads fatigue and bids his guest farewell. Benoist-Méchin returns to the Rhineland, witnesses the further decline of

Franco-German relations, and is too obsessed with his political tasks to assimilate the news of Proust's death in November. As the Germans lag in reparations payments, the French, to Benoist-Méchin's chagrin, decide to occupy the Ruhr. The night before that surprise military action, he finds himself at the opera in Wiesbaden, the only Frenchman in an audience tense with anticipation of bad times for Germany. The performance: *Die Meistersinger von Nürnberg*. As the lights dim, he is suddenly struck by the quality of the light in his box: "Les lumières s'éteignirent progressivement et, dans mon alvéole faiblement éclairée par une applique dont les ampoules étaient masquées par de petits abat-jour roses, s'établit une pénombre étrangement semblable à celle où s'était déroulé mon entretien avec Proust."[15] Whereupon he realizes the full import of Proust—and his death—for him. This will be Proust's night even as the chance resurrection of the ambience of their past encounter will mark Benoist-Méchin's consecration as a writer. The pink-shaded light, that is, is at some level his *madeleine*.

The political tension of the evening results in a second surprise. In Act III of the opera, as Hans Sachs intones his hymn to holy German art, affirms its virtue as consolation for every political humiliation, a febrile woman rises in the audience, her head erect; several rows away another strikes a similar pose. Soon the entire audience, group by group, row by row, has risen and remains standing in silent solidarity until the end of the performance. Whereupon, instead of the expected applause: "durant un long moment, la foule garda le silence, un silence enivré, total, vertigineux, comme si elle avait peine à retrouver le chemin de la terre. Et puis, un à un, les groupes se défirent et les assistants quittèrent le théâtre sans proférer un mot."[16] Benoist-Méchin is overcome with emotion, concludes that this is what Proust had in mind when he spoke of music in terms of a "communication of souls." He leaves the theatre determined to be a writer, and composes his first "complete piece" on "La Musique et l'Immortalité dans l'Oeuvre de Marcel Proust."

Consider, then, that for Benoist-Méchin to recount this sequence in 1957 was virtually to claim that Proust—French literature—was his path to collaboration. For whether or not he rose—with "les deux milles personnes de l'assistance"—the almost religious solidarity with the German community at the outbreak of a new phase of Franco-German hostility is read here as a scenario scripted by

Proust.[17] As though it were the novelist's "faisceau de lumière" which would bring Benoist-Méchin, in the fullness of time, to the light of that earliest of French symbols of fascism, *le faisceau.* . . .[18]

A "fascist" Proust? The most memorable pages of Benoist-Méchin's essay of 1922 are in the chapter, "La Communication des âmes." They elaborate as a vast metaphor for Proust's novel the glass wall of the entrance hall of the Gare d'Orsay. Through its semi-transparency one could see superimposed and subdivided into rooms the floors of the Palais d'Orsay: "Des grappes superposées [d'individus] se nouent, puis se dissolvent, séparées par la ligne horizontale d'un plancher invisible le long duquel défilent des processions de fantômes qui semblent avancer dans le vide. . . . On croirait assister à quelque rite obscur, à quelque sacrifice inhumain où chacun serait à la fois officiant et victime. . . ."[19] Benoist-Méchin's intuition is that the glass wall, with its magisterial clock, is the esthetic medium within which a new sociality is forged. As in the music of Proust, the compartmentalized existences of the denizens of the Palais can here unconsciously commune. Now Benoist-Méchin's preferred metaphor for Proust's novel is, of course, at a great remove from the reality of collaboration. Yet to seek out the specificity of Proust ("un changement de régime au sein de notre subconscient") in an idealist affirmation of the primacy of the collectivity over the individual is both to depart sharply from Proustian orthodoxy (what P. Sollers has called "le triomphalisme esthético-subjectif") and to link up with that spiritualist dream of a "socialism" shorn of specifically proletarian aspirations which was a crucial juncture on the path to fascism.[20]

The pinkish light at the Opera in Wiesbaden was the element through which the Proustian effect *took,* Benoist-Méchin's graft of the *madeleine.* But this is not the first occasion in his book in which a *rose* motif leads to the *madeleine.* We have already quoted Reynaldo Hahn's recollection of Proust pondering the hidden essence of a *rosier* and seen Benoist-Méchin's use of it to introduce a discussion of the *madeleine.* But rosier/Rozier brings us back to the Jewish *parvenu* Bloch and the rue des Rosiers, the anecdote—*S/Z*—with which we began. Even as the pinkish light in Wiesbaden returns us to the *taffetas rose* of the Ritz shading Proust's distinctly Oriental ("Assyrian") face. As the associations in our intertext proliferate, they will be seen to converge with devastating rigor on a single historical eventuality: had Proust lived long enough, he would have been slated for annihilation as a Jew by the very collectivity—the New Europe—he was being enlisted (in Wiesbaden) to underwrite.

But at this juncture, Benoist-Méchin begins sounding less like a reader than a character of Proust. Music in Proust? Consider that after Vinteuil, Proust's exemplary composer, dies, the narrator finds himself transfixed at a spectacle—or theatre—as well. Outside the window of the house where Vinteuil used to compose, Marcel peers in to see his daughter and her friend desecrating Vinteuil's portrait in a highly charged ritual of evil.[21] The humiliation, that is, which would in strict logic befall the deceased Jew Proust, mentor in music, at some level *repeats* the desecration of the dead father and musician Vinteuil.

Benoist-Méchin as a character out of Proust? The more one reads his account, the more one suspects that if the young man was searching for a mentor, the dying novelist was looking for materials for his book. It is in that light, perhaps, that Proust's letter to him should be read. After authorizing the German translation, Proust appends a curious request:

> Je me souviens d'avoir vu jadis Madame votre Mère. Je ne la connaissais pas, mais me la rappelle très bien. Elle était superbe et très grande. Est-ce que vous lui ressemblez? Comme je ne vous verrai probablement jamais, si vous pouviez me faire envoyer par la poste une photo de vous, je vous la renverrais aussitôt. Mais (vous avez dû voir cela par les considérations sur la ressemblance de Gilberte Swann avec son père et avec sa mère dans les *Jeunes Filles en fleurs*) je suis toujours très intéressé par les réincarnations d'un type admiré, dans un autre sexe."[22]

Benoist-Méchin is flattered, but embarrassed. For the woman Proust had seen was not his mother, but his father's first wife. He sends the photograph, nevertheless, without clarification. Proust responds that the resemblance is astonishing. Benoist-Méchin is obliged to disabuse him. Proust counters:

> . . . telles quelles, les choses sont infiniment plus intéressantes que vous ne pouvez l'imaginer, car votre photographie m'a confirmé le bien-fondé de mes conceptions de l'amour. Ne vous étonnez donc pas si je lui attache une grande importance. Je pense, en effet, que les hommes n'aiment pas telle ou telle femme isolée, mais un certain type de femme dont ils ne s'écartent jamais. Si, par suite d'un deuil ou d'une séparation, ils perdent la femme qu'ils aiment, ils courent après son type, qu'ils poursuivent obstinément, quoique souvent à leur insu. Si votre père a épousé en secondes noces Madame votre Mère, c'est qu'elle incarnait

ce type spécial qu'il aimait plus que tout. Elle devait ressembler, par quelque côté, à sa première épouse. Il n'est donc pas étonnant que je retrouve sur votre image quelques traits d'une femme qui n'était pas votre mère et que vous n'avez jamais vue. A travers elle, un reflet du type de femme qu'aimait votre père est venu se poser sur votre visage, créant en quelque sorte une ressemblance au second degré. Cela confirme tout ce que je pense . . .[23]

Benoist-Méchin can but submit to Proust's analysis: "Voilà ce qu'il en coûte de vouloir jouer au plus fin . . . on ne trompe jamais les esprits supérieurs."[24]

If the light in the Wiesbaden Opera reproduced the *madeleine* episode, the struggle over maternal identification (which Benoist-Méchin loses), the decisive imposition of a mother on this son, repeats another nodal episode of Proust's novel: the celebrated good night kiss scene of *Combray*. Marcel's father fails to separate mother and son; she is dispatched to spend the night with him; his will undergoes a decisive decline ("Ainsi, pour la première fois, ma tristesse n'était plus considérée comme une faute punissable mais comme un mal involontaire qu'on venait de reconnaître officiellement; comme un état nerveux dont je n'étais pas responsable . . .") Now as Marcel's father climbs the stairs, we see the reflection of his lamp flickering on the wall. In his white night gown, he is compared to Biblical Abraham in an Italian etching by Benozzo Gozzoli telling Sarah to get away from their son Isaac in anticipation of his sacrifice on Mount Moriah. But Marcel's father fails to, the symbolic sacrifice is avoided, and . . . the Jewish mother (Madame Weil?) swallows him whole. One result of that sequence, I have attempted to show elsewhere, is the obsessive assimilation throughout the novel of Jews and homosexuals as the two cursed races: the son, that is, *as* Jewish mother.[26] "Homosexuality is the truth of love" in Proust, writes Deleuze.[27] And our consideration of Proust's *S/Z* invites us to append—with reference to the other devouring passion in the novel, snobbery—that Jewishness is at some level the truth of snobbery. Together they form for Proust the disaster of life, which art—and the *madeleine*—alone can redeem.

With this linkage between Jewishness and homosexuality in Proust, our inquiry (into the literary fantasia of Benoist-Méchin) converges curiously with that of Hannah Arendt in her volume on *Anti-Semitism* in *The Origins of Totalitarianism*.[28] For in her effort to understand the roots of Nazism, the author on whom she draws most extensively is Proust, the "exemplary witness of dejudaized Judaism."[29] And the Proust she gives us is the virtuoso delineator of all the paradoxes informing the pariah status of Jews and "inverts." Arendt, of course, is a political theorist. Her strong suit, that is, is neither textual nor psychological analysis. (To reflect on the specific textuality of her *Anti-Semitism* would entail focusing on her rewriting of Marx's "farce" of Bonapartism as the "comedy" of the Dreyfus Affair, using Proust, for example, to bring *The Eighteenth Brumaire of Louis Bonaparte* an—anti-Semitic—step closer to the Hitler experience, with the "mob"—"the residue of all classes"—replacing Marx's *bohême*, and the anti-Dreyfusard Jules Guérin—"in whom high society found its first criminal hero"—replacing the Nephew.)[30] And yet Arendt's "political" analysis harmonizes eerily with our own comments on the structure of Proust's fable. For her subject is ultimately the degeneration of "Judaism," an ethical reality for both Jews and Christians, into the psychological essence—virtue or vice—of "Jewishness": "Jewish origin, without religious and political connotation, became everywhere a psychological quality, was changed into 'Jewishness,' and from then on could be considered only in the categories of virtue or vice. . . ."[31] And further on: "As far as the Jews were concerned, the transformation of the 'crime' of Judaism into the fashionable 'vice' of Jewishness was dangerous in the extreme. Jews had been able to escape from Judaism into conversion; from Jewishness there was no escape. A crime, moreover, is met with punishment; a vice can only be exterminated. . . ."[32] It will be perceived to what an extent this analysis prepares a comprehension of totalitarianism. But the degeneration of the ethical into the psychological, of a "faute punissable" into a "mal involontaire," was the upshot of the good night kiss scene in *La Recherche*. It is as though Arendt were taking her macropolitical cue from Proust's microtextual maneuver. At the end of which she is left to develop the imaginary reverberations of Proust's maternal identification into a sociology of Jews and/as "inverts."

*   *   *

The essential tenet of Proust's esthetic philosophy, as we have seen, posits a radical discontinuity between art and life, the realms epitomized in the novel by the *madeleine*, on the one hand, and the good night kiss scene on the other. For should the two overlap, should the esthetic blessings of involuntary memory be contaminated by the ethical curse of willlessness, Proust's idealism would be decisively stalled. Art could no longer reverse or redeem what would no longer be entirely distinct from itself. The most programmatic statement of that essential difference appears in *Contre Sainte-Beuve*, with its distrust of any appeal to an author's life in order to understand his art: "un livre est le produit d'un autre moi que celui que nous manifestons dans nos habitudes, dans la société, dans nos vices. . . ."[33] In *La Recherche,* the prototypal exemplification of the thesis is the inconceivability of any link between the wretchedness of Vinteuil's existence and the splendors of his music.

Yet in reading Benoist-Méchin on Proust—*Avec Marcel Proust* against *Contre Sainte-Beuve*—it was precisely that connection which interested us. The night at the Wiesbaden Opera, in our extrapolation, mapped the cult of art ("music in Proust," Vinteuil) on to the episode relating the horrors of degradation Vinteuil underwent at the instigation of his daughter. In that reading, Proust as guide in art is indistinguishable from Proust as victim in life. The project of *Contre Sainte-Beuve* would end in collapse.

In *A Structural Study of Autobiography,* in terms deriving from Lacan, I attempted to show that such a collapse was always already in effect in *La Recherche* itself, indeed in *Jean Santeuil.*[34] In the context of Benoist-Méchin's implicit apologia, and against the horizon of the political episode he has come to represent, I would like to expand that analysis—of the collapse of the thesis of *Contre Sainte-Beuve:* the radical autonomy of art—in the direction of the historical reality informing it. Against Sainte-Beuve? In the central chapter from which we have quoted, "La Méthode de Sainte-Beuve," Proust suggests that the future of Sainte-Beuve's thesis lay in its extrapolation to considerations of race by Taine ("Il considérait Sainte-Beuve comme un initiateur, comme remarquable 'pour son temps,' comme ayant presque trouvé sa méthode à lui, Taine").[35] The radicalization of Proust's argument, then, would read *Contre Taine,* or, in abbreviated form, art as opposed no longer to "life" so much as to "race." But that chapter is curiously framed by an anecdote imbued with a specific racial reference. Marcel reveals the idea of writing *Contre Sainte-Beuve* to his mother from a sickbed. Because of his extremes of mood, she hesitates to impinge on his privacy. In his affectionate largesse he finds himself reciting lines of Racine's Assuérus to his mother's Esther: the Gentile king and his Jewish bride. . . . On the one hand, then, in the frame we find an intrusive Jewish mother ("les belles lignes de son visage juif . . ."), and, on the other, in the chapter, an implicit desire to defend art from incursions of "race."[36] But the Jews of Racine's *Esther* will surface in *Sodome et Gomorrhe* as ironic metaphorical equivalents of the "inverts" who have secretly invested all the strategic positions of mainstream society. Again we find the link between the two "cursed races," but in this context as the figural train of Esther-as-Jewish-mother.

From *Contre Sainte-Beuve* (or the thesis of art opposed to life) to *Contre Taine* (or that of art opposed to—the Jewish—race). . . . That second formulation in fact brings us to the very end of the volume published posthumously as *Contre Sainte-Beuve suivi de Nouveaux mélanges* and the specific light it casts on Proust's essential distinction—even as it totters on the brink of collapse. The final entry in the book is entitled "Léon Daudet," and deals with the famous polemicist, aide to Drumont before becoming a leader of Action Française.[37] Daudet, arguably the most influential French literary critic of the century, launched the careers of Bernanos and Céline, and was responsible for the Goncourt Prize that marked Proust's consecration as a major figure in 1919. *Le Côté de Guermantes* was dedicated to him, presumably out of gratitude, but the ethical stake in Proust's homage to Daudet becomes clear only at the end of *Nouveaux mélanges*. From which:

> Ne pouvant plus lire qu'un journal, je lis, au lieu de ceux d'autrefois, *l'Action française*. Je peux dire qu'en cela je ne suis pas sans mérite. La pensée de ce qu'un homme pouvait souffrir m'ayant jadis rendu dreyfusard, on peut imaginer que la lecture d'une "feuille" infiniment plus cruelle que le *Figaro* et les *Débats*, desquels je me contentais jadis, me donne souvent comme les premières atteintes d'une maladie de coeur. Mais dans quel autre journal le portique est-il décoré par Saint-Simon lui-même, j'entends par Léon Daudet . . .[38]

Life and art are rigorously separated here, but life, in this case, is Jewish suffering (Dreyfus), and art, in a word, is French style. Might the latter redeem the former?

In his next gust of praise for Daudet, Proust almost stumbles over his own distinction:

> Cet homme si simple, si ami des "petits," du peuple, le moins snob en vérité des hommes, et qui a écrit, contre la richesse et le monde, les pages les plus délicieuses, cet homme qui semble s'être donné par patriotisme la tâche "héroïque" de détester, dans le sens où il dit le "faux

héroïque" du colonel Henry (que je ne trouve pas héroïque du tout, si revenu que je sois depuis longtemps de tous les dreyfusards nantis qui essayent de se faire une position dans le faubourg Saint-Germain) . . .[39]

Here we find Proust backing into a realization that the prose he admires is inseparable from the injustice (Henry's forgeries) it espouses and then latching on to the fact of the subsequent corruption of the cause of justice as a pretext for half-heartedly disavowing his discovery.[40] Finally, the distinction between art and life, the cult of French style and the torments of Jewish suffering, evaporates. Of Daudet's prose, he asks: "Qu'est-ce que cela doit être pour les victimes?"[41] And he answers: "Eux-mêmes, lisant le livre, doivent croire que les articles sont un affreux cauchemar, ou en lisant les articles que le livre est un rêve béni auquel on ne peut ajouter foi."[42] Art and life, the devotion to French style and the rigors of Jewish exclusion are, then, the *same* script, with a change of sign. But at this point, reverie takes over ("un rêve béni auquel on ne peut ajouter foi"), as though any fantasy would do to defend against the collapse of the assimilationist wish—French style as a balm for Jewish suffering—which the essay portends.

*   *   *

Toward the middle of *Le Côté de Guermantes,* the narrator offers a fable of redemption so complete as to resemble, in genre, a fairy tale.[43] The scene is a restaurant in Balbec, divided into two rooms by the slimmest of partitions. On one side, the Hebrews; on the other, "les jeunes nobles." Marcel enters unaccompanied and is subjected to a rude surprise: "Pour comble de malchance j'allai m'asseoir dans la salle réservée à l'aristocratie d'où il [le patron] vint rudemement me tirer en m'indiquant, avec une grossièreté à laquelle se conformèrent immédiatement tous les garçons, une place dans l'autre salle. Elle me plut d'autant moins que la banquette où elle se trouvait était déjà pleine de monde et que j'avais en face de moi la porte réservée aux Hébreux qui(. . .), s'ouvrant et se fermant à chaque instant, m'envoyait un froid horrible. . . ."[44] His humiliation seems total when Saint-Loup enters and sweeps him blissfully into the warmth of the aristocratic room, even commandeers the cloak (*manteau*) of the Prince de Foix to assure his comfort.[45] Marcel's triumph is complete. In the reading of Proust sketched in these pages, the autonomy of art, the new-critical prize presumably won *contre Sainte-Beuve,* is a transformation of the

room in the restaurant reserved for aristocrats. The ultimate argument against the redemptive interpretation of *La Recherche*, that
is, is its incoherence. "Art" cannot redeem the torments of "life"
because it is their cause. French (literature) will not absolve from
(Jewish) suffering because it is its enabling condition. . . .

Perhaps we should imagine the encounter (in the Ritz) between
Proust and Benoist-Méchin as an audition: the author secretly tries
out his future critic for a role in the drama of his redemption from
"Jewishness." The future collaborator with the Nazis waits thirty
years to accept the role, but interprets it as his own absolution from
collaboration. . . . The "unconscious" of their transaction is perhaps the muteness of that unformulated pact. It is a silence in
whose margins Hannah Arendt was able to read Proust as the
exemplary sociologist of the world that would culminate in Nazism.

This analysis, it may be perceived, is a transformation of an
effort to read Proust with Lacan undertaken ten years ago. To
immerse an interpretation born of Lacan in the medium of European Jewish pariahdom at the beginning of the century is arguably to expose that discourse to its own most radical roots in
Freud.[46] If this reading, that is, has allowed us to move further
into Proust's narrative, it is my suspicion that in the proper light
it might well take us further into Lacan as well.[47] In the interim,
it is hoped that the substitution of a fantasy of "French exclusion"
for "esthetic autonomy" at the manic pole of imaginary speculation
in Proust will not be perceived as lacking in implication for an
understanding of the vicissitudes of French thought in this country
in general.

Boston University

NOTES

1 This essay grew out of comments on a paper by Michael Weaver of Oxford
   University on "Right-wing Intellectuals and Racialism in the 1930's," delivered
   at a colloquium on *The Jews in Modern France* at the Tauber Institute of Brandeis
   University in April 1983.

2 D. Sibony, "Mais qu'est-ce qu'une histoire juive?" in *La Psychanalyse est-elle une
   histoire juive?: Colloque de Montpellier*, ed. A. & J.-J. Rassial (Paris: Seuil, 1981),
   pp. 142-143.

3 *A la recherche du temps perdu* (Paris: Pléiade, 1954), III, p. 952.

4 Ibid., II, p. 1107. In *The Proustian Community* (New York: New York University
   Press, 1971), p. 205, S. Wolitz comments provocatively on this reference, but
   mistakenly locates it in *Le temps retrouvé*. It occurs in *Sodome et Gomorrhe*.

5 *Avec Marcel Proust* (Paris: Albin Michel, 1977), pp. 53-54.

6 Ibid., p. 54.

7 See M. Weaver's Brandeis manuscript (unpublished), p. 43.

8 R. O. Paxton, *Vichy France: Old Guard and New Order, 1940-1944* (New York: Norton, 1972), pp. 387-390.

9 Ibid., p. 50.

10 See M. Weaver's manuscript.

11 Benoist-Méchin's most elaborate projects in European history were his *Histoire de l'armée allemande* (Paris: Albin Michel, 1936-1938) and *Soixante jours qui ébranlèrent l'Occident* (Paris: Albin Michel, 1956). The tendentiousness of the second project, a history of Europe from 10 May to 10 July 1940, is severely criticized in P. Dhers, "Comment Benoist-Méchin écrit l'histoire" in *Regards nouveaux sur les années quarante* (Paris: Flammarion, 1970).

12 Benoist-Méchin was responsible for the serialization in *Paris-Match* of *Mein Kampf* during the 1930's. His *Eclaircissements sur 'Mein Kampf'* (Paris: Albin Michel, 1939), p. 185, chose to avoid all "criticism" of or "personal commentary" on Hitler's positions.

13 *Avec Marcel Proust*, p. 134.

14 Ibid., p. 127.

15 Ibid., p. 167.

16 Ibid., p. 171.

17 Ibid., p. 170.

18 On the symbol of the *faisceau*—integrating nationalists and socialists—in the politics of the Marquis de Morès, see Z. Sternhell, *La Droite révolutionnaire: Les origines françaises du fascisme, 1885-1914* (Paris: Seuil, 1978), p. 180.

19 *Avec Marcel Proust*, p. 94.

20 On the emergence of such a "post-Marxian" socialism in the work of Henri deMan, see Z. Sternhell, *Ni droite ni gauche: L'idéologie fasciste en France* (Paris: Seuil, 1982), p. 136-159. Concerning "la primauté de la collectivité sur les individus qui la composent" in emerging French fascism, see Sternhell, "Les origines de l'antisémitisme populaire sous la IIIᵉ République" (unpublished paper delivered at the Brandeis colloquium on *The Jews in Modern France*, April, 1982). Concerning Proust and "fascism," it may be noted that Benoist-Méchin's sole criticism of *La Recherche* is ultimately the same as the criticism lodged against France itself by Drieu la Rochelle in *Mesure de la France* (Paris: Grasset, 1964). Benoist-Méchin: "Aucune génération nouvelle ne vient assurer la relève de celle qui disparaît progressivement sous nos yeux, si bien qu'une fois morts tous les personnages du *Temps perdu*, la France serait dépeuplée (pp. 131-132). Drieu la Rochelle: "La France n'a plus fait d'enfants. Ce crime d'où découlent les insultes, les malheurs qu'elle a essuyés depuis cinquante ans, elle l'a mûri à la fin du XIXᵉ siècle et consommé au début du XXᵉ siècle" (p. 42).

21 For a discussion of this passage in a Lacanian context, see my *A Structural Study of Autobiography: Proust, Leiris, Sartre, Lévi-Strauss* (Ithaca: Cornell University Press, 1974), pp. 32-35.

22 *Avec Marcel Proust*, pp. 147–148.

23 Ibid., pp. 150-151.

24 Ibid., p. 151.

25 *A la recherche du temps perdu*, I, p. 38.

26 See my *A Structural Study of Autobiography*, pp. 20-31.

27 G. Deleuze, *Proust et les signes* (Paris: P.U.F., 1970), p. 97.

28 *The Origins of Totalitarianism* (New York: Harcourt Brace Jovanovich, 1951).

29 Ibid., p. 80. Arendt borrows the phrase from J. E. van Praag, "Marcel Proust, témoin du judaïsme déjudaïsé" in *Revue juive de Genève*, 1937, Nos. 48, 49, 50.

30 Arendt, pp. 107, 111. For a discussion of the textuality of *The Eighteenth Brumaire of Louis Bonaparte*, see my *Revolution and Repetition: Marx/Hugo/Balzac* (Berkeley: University of California Press, 1977), Chapter I.

31 Arendt, p. 83.

32 Ibid., p. 84.

33 Proust, *Contre Sainte-Beuve* (Paris: Gallimard, 1954), p. 137.

34 *A Structural Study of Autobiography*, pp. 20-64. The chapter in *Jean Santeuil* analyzed to this end is "Querelle de Jean avec ses parents" (Part 3, Chapter 7).

35 *Contre Sainte-Beuve*, p. 134.

36 Ibid., p. 128.

37 Concerning Daudet, see P. Dominique, *Léon Daudet* (Paris: Vieux Colombier, 1964). Concerning his most successful novel, *Les Morticoles* (1894), E. Roudinesco, in her excellent *La Bataille de cent ans: Histoire de la psychanalyse en France* (Paris: Ramsay, 1982), p. 61, has written: "On trouve dans *Les Morticoles*, à l'état naissant, l'emphase, la redondance, la rhétorique accumulatoire, et le balancement de la parole alexandrine, qui vont caractériser, pendant tout le siècle suivant, le phrasé spectaculaire du pamphlet antisémite."

38 *Contre Sainte-Beuve*, pp. 439-440.

39 Ibid., p. 440.

40 In the awkward blatancy of its contradictions, the sentence calls to mind Freud's statement in the famous letter (21 September 1897) to Fliess renouncing the theory of seduction: "It is curious that I feel not in the least disgraced, though the occasion might seem to require it. Certainly I shall not tell it in Gath or publish it in the streets of Askalon, in the land of the Philistines—but between ourselves I have a feeling more of triumph than of defeat (which cannot be right)" (*The Origins of Psychoanalysis*, ed. M. Bonaparte, A. Freud, E. Kris; New York: Basic Books, 1954, p. 217). Much of psychoanalysis may be construed as a working through of those contradictions. One can only speculate on what Proust's novel would have been had he "worked through" the contradictions of the text on Léon Daudet.

41 *Contre Sainte-Beuve*, p. 441.

42 Ibid., p. 441. For Daudet's evocation of Proust as a simpering Dreyfusard in the Restaurant Weber (Proust: "Vous comprenez, monsieur, monsieur, il peut supposer que sa force aux armes m'intimide. Il n'en est rien"), see his *Paris vécu* (Paris: Gallimard, 1969), p. 103.

43 The sequence is well discussed in J. Recanati, *Profils juifs de Marcel Proust* (Paris: Buchet/Chastel, 1979), pp. 54-56.

44 *A la recherche du temps perdu*, II, pp. 401-402.

45 On the role of a *manteau* (in *Jean Santeuil*) as anticipation of the *madeleine*, see my *Structural Study of Autobiography*, p. 61.

46 On Freud's relation to Judaism, see M. Robert, *D'Oedipe à Moïse: Freud et la conscience juive* (Paris: Calmann-Lévy, 1974).

47 See, for instance, my "Suture of an Allusion: Lacan with Léon Bloy" in *Legacies: Of Anti-Semitism in France* (Minneapolis: University Press, 1983) as well as E. Roudinesco, *op. cit.*

Lacan, Poe, and Narrative Repression

ॐ

Robert Con Davis

There is one word which, if we only understand it, is the key to Freud's thought. That
word is "repression."[1]

Norman O. Brown

The [literary] work poses the equivalent of
the Unconscious, an equivalent no less real
than it, as the one forges the other in its
curvature. . . .[2]

Jacques Lacan

Recent thinking about psychoanalysis has led literary theory res-
olutely back to the concept of repression as one of the most important tropes in the Freudian interpretation of literature. This
move runs clearly counter to the tradition of psychoanalytic criticism in America—based on ego psychology—which all but vanquished repression and the unconscious processes that attend it
and has kept both from having any import in interpretation.[3] In
1959 Norman O. Brown does call for a return to the concept of
repression, but he is little concerned with the implications for interpretation. In the Continental tradition newly influential in
America, owing to Jacques Lacan and the French Freudians,
repression is the principal figure without which psychoanalysis
sinks into what Edmund Husserl called, pejoratively, "psycholo-
gizing"—the mere privileging of psychological concepts and terms
without a corresponding development in analysis. The Lacanian
claim to a legitimate psychoanalytic reading is based on Freud's
ideas about transformation in language, in which repression is a
functional principle within systems of discourse; those systems,
taken together, constitute textuality. By functional principle, I
mean that repression is not a simple event (as traditional Freudian

analysis has it) but an ongoing process of marking and suppressing differences, a process which, as Ferdinand de Saussure and others have suggested, is the basis of signification. In this view, repression, in turn, creates a textual unconscious—a linguistic system—that can be regarded neither as a simple addition to an already manifest text nor as an added dimension of enriched symbolism. Such, as Lacan claims, are misreadings and a reductive containment (ultimately a making safe) of Freudian thought. Rather, Lacan claims that the notion of repression and a textual unconscious demands that we think of textuality *and* interpretation in the precise terms of a writing system. In so doing, he decisively cancels the special privilege of narration as a manifest order (and on this point Lacan's work, in fact, may be *decisive*) and therein opens interpretation to a psychoanalytic reading situated within unconscious discourse. Thus, Lacan's analysis "returns" to (or reconceives) Freud's idea of repression as that which makes signification and narration possible, repression as the figure for the difference—in a text—that makes a difference. Lacan, in this way, presents us with his version of a semiotic Freud.

One sure way to follow this important "return to Freud"—and to go forward to the significance of Lacan's view of narration—is to read a key Freudian text on repression, "Instincts and Their Vicissitudes," with Lacan's assistance and then to interpret a literary text, Poe's "The Tell-Tale Heart," as Lacan might do it, situating the text within the discourse created by repression. The main question will concern repression's function in a text and the kind of interpretation that follows repression's retrieval as a central concept in psychoanalytic reading. Such a "retrieval" of repressed material, in texts as well as in psychoanalytic discourse, is occasioned, as we shall see in Poe, by a certain discontinuity and by important "gaps" in discourse. At stake here is the very possibility of Freudian interpretation, not of neurosis merely, but of literary texts.

I

Freud's "Instincts and Their Vicissitudes" follows several changes in language primarily related to the dynamics of visual experience, to seeing. He wrote it in 1915, just prior to an essay on repression, and there are indications that he planned other similar articles in this period, articles that evidently were not written. In any case, it is clear that during this time Freud thought intensely about the complex of operations later grouped by Jacques Lacan under the idea of metaphor: the action of exchange—through linguistic processes—between the conscious and the unconscious. In "Instincts," Freud addresses repression by turning to one of its effects, the "reversal of an instinct into its opposite," making specific connections to two of the three great polarities of mental life: subject/ object and active/passive (the third is pleasure/pain).[4] In various stagings of theory in this essay he shows these polarities to be actual linguistic "positions" within a discourse, structural positions from which a narrative system is elaborated. This system is wagered directly against conventional notions of the subject as a unified entity—that is, against its status as a discrete being. His central exhibit is the scopic (visual) drive and the "waves" or "vicissitudes" it undergoes as it is repositioned through the operation of metaphor. Freud creates a surreal theatre of masochists, sadists, significant looks, voyeurs, and exhibitionists, and eventually he shows visual experience to be governed by an unconscious mechanism that is inscribed through a process of looking and being seen. Freud theatricalizes this mechanism in various ways as a linguistic process and as a series of shifts and substitutions among the subject and object, active and passive positions he sets forth.

Freud demonstrates, for example, that the simple concept of "looking" is but one part of visual experience, in fact, only the first and most limited in three scenes of seeing. In the first scene, "looking" is a gesture toward control, visual "possession" or "mastery" of an object. It is discrete and without any reciprocal response, a frozen act. After this initial look takes place, there is a reversal, a seemingly impossible shift from a subject's viewpoint to an object's. This shift entails a virtual "giving up of the object" as a thing to be seen and mastered and a repositioning of "seeing" from a different position. The looker, in effect, becomes an object.[5] In one sense, what happens here is that the looker first looks and, as a part of looking, as a kind of culmination of possessing the object, becomes that object; as a result, the subject surrenders visual mastery as it then enters the field of vision as an object in a different position. In reality, the "single" act of looking has created two positions, that of looking and of being seen. Simultaneously, to be understood, one position at a time must be "repressed" or cancelled. And with this cancellation of an opposing position, a kind of surrender of sight is effected. Seeing, hereafter, is not

"single," a totally masterful (and sadistic) activity taking place for
a subject, but a construct that includes a lost object of vision. After
this surrender comes the introduction of a new position—a new
viewer—who watches, one who takes the position left vacant by the
subject who looked initially and "to whom one displays one self in
order to be looked at by him."[6] The object position here—as if
occult—virtually looks back at the (former) subject. With this elaboration of subject and object relations, wherein the direction of
sight has been reversed, and wherein the complete expression of
seeing has become necessarily twofold—seeing and being seen—
the whole process of "seeing" has gone, additionally, through a
middle range, neither active nor passive, in which the looker—in
the stage of becoming an object—is a partial object, one looking at
itself, part subject and part object. This is a "mirror-stage" development in which subject and object are held, as if on the brink of
dissolution, in an imaginary and ideal equivalence—as if perfect
doubles of each other. Finally, in the last scene, the looker is made
passive, fully an object for another watcher. Whereas the process
starts with the power of a subject to see, the subject afterwards
straddles the subject-object relationship by becoming a partial object of contemplation. In the third scene subjectivity is abandoned
altogether and is replaced by an object exclusively for another's
scrutiny.

We see in this set of scenes Freud's theatricalization of positioning in a text—largely a process of alternation between active
and passive, a kind of spiral that continually twists deeper into
experience—first active, then passive, then active, and so on—always claiming new territory through the repositioning of the subject. More accurately, since the spiral is a relationship and not a
thing, the spiral virtually *is* the contour of experience as it revolves.
This decentered set of positions never—at any stage—reaches an
end or comprises a totality. There are, however, extremes of relations that Freud calls voyeurism and exhibitionism, types of optical illusions. In voyeurism is a "refusal" to be seen as an object
and, thus, a negation of object loss. It is an exclusive concentration
on visual mastery, on the first position. In it is a figurative insistence on the "single" position of mere looking, whose practical
consequence, possibly, is an attempt to escape the eyes of others
who necessarily will reposition a masterful subject as a mastered
object. Thus, voyeurism—mere looking—can be interpreted as a
resistance to ongoing repression, which, taking the position of mastery as substantial truth, is the gesture of ego psychology. Voy-

eurism is a move always to see and never to be seen. Lacan makes precisely this point about voyeurism—much as folklore and myth often do—when he comments that the drive to see may "completely [elude] the term castration" (Lacan's term for being bound within the system of shifts) and can function, or can seem to function, outside of the shifts from one position to another, outside of substitution.[7] Mere seeing, then, is potentially a perverse activity. Conversely, exhibitionism is equally a denial of object loss; Freud sees it as an idealization of loss in the illusory form of a *thing* rather than as an acceptance of loss as a structural absence. In this idealization, an hysterical concern with the nature of object loss, exhibitionism enshrines loss as a phantom presence—a fetishistic totem—that, in reality, negates ("forecloses," as Lacan would say) the structural position the loss should have created. Exhibitionism is a positioning whose significance is always to show and never to be shown—that is, never to be shown any loss.

Each of these optical extremes in Freud's text takes on especial significance in light of Lacan's version of the unconscious and ultimate aim of visual experience. We have noted that the process of seeing effects a series of reversals, the result of which is to bind together the subject and the visual object in a series of shifting relationships. But beyond recounting this function, Lacan has shown that seeing's true aim cannot be visual in any immediate sense: seeing is but a function in a largely unconscious discourse that can be glimpsed in what Lacan calls (extending Freud's discussion) the "Gaze"—the functioning of the whole system of shifts. The theoretical leap outside of the strictly "visual" terms of Freud's essay is obligatory, as Lacan shows, because visual experience—always positioning—is but a staging for the intersection of the line of sight and the trajectory of unconscious desire expressed in the Gaze. The subject who looks, in Lacan's scheme, is the one who precisely is "seen"—that is, is implicated—by the desire of unconscious discourse. That is, in looking one always is "seen" by the nonvisual Gaze, in Lacan's meaning of "seen," since visual experience—in fact, any text—theatricalizes an "Other" desire in the shifting from one position to another. The positions actually signify the "Other" system as a supplement to the manifest system. The Gaze, in this way, encompasses the voyeuristic wish not to be seen and the exhibitionistic wish not to be shown, and the relationship of these "perversions" (as Freud calls them) points up rather directly the positionality of visual experience *as a text*.[8]

To sharpen Lacan's insight concerning Freud's essay—and to see why Lacan's move is a "return to Freud" in a radical sense—we must see that Freud's text, in staging the visual relationship, has already situated the Lacanian Gaze in the term "desire." Freud's staging of theory shows that desire cannot belong to any single position or subject, a point on which Freud is adamant. Desire, therefore, is not in the text or reader, or in any combination of the two; so, meaning cannot be guaranteed by any subject. Rather, desire exists, in Freud's view, in the province of the unconscious, in the very system of substitution and shifts; and, thus desire always escapes being manifested "positively" in a "single" and determinant meaning or position. Freud locates desire always in the place of the Other (the unconscious), in the structural otherness of the system of positions and shifts. Accordingly, the textual system carries on an unconscious discourse that is always more than the significance of any position or viewpoint in it. In this way, Lacan's "return to Freud" is one that demands a focus on textuality as the production of desire. And in this perspective desire is captured most accurately in relation to the profoundly paradoxical situation of reading, where the line of sight and the Gaze meet most dramatically. That is, we turn to and read a text as if, by giving attention to it, we look into it and master or possess it *as an object.* But while reading, in fact, we are focused upon and held by a Gaze that comes through the agency of the object text. Thus held in the act of reading—in what Frank Kermode calls the dimension of *kairos*—we are not masterful subjects; we—as readers—then become the object of the Gaze. The Gaze—which inscribes the Other's desire in a discourse of positioning—is trained on readers from the outside as they read, and through the willing surrender to the active/passive alternations of reading, readers (subjects who become objects) play within and also escape the confines of voyeurism and exhibitionism. In this view of textuality and desire, with Lacan's help, we decisively place ourselves as readers (objects) under Freud's gaze—more strictly, under the Gaze, as Lacan has taught us, that comes through the agency of Freud's text.

Along these lines in "Instincts and Their Vicissitudes" Freud shows a metaphoric operation at work—or rather, its *representation*—as a text virtually writes itself in structural positions. We see in Freud's essay that the text at one moment inscribes the exhibitionist and suppresses, but in this sense also "writes," a voyeur; at another it inscribes passivity and suppresses, but also "writes," activity. In each case the text marks the changes controlled by metaphor in a process of linguistic substitution among structural positions. A text has authority to be a text, in this view, precisely insofar as it marks these differences—positions and their shifts. Guarantees of meaning, continuity, or unity are not built into the text as Freud depicts it, but then neither (in Lacan's phrase) does the text "come a cropper." The text—no mere cropper—stands in for (signifies) the Other's desire according to the shifting of positions within the discourse of substitution. Freud, thus, explores textuality in "Instincts and Their Vicissitudes" by staging the drama of alternation between voyeurism and exhibitionism. Further, he underscores the existence of a nonmanifest text, a text that has no positive terms—a textual unconscious—in which positions exist in a decentered system by virtue of differing from each other.

Lacan's primary contribution to psychoanalysis—and, by extension, to narrative theory—has been to elaborate this notion of the text: an economy of conscious and unconscious systems in various stages of disunity—a text/system governed, as Lacan shows, by metaphor. A primary assumption underlying Lacan's reading of the Freudian text is that in it words as such exist only in a "conscious" system where signifiers in one constellation (or chain) of association continually stand in for signifiers in another. While we cannot examine these substitutions directly, we can see what Lacan means if we set in motion a few linguistic changes and observe the results. For instance, we can take at random the utterance "Moriarty is a snake," a simple sentence and overtly metaphorical, and surmise that "snake" forms a chain of association with an array of similar nouns—lizard, reptile, etc. At the same time we can posit that a "repressed" term, one left out of the utterance, exists in a separate chain, say, of human character descriptions. We can identify the sentence's missing term (arbitrarily) as "untrustworthy." Further, "snake" and "untrustworthy" are signifiers that could fit in many other possible chains, the total system of which would be quite literally impossible to trace. However, we can speculate that there is a substitution taking place already in the original sentence that allows "snake" to stand in for (or for something similar to) "untrustworthy," a metaphorical substitution of one term for another: a word in one chain takes another's place in a different chain. To represent this process, Lacan uses the notation ("little letters," as he calls them) of Ferdinand de Saussure, $\frac{S}{s}$—signifier over signi-

fied.[9] In Lacan's notation my sentence would be shown in this
form:

$$\frac{\text{snake} \quad\quad S'}{\begin{array}{l}\text{Moriarty's} \quad s \\ \text{bad} \\ \text{character}\end{array}}.$$

Here "snake" (S') substitutes for another signifier, "untrustworthy"
(S), that must be deleted for the sentence to make sense. In this
substitution the new signifier (S') has turned the old one (S) into
its signified. Hence, in $\frac{S'}{s}$ there is a missing but retrievable term (S).

In this example it could seem that the metaphoric substitution
of terms is carried out completely "consciously" and is a matter
with merely discursive implications. This conclusion is tempting
only if we accept various reified versions of the unconscious as a
"dark" and "closed" place. In the semiotic reading of this sentence—which promotes a quite different version of the unconscious—we find the suppression of some terms—more than may
be apparent initially—while others are being directed into a manifest text. Moreover, this sentence illustrates that signifiers have
meaning because they have a position in discourse in relation to
each other. Meaning's meaning, in this sense, is precisely positionality, ultimately a relationship between manifest and repressed discourses. Lacan's rather compact account of metaphoric substitution—an elaboration of the system of positions in "Instincts and
Their Vicissitudes"—is as follows[10]:

$$\frac{\text{snake} \quad S'}{\begin{array}{l}\text{untrust-} \quad S \\ \text{worthy}\end{array}} \cdot \frac{\text{untrustworthy} \quad S}{\begin{array}{l}\text{Moriarty's} \quad s \\ \text{bad} \\ \text{character}\end{array}} = \frac{\text{snake} \quad\quad S'}{\begin{array}{l}\text{Moriarty's} \quad s \\ \text{bad} \\ \text{character}\end{array}}.$$

In this algorithm Lacan has complicated but also organized Freud's
formulation substantially. At the extreme left "snake" (S') is a signifier for another signifier—"untrustworthy" (S)—that is left out
of the utterance and yet is retained in the unconscious system—
"unconscious" in the sense, simply, of belonging to textuality
without being marked as part of the manifest text. Then, on the
extreme right in the formula's quotient ($\frac{S'}{s}$), "Moriarty's bad character" (s) again is below the bar, while the term "snake" has been
placed as a substitute for it in the chain that s belongs to. The

movement, then, from "Moriarty is untrustworthy" to "Moriarty is
a snake" involves the substitution of some terms at the manifest
level of the sentence/text—above the bar—for others at the unconscious level—below the bar. This process of substitution, in short,
creates two distinct levels of textuality in the manifest (conscious)
and unconscious systems.

Jean Laplanche and Serge Leclaire show that the operation of
this formula expresses the very substance of textual repression in
that it functions only through a connection with the unconscious.[11]
As they explain, for metaphor to operate it must be assumed that
repression already has happened at least once (Freud's myth of a
"primal repression")—otherwise, there could be no bar *already in
place* between "Moriarty" and "untrustworthy," or between "snake"
and "untrustworthy," no possible pinning of one signifier to another. The presence of the bar in each part of the formula is (in
Lacan's revision of Saussure) a sign of the prior existence of repression as a function and, as it follows, of a chain of unconscious
signifiers. In Lacan's notation, the unconscious chain can be designated as $(\frac{S}{S})$—the merely metonymic relationship of a signifier to
another signifier (the special sense of unconscious signifiers—in
Lacan's term—as nonsignifying "thing representations"). To the
formula for repression, Lacan includes this specific notation for
the unconscious chain:

$$\frac{S'}{S} \cdot \frac{S}{s} = \frac{S'}{\dfrac{s}{\dfrac{S}{S}}} \cdot {}^{12}$$

In this revised formula the designation $(\frac{S}{S})$ in the quotient is a no-
tational reminder that signification is a discourse carried on by
virtue of the nonsignifying bar of repression that makes the sign
possible. In fact, the formula shows a notation for three systems:
in the quotient, S' stands for the manifest (conscious) system; s
stands for the preconscious system (capable of becoming conscious), and $(\frac{S}{S})$ stands for the unconscious.

What we see here is an account of repression's function in a
metaphoric operation, an algorithm that accounts both for the separation of the three systems and for their being bound together.
Moreover, the metaphoric operation—the manner of exchange between the conscious and the unconscious—at once institutes sig-

nification and creates linguistic positions within a text. And in Lacan's formula the nonsignifying bars separating the "little letters"
(the effects of repression that Lacan calls "points de capiton") buoy
up narration even as they create it. In other words, the metaphoric
system functions as an unconscious writing agency, inscribing differences in two texts at once. Metaphor, therein, creates systems
of discourse and in so doing governs textuality.

Lacan's formula for repression points to an "end"—in a sense,
a product—of that which is begun in "primal repression," the bar's
mythical origin. The unconscious discourse in turn situates repression in a signifying system, and there the "end" of repression virtually "speaks" of unconscious desire—that is, "speaks" of repression as a law inscribed in the positioning of textual systems. In
effect, discourse elaborates and bodies forth the meaning of textual
law, the law not merely as a repressive interdiction but as a principle of function, the rule according to which the narrative subject
(and object) comes to be in discourse. In the metaphoric vision of
Freud's "Instincts and Their Vicissitudes," and in Lacan's view of
Freud's text, floating on the surface of unconscious discourse, narrative is virtually buoyant with repression. And in floating—thus
positioned—rather fragilely on discourse's surface, the manifest
text takes on, a little romantically perhaps, the momentary appearance of being inherently meaningful as its own discourse—as
if the manifest text contained and sent forth its own meaning as a
substantial presence. However, this illusion of presence and centrality, harmless in itself, is an imaginary effect of signification and
discourse, an imaginary centering in a discourse that is centered
always elsewhere in an "Other" desire. If we look closely at the
manifest text, we see something else, a hollowness that inhabits the
text—a mere inscription—through and through.

II

Edgar Allan Poe's texts, like Freud's, tend to explore the structural
positions within visual experience, and perhaps for this reason
Lacan has used Poe's work as a staging for various psychoanalytic
scenes. We can restage several of these scenes à la Lacan—in a
theatre of unconscious discourse—if we can challenge the fixity of
"reading" as interpretation (even a "Lacanian" interpretation) in
order to theatricalize a set of positions in a particular text by Edgar

Allan Poe. With Lacan's guidance, for instance, one notes initially that the tendency to see without being seen—voyeurism—is a dominant pattern in Poe's tales; its devastating effects are everywhere. In Poe's obsessive stories the eye's power to control, to master, becomes demonic and, at base, expresses an hysterical response to the eye's power to implicate the looker in the fate of the seen. Hysterical about being looked at and turned into an object, Poe's narrators busy themselves by walling up, burying, dismembering, analyzing, and rationalizing in a furious attempt to remain active and, thus, elusive. Ultimately, they wish to escape the gaze of another who, in turn, in a nightmare of victimage, would transform them into being mere objects of attention. The typical Poe narrator wagers, dangerously of course, that the person walled up or killed afterwards will not be able to look back and that the world's eyes can be walled over permanently.

Such a daring gambler is the nameless narrator of "The Tell-Tale Heart," who is, he insists, not vexed at all by the kindly old man he lives with, but simply by what he identifies as the old man's "Evil Eye." Because of his professed hatred for the eye, he vows "to take the life of the old man, and thus rid myself of [that] eye for ever."[13] The story, however, not only focuses on the narrator's response to the eye and the old man's murder, but by allowing no preparatory circumstances or motives for the murder to arise, the story also highlights the Evil Eye motif and the narrator's response to it in perhaps the starkest manner imaginable. That is, first, after giving details of how the eye looked to him (it "resembled that of a vulture—a pale blue eye, with a film over it" 303), the narrator describes his own dread of being looked at by the eye. The narrator then tells how he previously dissembled with the old man he lived with, appearing jovial when angry and peaceful when agitated, so that his true nature in effect would be hidden from inspection by the dreaded eye under a mask of conviviality. However, when he does kill the old man and, shortly afterwards, delirious, confesses the crime to only mildly-suspicious policemen, the narrator in fact directs himself into just the sort of subservient position as an apprehended criminal (object-like) that he sought to avoid while he was the old man's friend. Supposedly, as the story shows, the sole motive for the murder is the narrator's fear of the old man's Evil Eye and of becoming a mere object for the eye's gaze. But, paradoxically, while the narrator cannot abide being looked at and made an object, he chooses to make himself an object for the eye of the law when he is caught; as a criminal he is an object of prosecution—of, as he fears, persecution. In the first version of being seen, the old man could decide to look at, to expose, the narrator at will; in the second, the narrator-turned-murder can control—or can seem to control—the moment for his own exposure to the law. The difference between the two is crucial in that it points to the narrator's fundamental wish to resist the passivity inherent in becoming an object for an other's sight. That is, he wishes to perform the impossible by actually directing when he will be looked at by others and by remaining in complete control, active, even if doing so means death. His resistance to being seen points to a desire to escape subjugation absolutely and to choose death rather than to become passive while alive.

Such thematic material suggests the Lacanian interpretation of the Gaze, but it also illustrates, if indirectly, aspects of textual repression. We know, for instance, that repression is responsible for organizing different systems of signification, an economy of functions that can be expressed in Lacan's formula for the operation of repression:

$$\frac{S'}{S} \cdot \frac{S}{s} = \frac{S'}{\dfrac{s}{\dfrac{S}{S}}}.$$

Starting at the formula's far left ($\frac{S'}{S}$), we can experiment and say that the most prominent event in the story, the one that is connected to all of the events leading up to the murder, the murder itself, and the denouement, is the narrator's voyeurism—his attempt to see without being seen. Similarly, it is clear that the narrator, as a voyeur, is fearful of being looked at. Now it follows in Freud's analysis, as we know, that voyeurism and the fear of being seen can be linked as signifier and signified; Poe's tale also suggests this. In Lacan's notation, this relationship would be shown as

$$\frac{\text{voyeur}}{\substack{\text{fear} \\ \text{of being} \\ \text{seen}}} \quad \frac{S'}{S}.$$

But the "fear of being seen" (S) is also a signifier in itself, a representation of who this character is at the story's manifest level—

the old man's obsessed and paranoid friend. Here we uncover
another signifying relationship, one that can be expressed as follows:

$$\frac{\text{fear of being seen}}{\substack{\text{narrator's} \\ \text{obsession with} \\ \text{the old man}}} \quad \frac{S}{s}.$$

The formula for repression, as we connect these possibilities, shows
the signifying relationship of these terms to the manifest characteristics of the tale; the result is

$$\frac{\dfrac{\text{voyeur}}{\substack{\text{narrator's} \\ \text{obsession} \\ \text{with the} \\ \text{old man}}}}{\dfrac{\substack{\text{fear of} \\ \text{being seen}}}{\substack{\text{fear of} \\ \text{being seen}}}} \quad \frac{\dfrac{S'}{s}}{\dfrac{S}{S}}.$$

The top section of this quotient is what we might expect: the
"narrator's obsession with the old man" is signified by his being a
"voyeur." But far below the line of repression in the unconscious
system is the chain of "fear of being seen" and "fear of being
seen"($\frac{S}{S}$). This—as the formula suggests—deeply repressed material is more difficult to account for. In what way, for example, can
this repressed material hold the place of the Other—creating the
repressive bar that separates "voyeur" from the "narrator's obsession with the old man"?

The most nearly adequate answer—one of interest to practical
criticism—would be worked out in great detail in an exhaustive
examination of the narrative details, the *lexias* (as Roland Barthes
calls them) of the whole story. However, it will suffice here to focus
on the positioning of the unconscious chain in the narrative, the
chain's function if not precisely its detailed constitution. For instance, in addition to the narrator's voyeurism in regard to the old
man, there are three revealing aspects of their relationship: (1)
their mutual obsession with the evidence of the senses, hearing as
well as seeing; (2) their mutual insomnia, and (3) their shared

nightly fear of the figure of a stalking "Death." In these ways the two men are much alike, doubles. The narrator's sense of hearing, for instance, comes up in the story's opening lines when he asserts that his obsession "had sharpened my senses . . . not dulled them. Above all was the sense of hearing acute. I hear all things in the heaven and in the earth. I heard many things in hell" (303). The old man, too, has sensitive hearing and wakes at the slightest sound of the narrator's movement in his room. The old man listens most closely at night when, like the narrator, he sits "up in bed listening;—*just as I have done,* night after night, hearkening to the death watches in the wall" (emphasis added, 304). Then when the old man hears the narrator moving stealthily around his room he makes a "slight groan." The narrator testifies to his own familiarity with this fearful sound:

> I knew it was the groan of mortal terror. It was not a groan of pain or grief—oh, no!—it was the low stifled sound that arises from the bottom of the soul when overcharged with awe. I knew the sound well. Many a night, just at midnight, when all the world slept, *it has swelled up from my own bosom,* deepening, with its dreadful echo, the terrors that distracted me. I say I knew it well. I knew what the old man felt, and pitied him, although I chuckled at heart. (emphasis added, 304)

Sharing an obsession with death, as these details show, the narrator and the old man express their fears through similar hysterical symptoms. An important difference between the men is that, in choosing to heighten the old man's fear of death and to kill him, the narrator controls—just as a voyeur sadistically controls—a situation *like his own,* as if subject and object could be merged in a mirror phase of complete identification.

In fact, most important about the narrator's sadism/voyeurism is the fact of his similarity to and deep involvement with the old man. "I loved the old man," he attests, and "for his gold I had no desire." There is no "object" to the murder, the narrator swears; "there was none" (303). The narrator is motivated in the murder by, rather, a missing object, one that stands for death. That is, both the narrator and the old man have a singular fear—that they will be *seen* at night by the "Death . . . [who stalks] the halls with his black shadow before him" (304). In this depiction, Death—like the narrator and like the old man, at least in the narrator's view—is a sadist/voyeur who watches from hidden recesses (from behind a "black shadow") and, therein, can master and "envelop the victim"

at will (304). The Death with a voyeuristic tendency, the narrator
laments, is apprehended and mastered as an *object "all in vain"*
(304) because it hides and only manifests itself negatively in darkness, as an absence. The narrator's subsequent strategy for overcoming Death is simple and insane: Death is elusive as an absence,
so he reifies it (impossibly) *as a presence,* as a totemic presence, an
imaginary object. Which is to say, the two men are friends with
the same fears, so the narrator will locate absence (Death) as an
object in a double, in someone—like a mirror image—the same yet
different. In the terrified old man's "vulture eye," "his Evil Eye"
(304), Death will emerge as an object visible and present to the
narrator—capable of being mastered. The narrator follows this
strategy, but to his horror, the missing object fails to appear in the
old man's Evil Eye. There in the eye, past the room's darkness and
supposedly behind the "black shadow" that shields death, where
the thing itself seemed certain to dwell and to emerge, is yet another veil, a darkness within the darkness. Finally, staring at the
eye, the narrator says, "I saw it with perfect stillness . . . a hideous
veil over [the eye] that chilled the very marrow in my bone; but I
could see nothing else of the old man's face or person: for I had
directed the ray [of my lantern] as if by instinct, precisely upon
the damned spot" (305). The eye itself is veiled, and the narrator
finds yet an absence. At this furthest reach of the power to control
through mere looking, to master an object, the narrator is stymied
by the "black shadow" and held in the gaze of that which he sought
to grasp.

The repressed material in this narrative is evident as we retrieve
the unconscious chain where the two men stand in relation to
Death. In the story the old man embodies a forbidden satisfaction
and exercises an obsessional attraction for the narrator. Conversely, Death, like the figure zero, is without features and merely
holds a position in the tale—as an object of the narrator's fear.
The narrator's specific function in the tale is to tell of his forbidden
desire and his crime. The triadic relationship of these three figures
is marked by the narrator's attempt to destroy all difference in
seeking to possess Death directly as an object in the old man's eye.
In Lacan's terminology, in rejecting Death (an irreducible difference), the narrator "forecloses" the law—that is, covers over difference. This crime's implications are suggested in the tone of the
narrator's sexualized pursuit of the old man. In the murder scene,
for example, sneaking into the old man's room "so gently!" the

narrator "made an opening sufficient for my head . . . then I thrust
in my head. Oh, you would have laughed to see how cunningly I
thrust it in! I moved it slowly—very, very slowly. . . . It took me an
hour to place my whole head within the opening so far that I could
see him as he lay upon his bed" (303). The overtones of such
intense (and otherwise pointless) sexual pursuit, violation, and possession tell much about the psychic event underlying the murder:
in seeking a forbidden satisfaction in what appears to be a mater-
nalized old man, the narrator creates for himself a dyadic trap—
an exclusive relationship between two—wherein the law, the term
of difference (here marked by the figure of Death), has no allotted
place. Positions without the marks of difference—this story implies—are outside the law (of relationship)—illicit. The third term's
position mediates these two terms and creates a (triadic) relationship—a system marked by difference. The law does return in the
tale but in a different form—in a hallucination—as it opens the
trap: an exaggerated figure of law returns at the tale's end in the
accusatory pounding of the tell-tale heart and in the narrator's
fantasy about police authority and vengeful pursuit. Whereas the
narrator's function was to repress difference between himself and
the old man, here difference returns with a vengeance in the story's
conclusion as the inquisitional (police) version of the law. With this
turnabout—wherein the narrator who wishes not to be seen, a
voyeur, exposes himself in an exhibitionistic manner—the text inscribes and suppresses the positions of the optical illusion—the
"perversions" (of voyeurism and exhibitionism) that mark the extremes of positionality.

   This thematic and somewhat arbitrary rendering of the tale is
sufficient to establish several "gaps" of reference and several positions within the text. We glimpse the text in a stage of produc-
tivity when we retrieve the unconscious chain—rather, as Lacan's
algorithm suggests, its representation—in the association of two
positions marked as "the fear of being seen"($\frac{S}{S}$): the narrator's and
the old man's fear of being seen by Death. The narrator seeks
recognition and mastery of his fear in the old man, and in seeking
that recognition, the narrator—a double of the old man—expresses
what amounts to a desire for death. The killing of the old man
simultaneously negates this desire and satisfies it in that the narrator destroys difference by deferring its inscription. Here a gap
is created—really, a series of gaps—in relation to which the tale's

lexias are made signifiers in an unconscious discourse. Thus, as we have seen, the "events" of entering the room become signifiers in which is inscribed another "drama," another set of relationships altogether. The desire for death in this narration is made a ward of the foreclosed law of repression, and it returns with the law in repression's staging in the tale's conclusion. In this way, a reading of the manifest and unconscious texts opens into the activity of textual production.

Repression, of course, is never actually inoperative in the text; for the text to be a text, repression already is in place. The tale can be read from the perspective of the end (as readers always do), and gaps appear distinctly like hatchmarks across the narrative to mark what is repressed—what has been pushed down from the surface level of narration and relegated to the unconscious system. A gap appears in the narrator's mysteriously frenzied state, in a strikingly intense obsession that has no object in the manifest text. Another opens in the narrator's compulsive concern with the old man's Evil Eye, an apparently cataract eye with no obvious manifestation of evil intentions. Another is the narrator's need to manipulate the old man and to kill him, neither of which is motivated in the manifest text. And last is the narrator's hallucination of the pounding heart and police suspicion. In each case the narrative event is peculiar, seemingly unmotivated and unattached, a holder for a position that somehow goes unfilled. In fact, such marks do indicate the positioning of the unconscious in relation to the manifest system and signal an activity of exchange between the two systems. Each such event marks a gap, a kind of "trace," that "represents [what cannot] enter the domain of the signifier without being *barred* from it."[14] Lacan's meaning for *barred* here has the double sense of being blocked and of being signified by virtue of (the bar of) repression. These traces indicate a repressive activity that makes manifest narration possible by separating it from an unconscious discourse. The unconscious material, theoretically, could be raised to the manifest level (above the bar), but the text as it is then would collapse and would be repositioned as a different story with different repressed material. Rather, it is because repression creates the syncopated structure of manifest narration—marked with the traces of the unconscious system—that the text can exist at all. Poe's story shows, as does "Instincts and Their Vicissitudes," that the unconscious is a system positioned in relation to a manifest text, like a language. Not at all a depository of meaning (the reified notion of the unconscious), the unconscious is a system of discourse and the component of a writing agency.[15]

III

This psychoanalytic reading of "The Tell-Tale Heart" depicts two somewhat opposed versions of reading under the Gaze. We begin with a "single" version of narrative events (as Lacan does in his reading of Poe's "The Purloined Letter"[16]), a thematic progression (a prior interpretation) that poses as a unity—a sequence whose already-existent meanings we discover through mere articulation. But then we proceed to read the gaps in the narration—Poe's tale as not equal to itself and not a unity. The text then gradually opens itself to a discourse of conscious and unconscious systems, systems (in Saussure's and Lacan's view) without positive terms or a fixed reference. This view of textuality and reading, while it certainly does not cancel out the manifest text, cancels the traditional privilege of the manifest order as a sole determiner of meaning in so radical a way as to question the possibly corrosive influence of Lacanian reading. Jacques Derrida has even asked if Lacanian reading is not an invalid practice of brutalizing the text, of doing violence to the text as it forges its own image as a psychoanalytical allegory. Derrida claims that psychoanalysis actually elaborates itself through its own synthetic (textual) creation in what amounts to a critical act of doubling. Such counterfeit reading, he argues, betrays the true function of narration because, in Barbara E. Johnson's words, "the *textual* signifier . . . [always] resists being thus totalized into meaning" and leaves "an irreducible residue" outside of signification.[17] The question is whether or not psychoanalysis can look into a text and see anything other than itself, see more than its own reflection.

Derrida's criticism of Lacan is important, but it is directed more appropriately to a different version of psychoanalytic reading in reader-response criticism. Norman Holland, for example, attempts—quite unlike Lacan—"to understand the combination of text and personal association."[18] "Instead of taking the text as a fixed entity," he proposes, "let us think of it as a process involving a text and a person. Let us open up the text by assuming the person brings to it something extrinsic. It could be information from literary history, biography, or an archaic ritual like the flyting between primitive bards. It could even be some quite personal fact like my reading this story in Pocketbook No. 39 or my finding it at a time in my life when I had something sexual to hide."[19] Working from these assumptions, Holland proceeds to "re-cover" a story from the overly "abstract, intellectual reading" of Lacan. He strategically consults his own idiosyncratic responses to a text and finds a personal order of meaning and unity, a personality theme. By introducing this element of personal subjectivity into interpretation, Holland attempts to push aside Lacan's intellectual apparatus in order to go—supposedly—to the heart of a story. Yet on closer examination Holland's "transactive criticism" is caught in an impossible contradiction about textuality—precisely the contradiction that Derrida charges to Lacan. In Holland's essay about Poe's "The Purloined Letter," he says, "instead of taking the text as a fixed entity, let us think of it as a process involving text and a person." In the first half of his sentence, surely, the text-as-fixed-object is rejected. It is not an object "out there." But in the sentence's second half the fixed object hastily returns in relation to a person's changing response, as a separate partner in an interpretive relationship. What then is this text that the person responds to?

The question is difficult to answer because in Holland's formulation there is an absolute separation of text and interpretation, a separation central to his theory of textuality. "According to Holland," as Steven Mailloux points out, "the reader makes sense of the text by creating a meaningful unity out of its elements. Unity is not in the text but in the mind of a reader."[20] So, if the text is devoid of meaning, what is the status of this mysterious text? Holland's answer, as Mailloux shows, simultaneously affirms an object text and then ignores it.[21] More pointedly, in *5 Readers Reading* Holland says that "the reader is surely responding to *something*. The literary text may be only so many marks on a page—at most a matrix of psychological possibilities for its readers."[22] For Holland textuality actually vanishes from the text and leaves an empty "matrix" of "marks on a page." Holland then relocates textuality in the "mind of the reader." The reader—independent of the text—contains meaning and *brings* it to the supposedly empty text, just as Holland *brings* his own meaning to Poe's story. The transparent text, in the process, has been turned into a mirror for its reader and a permanent mystery for the critic. Textual law has no allotted place in this version of the text and vanishes only later to reappear in the reader's mind. The loss of textuality from the text in Holland's thinking is a virtual instance, in Lacan's terms, of foreclosure—of textual psychosis, as it were. Such ego psychology takes, as I mentioned earlier, a position of mastery as a substantial truth.

This is not the situation with Lacan for whom reading under the Gaze means canceling the special privilege of the manifest order, whether in the "mind of the reader" or in the "marks on a page," and a repositioning of the manifest text within an unconscious discourse. Going in precisely the opposite direction from Holland (and from other versions of ego psychology), Lacan shows that the reader's mind is not an independent agent, a separate and discrete entity that so simply may respond to, accept, reject, or assess a pre-existent text. In a sense crucially important for literary theory, the text is not a thing to be responded to; rather, it is a structural site where positions are inscribed in two texts (manifest and unconscious) and where interpretation and subjectivity are always at stake. Textuality and reading exist in double dimensions in that they both can represent a text as product and as production—as an object to look into and, simultaneously, as the agency through which the reader is looked at by the Gaze. Lacanian reading, in this way, continually throws into question (decenters) the object-text and the authoritative reading.

In response to Derrida's charge, Lacan shows that psychoanalysis indeed does find itself in its texts—in a productive way—because interpretation, too, is a text and one split radically by an otherness that inhabits the same—by the presence of an absence. Johnson answers Derrida's charge about interpretive fakery when she explains that "if the act of (psycho)analysis has no identity *apart from* its status as a repetition of the structure it seeks to analyze (to untie), then Derrida's remarks *against* psychoanalysis as being always already *mise en abyme* in the text it studies and as being only capable of finding *itself,* are not *objections* to psychoanalysis but in fact [are] a profound insight into its very essence."[23] Psychoanalysis does assume that every finding of an object is the refinding of an object (-position). And the "already" nature of textuality and reading that Johnson mentions points up exactly what is missing from Holland's reader-response version of the text—the unconscious. What is already there, positioned "within" and yet "before" any one text, is not a brute matrix on the page, but language. And what is in language "before" anything else is the Other—the un-

conscious as a chain of signifiers. A text without the insistence of
the unconscious (such is not easy to imagine) is, in Freudian terms,
a psychotic text, a text locked permanently in the imaginary order
and bound perpetually in a struggle for legal right in a realm
where the law has been foreclosed.

Lacan also shows, as we have seen, that textual economy inhabits
interpretation, and with this insight we again circle around the
point we are using as a structural origin—that is, as a substitute
for an origin: repression. The repetition of repression, of the "passage into the semiotic triangle of Oedipus,"[24] takes place in interpretation as well, in the mediatory coils of textuality/interpreta-
tion—in reading. This repetition of repression, in Geoffrey H.
Hartman's words, circles in a "contagious orbit," the "epidemic of
soul-(un)making,"[25] the epidemic of continual passage through unconscious discourse. Such passage is signalled in the bar's existence
and in the insistence of the unconsious chain as separate from the
manifest text in every narrative. Properly considered, this sense of
the importance of textual repression is a powerful inducement for
understanding textuality/interpretation as the inscription of an unconscious writing agency—as a text to be read radically Otherwise.[26]

University of Oklahoma

NOTES

1 *Life Against Death* (New York: Vintage Books, 1959), p. 3.

2 In Robert Georgin, *Lacan,* Cahiers Cistre No. 3 (Lausanne: L'Age d'Homme, 1977), pp. 15-16.

3 This line of development can be followed in Edmund Wilson's *The Triple Thinkers* (New York: Harcourt, Brace and Co., 1938) and *The Wound and the Bow* (Boston: Houghton Mifflin Co., 1941); Lionel Trilling's *The Liberal Imagination* (New York: The Viking Press, 1951) and *Freud and the Crisis of Our Culture* (Boston: Beacon Press, 1955); Simon O. Lesser's *Fiction and the Unconscious* (Boston: Beacon Press, 1957); Frederick J. Hoffman's *Freudianism and the Literary Mind,* 2nd ed. (Baton Rouge: Louisiana State Univ. Press, 1957); Norman H. Holland's *The Dynamics of Literary Response* (New York: Oxford Univ. Press, 1968), *Poems in Persons* (New York: W. W. Norton and Co., 1973), and *5 Readers Reading* (New Haven and London: Yale Univ. Press, 1975); and Frederick C. Crews' *The Sins of the Fathers* (New York: Oxford Univ. Press, 1966), *Psycho-analysis and Literary Process* (Cambridge, Ma.: Winthrop Publishers, 1970), and *Out of My System* (New York: Oxford Univ. Press, 1975). This line of American Freudian interpretation culminates in Crews, who in the end repudiates it, and in Holland, who exclusively analyzes readers' responses to literature.

4 "Instincts and Their Vicissitudes," *The Standard Edition of the Complete Psychological Works of Sigmund Freud,* Vol. 14, trans. James Strachey (London: The Hogarth Press, 1955), p. 127. Maurice Merleau-Ponty's very similar approach to the phenomenology of seeing is presented succinctly in "Eye and Mind," *The Primacy of Perception,* ed. James M. Edie (Evanston: Northwestern Univ. Press, 1964), pp. 159-190.

5 "Instincts and Their Vicissitudes," p. 129.

6 Ibid.

7 *The Four Fundamental Concepts of Psycho-Analysis,* ed. Jacques-Alain Miller, trans. Alan Sheridan (New York: W. W. Norton, 1978), p. 78.

8 I made some of these points about voyeurism and discussed a voyeuristic tendency in American literature in "*Other Voices, Other Rooms* and the Ocularity of American Fiction," *Delta,* 11 (1980), pp. 1-14. From that discussion, a comment about Ralph Waldo Emerson is particularly relevant here: "There are other major American writers in this voyeuristic tradition. F. O. Matthiessen refers to 'the special stress that the nineteenth century put on sight' and to the intense expression of this tendency in Ralph Waldo Emerson's work. Such intensity is shown in what Matthiessen calls 'the exalted climax' as Emerson rhapsodizes in the first chapter of *Nature:* 'Standing on the base ground,—my head bathed by the blithe air and uplifted into infinite space—, all mean egotism vanishes. I become a transparent eyeball; I am nothing; I see all; the currents of the Universal Being circulate through me; I am part or parcel of God.' Emerson's figure for American character as a transparent eyeball, whose gaze is fixed—really transfixed—on the possibilities of a new world, precisely captures the essential qualities of voyeurism. The eyeball metaphor exaggerates the importance of mere looking and heightens the power of simple visual apprehension as if—like the young Isabel Archer—the American were especially capable, and only capable, of detached appreciation in the exercise of an uncorrupted ability to see. And—and here lies the crucial point—because it is transparent, the eyeball itself provides—rather impossibly—no substance that may be gazed upon in return as it looks. So, like the voyeur who stares out from a place hidden in darkness, the transparent eyeball metaphor embodies a version of seeing in which the masterful side of looking predominates, as if seeing did not also necessitate being seen, and as if seeing itself were not a *process* of apprehension. Instead of processes, Emerson speaks of 'occult facts in human nature,' and, as he writes in his journal, 'the chief of these is the glance (*oeillade*).' Such emphasis on sight leads Emerson in *Representative Men* to define 'genius' literally by the measure of 'the first look he casts on any object,' as if that precious look could reveal everything" (p. 11).

More recently, Carolyn Porter has done an extensive investigation of visual experience in American literature in *Seeing and Being: The Plight of the Participant Observer in Emerson, James, Adams, and Faulkner* (Middletown, Ct.: Wesleyan Univ. Press, 1981).

9 *Écrits: A Selection,* trans. Alan Sheridan (New York: W.W. Norton and Co., 1977), p. 163.

10 *The Four Fundamental Concepts of Psycho-Analysis,* p. 248. See also *Écrits,* pp. 164 and 200.

11 "The Unconscious: A Psychoanalytic Study," *Yale French Studies,* 48 (1972), p. 158. Lacan disagrees with the priority that Laplanche, in particular, gives to the unconscious as somehow coming before language. As Lacan explains:

My statement that the unconscious has the structure of a language positively cannot be understood other than in accordance with what I was saying a moment ago, namely that language is the condition of the unconscious.

The unconscious is purely and simply a discourse and it is as such that it necessitates the theory of the double inscription. This is proved by the fact that there may be two completely different inscriptions, although they operate on and are supported by the *same signifiers*, which simply turn their battery, their apparatus, in order to occupy topographically different places. For, in any case, these inscriptions are strictly dependent upon the site of their support. That a certain significant formation be at one level or the other is exactly what will ensure it of a different import in the chain as a whole." Quoted in Anika Rifflet-Lemaire, *Jacques Lacan*, trans. David Macey (London, Boston and Henley: Routledge and Kegan Paul, 1977), p. 118.

12 *The Four Fundamental Concepts of Psycho-Analysis*, p. 248.

13 *The Complete Tales and Poems of Edgar Allan Poe* (New York: The Modern Library, 1965), p. 303. Subsequent page references to this work will be noted in the text.

14 Quoted in Anthony Wilden, *The Language of the Self* (Baltimore: The Johns Hopkins Press, 1968), p. 187.

15 For a discussion of the "textual unconscious," see Jean Bellemin-Nöel's *Vers l'inconscient du texte* (Paris: Presses Universitaires de France, 1979). For a discussion of Bellemin-Nöel's book, see Jerry Aline Flieger's "Trial and Error: The Case of the Textual Unconscious," *Diacritics*, 11 (1), pp. 56-67. See also Fredric Jameson's Marxist version of the textual unconscious in *The Political Unconscious: Narrative as a Socially Symbolic Act* (Ithaca: Cornell Univ. Press, 1981).

16 "Seminar on 'The Purloined Letter,'" trans. Jeffrey Mehlman, *Yale French Studies*, 48 (1972), pp. 38-72.

17 What I have quoted here is Barbara E. Johnson's succinct and clear version of Derrida's position in her "The Frame of Reference," *Yale French Studies*, 55/56 (1977), p. 483. What Derrida actually says, among other things, in his comment on Lacan's reading of "The Purloined Letter," is that "the letter would have no fixed place, not even that of a definable gap or void. The letter would not be found; it might always not be found; it would in any case be found less in the sealed writing whose 'story' is told by the narrator and 'deciphered' by the Seminar, less in the context of the story, than 'in' the text escaping on a fourth side the eyes of both Dupin and the psychoanalyst." "The Purveyor of Truth," trans. Willis Domingo, James Hulbert, Moshe Ron and M.-R. Logan, *Yale French Studies*, 52 (1975), p. 64.

18 "Re-Covering 'The Purloined Letter': Reading as a Personal Transaction," *The Reader in the Text*, eds. Susan R. Suleiman and Inge Crosman (Princeton: Princeton Univ. Press, 1980), p. 364.

19 Ibid., pp. 363–364.

20 "Reader-Response Criticism?" *Genre*, 10(3), 417.

21 Ibid., p. 419.

22 (New Haven: Yale Univ. Press, 1975), p. 12.

23 "The Frame of Reference," pp. 498–499.

24 Gayatri Chakravorty Spivak, "The Letter as Cutting Edge," *Yale French Studies*, 55/56 (1977), p. 222.

25 "Psychoanalysis: The French Connection," *Psychoanalysis and the Question of the Text*, ed. Geoffrey H. Hartman (Baltimore: Johns Hopkins Univ. Press, 1978), p. 91.

26 I wish to thank Ronald Schleifer, Isaiah Smithson, and Melanie Ruth Collins for their helpful comments as I wrote this article.

"Alas, Poor Yorick": Sterne Thoughts

❧

Richard Macksey

> Ce *to be or not to be* est une histoire complète-
> ment verbale.
> —Jacques Lacan, *Le Séminaire: livre II,*
> p. 272

> Be hamlet. Be the property plot. Be Yorick
> and Lankystare. Be cool. Be mackinamucks
> of yourselves. Be finish.
> —James Joyce, *Finnegans Wake,*
> p. 465

> En racontant une histoire je fais parler le
> mort.
> —Louis Marin

I hope that the rubric for this collection of essays, "Lacan and Narration," licenses me to begin with an anecdote of the Master abroad.[1] Although there had been some antecedent correspondence, my first encounter with Jacques Lacan was in a hotel lobby as he arrived for the Baltimore "structuralist" symposium of October 1966. He had come down from a prelusory reconnaissance of New York with his then translator and disciple Anthony Wilden. No time was wasted on politesses; he wanted to confirm the names and sequence of the participants at the sessions. Already an old campaigner in the Parisian wars, he had been careful in earlier correspondence to select his own terrain and place in the order of events, but he also recognized that there were certain instabilities in the program for an occasion such as ours. When I mentioned that another speaker had joined the group—a young philosopher named Jacques Derrida—a little cloud, like a man's hand, passed over the Master's face. As I waited for worse to come, he remarked that I was carrying a book and asked me what it was. When I replied that it was a copy of *Tristram Shandy,* his manner changed abruptly, he sighed and said, "*Tristram Shandy* est le roman le plus analytique de la littérature universelle." (The allusion to the outrageous last sentence of Victor Shklovsky's pioneer essay on "the parodying novel" was, I assume, deliberate.)[2] This judgment led to a too brief discussion of the peculiar way in which all of the "characters" in the novel constitute themselves as "modes of discourse" and the equally peculiar way in which the novel constitutes itself around a notorious "lack."

Lacan soon enough returned to the tactical maneuvers of the symposium and, as far as I know, never returned in his seminars to the challenge of reading (and being read by) this "most analytic" of all novels. As a number of the contributors to this collection observe, Lacan in his teaching made ample use of a few privileged or model texts: certainly the "key narrative" of Oedipus, both at Thebes and in the analytic extremity of Colonus (at which latter venue Lacan contrives to win back from Freud the primacy of the psychoanalytic *praxis,* the efficacy of the speech act, as Shoshana Felman observes—in interpreting the Freudian *theory* of wish-fulfillment figured in the earlier narrative). But he also turned at critical moments in the elaboration of his theory to the reading of exemplary narratives drawn from the canon of English literature: that supreme act of interpretive larceny that serves as the overture to the *Ecrits,* the seminar on "The Purloined Letter," and the discussion of desire, mourning, and melancholia in the spring 1959 seminars on *Hamlet.* We can only regret that Sterne's novel, so reminiscent of Lacan's own rhetorical flights juxtaposed with unbuttoned colloquialisms, where—in Shklovsky's terminology— such a monument of *syuzhet* is spun from so little *fabula,* did not join this short list of favored texts.

Sterne like Lacan writes texts (at once "written" and "spoken") that displace and deconstruct themselves in the very process of their production. His style, quirky, discontinuous, and deliberately odd like Lacan's, inhabits time and triumphantly accepts its own incompleteness. And Sterne, availing himself in his eccentric way of Locke's "story-book" and Hume's *Enquiry,* advances a program of exploring the same "intersubjective logic" and "temporality of the subject" that Lacan announces in the *Ecrits* (the terms are Lacan's). Like Lacan he seems in all his turnings and digressions to be in search of "une vraie parole," what from a twentieth-century perspective appears as a celebration of the linguistic mediation in

the place of the narrating subject and in the discourse of interpretation. (Sterne would no doubt have had a parodic turn at the
descriptive vocabulary currently available to us.) In summary, *Tristram Shandy*, that novel in which the narrator seems always in search
of inventing the conditions in which he can invent himself, in its
duplicitous compact with the reader anticipates the analytic dialogue itself.

Superficial similarities are all too easy to enumerate in comparing Lacan's "return to Freud" with Stern's isolated performance: the word play and *mots d'esprit*, the rhetorical games and
parodic appropriations, the calculated lapses and sylleptic con-
junctions. But in a more pervasive sense *Tristram Shandy* addresses
topics central to Lacan's enterprise; it is an extended meditation
on thwarted paternity and its consequences, on a theory of reading
that attends to the subversive possibilities of signification, on proto-
Freudian topics like the primal scene, castration, and verbal wit,
and supremely on a comic narrative that elaborates the cross-im-
plications of sexuality and language—inscribed under the sign of
the death's head. It is a novel rising from the symbolic triad of the
family. As a most peculiar case history it can be seen as either a
congeries of symptoms or a narrative: the history of desire manifested through language. it is also a novel of wounds, scars, and
manque (Uncle Toby, we need hardly be reminded, was "wounded
in language"). Most of all it is a system of marks and repressions
that offer a model for contemporary analysis of the situation and
temporality of the subject.

THE ABSENT FATHER

> I know that it will be said, continued my father (availing himself of the
> *Prolepsis*) that in itself, and simply taken—like hunger, or thirst, or
> sleep—'tis an affair neither good or bad—or shameful or otherwise.
> —*Tristram Shandy*, IX, 33

For a novel haunted by so many gaps and discontinuities, *Tristram Shandy* appears to be a work remarkably precise about its
narrator's point of origin. The narrator ignores the wisdom of the
ancients and, while misquoting Horace, asserts that he will begin
"ab Ovo." The exemplary precision with which Tristram alleges to
establish the moment of his conception introduces the anecdote of
the senior Shandys and the clock; and in a narrative in which sex
and temporality are so intertwined, this has a certain initial aptness.
Further, it is on the most cursory examination, in a novel so gov-

erned by the rhetorical figure of aposiopesis, but the first of many interruptions that will punc.uate the work with maddening ingenuity.

Having excused all save the "curious and inquisitive," Tristram "shuts the door" in chapter 4 and asserts with an uncharacteristic lack of ambiguity, "I was begot in the night, betwixt the first *Sunday* and the first *Monday,* in the year of our Lord one thousand seven hundred and eighteen. I am positive I was." (I, 4) He then describes the monthly regularity of Walter's connubial and horological duties (always discharged "on the first *Sunday night* of every month throughout the whole year," adding, however, that he had remained chaste through December, January, and February while laid up with a Sciatica, and that he had departed for London on March 25th, where he remained until "the second week of the May following." This would seem to fix the night of Tristram's conception with some exactitude. He drives the final nail in the first sentence of the next chapter: "On the fifth day of *November,* 1718, which to the aera fixed on, was as near nine kalendar months *as any husband could in reason have expected,*——was I *Tristram Shandy,* Gentleman, brought forth into this scurvy and disasterous world of ours. (I, 5; second italics added) This is a precision that opens a considerable gap, since by any arithmetic the figure adds up to *eight* months, and here as elsewhere in the novel the point is made that Tristram was a term baby.

I have earlier argued that the novel thus begins with a considerable *méconnaissance,* one that is glossed at various critical points throughout the narrative.[3] In the opening pages the relationship of the father to the symbolic triad of the family is already one of absence. The insistence on the precise calculation of Tristram's putative gestation also forces the reader back to a re-reading of the riddle that concludes the first chapter: *"Did ever woman since the creation of the world, interrupt a man with such a silly question?* Pray, what was your father saying?——Nothing." (I, 1) It now appears that he was accomplishing nothing as well, although possessed by words. (Lacan offers an appropriate marginal comment in "Fonction et champ de la parole et du langage en psychanlyse": "Through the word—already a presence made of absence—absence itself comes to giving itself a name in the moment of origin.") The signs of Tristram's unrelatedness to Walter physically abound in the chapters that follow his ultimate arrival in the world; yet absent in the "first scene" (which is also absent from the book),

Walter does assume with his language-haunted theories of ped-
agogy and his doctrine of names the role of the *nom-du-père*.
Writing of Telemakhos' predicament in the *Odyssey*, Robert Con
Davis observes, "Instituted by the discovery of absence, the desire
for the father will be articulated in what is essentially a narrative."[4]
Walter's role in the narrative is thus generated out of "nothing"
but it serves, from the mangled naming of Tristram on through
his other misadventures, as constitutive of the symbolic order of
language.

There is, however, within the narrative another character who
in terms of appearance, temperament, and status as author has a
larger claim on the role of Tristram's natural father. This is the
character whose name Sterne actually purloins for the signature
of his other works, parson Yorick. And, like his precursor in
Shakespeare's play, he presides over much of the action of the
narrative from the grave—and yet, in *Tristram Shandy's* last
chapter, when Walter and his wife once again come together in a
discussion of perplexed paternity (IX, 33), he has the last words
of the book. Two passages from the chapters between these first
and last will perhaps serve for a summary of Walter's absence and
Yorick's involvement. Thus from the middle of the novel one of
the shorter chapters in Book IV in its entirety, where the question
of the mother's relation to her child has earlier been in learned
dispute:

CHAPTER XXX

—And pray, said my uncle Toby, leaning upon Yorick, as he and my
father were helping him leisurely down the stairs—don't be terrified,
madam, this stair-case conversation is not so long as the last—And pray,
Yorick, said my uncle Toby, which way is this said affair of Tristram at
length settled by these learned men? Very satisfactorily, replied Yorick;
no mortal, Sir, has any concern with it—for Mrs. Shandy the mother
is nothing at all a-kin to him—and as the mother's is the surest side—
Mr. Shandy, in course, is still less than nothing——In short, he is not
as much a-kin to him, Sir, as I am.—
        ——That may well be, said my father, shaking his head.
        ——Let the learned say what they will, there must certainly, quoth
my uncle Toby, have been some sort of consanguinity betwixt the
duchess of Suffolk and her son.
The vulgar are of the same opinion, quoth Yorick, to this hour.

The second passage, from Book VI, is a prime example of one of
Walter's ritual "beds of justice" investigations, this one conducted

the reader finally learns of a Sunday night. As in the earlier chapter, the allusions to the tall and lanky Yorick are obvious enough. Mrs. Shandy, the supreme "non-character" in the novel, through her silences and, here, echolalia draws Walter closer and closer to the reluctant possession of truth. The scene could be read as an anticipation of a psychoanalytic session. At issue is the "breeching" of Tristram, that social ritual when the child's gender (about which there has been some dispute following exaggerated accounts in the village of his accident with the window sash) is unambiguously declared:

CHAPTER XVIII

We should begin, said my father, turning himself half round in bed, and shifting his pillow a little towards my mother's, as he opened the debate—We should begin to think, Mrs. Shandy, of putting this boy into breeches.—

We should so,—said my mother.—We defer it, my dear, quoth my father, shamefully.——

I think we do, Mr. Shandy,—said my mother.

—Not but the child looks extremely well, said my father, in his vests and tunics.——

——He does look very well in them,—replied my mother.——

—And for that reason it would be almost a sin, added my father, to take him out of 'em.—

—It would so,—said my mother:—But indeed he is growing a very tall lad,—rejoined my father.

—He is very tall for his age, indeed, said my mother.—

—I can not (making two syllables of it) imagine, quoth my father, who the deuce he takes after.—

I cannot conceive, for my life,—said my mother.—

Humph!—said my father.

(The dialogue ceased for a moment.)

—I am very short myself,—continued my father gravely.

You are very short, Mr. Shandy,—said my mother.

Humph! quoth my father to himself, a second time: in muttering which, he plucked his pillow a little further from my mother's,—and turning about again, there was an end of the debate for three minutes and a half.

If the question is not clear enough at this point, the reader is invited to listen further to Walter when he revives sufficiently to pursue the "debate":

—When he gets these breeches made, cried my father in a higher tone, he'll look like a beast in 'em.

He will be very awkward in them at first, replied my mother.—
—And 'twill be lucky, if that's the worst on't, added my father.
It will be very lucky, answered my mother.
I suppose, replied my father,—making some pause first,—he'll be
exactly like other people's children.—
Exactly, said my mother.——
—Though I shall be sorry for that, added my father: and so the
debate stopped again.

Walter's attachment to language and to the erection of new linguistic theories cannot, of course, be silenced by such momentary
defeats as these, any more that Toby's campaigning and efforts at
precise representation can be terminated by his wound. Walter
would seek to order the articulation of the "auxiliary verbs" with
the same passion that Toby would seek to keep pace with the wars
in Flanders. In a world of radical unrelatedness they both strive
for some symbolic stay against disorder.

THE PURLOINED SERMON

—Here are two senses, cried Eugenius, as we walk'd along, pointing
with the fore finger of his right hand to the word *Crevice*, in the fifty-
second page of the second volume of this book of books. . . .
                                        —*Tristram Shandy*, III, 33

Authors and their critics, analysts and analysands, must all attend to the strategies of reading and to the challenges that they
raise. *Tristram Shandy* is a novel, perhaps above all others, that
concerns itself with the reciprocal and highly suspect relations of
author and reader. The reader is here again and yet again invited
to participate in the subversive act of the book's creation, to uncover the sub-text of the repressed read under the gaze of the
Unconscious. And the signature of the author or his surrogate,
insofar as he is embodied as a character within the book albeit a
dead character (who may, as I have argued, have begot the narrator
himself), is "read" by his own creations. We are reminded again
and again that the reader's "mind" is not an independent entity;
it exists and is constituted within language, which is itself a shared
experience described by the symbolic triangle. The strategy of
"Slawkenbergius' Tale" should be enough to catechize any reader
about the limits of his autonymy.

Trim, but one of many eccentric readers within the novel, was
caught by Hogarth in his plate for the second edition as the Cor-
poral adjusted himself to the "laws of gravity" (physical and rhe-

torical) and began to read that text of a sermon just fallen from a copy of Stevinus (II, 15). But what is the text that Trim begins, twice, to read? We learn that it is a sermon from the pen of Yorick, who has been memorialized some chapters earlier by the famous "black page," an invitation to mourn and a literal representation of that beance opened by death and ink. At least it *seems* to be Yorick's work, since Walter Shandy definitely recognizes his "stile and manner." And yet the authorship of the text within a text is further confounded, since the narrator tells us that this very sermon was "preach'd at an assize, in the cathedral of York, before a thousand witnesses, ready to give on oath of it, by a certain prebendary of that church, and actually printed by him when he had done,—and within so short a space as two years and three months after Yorick's death." (II, 18) "Yorick's death" is doubly ambiguous, since he is in one intertextual sense already dead and decayed when Hamlet's antecedent drama begins. Yorick as the presence of an absence is surely the most famous talking skull in literary history.

The prebendary of York was, of course, Laurence Sterne, who had preached the sermon at the close of the summer assizes on July 29, 1750, and who did indeed publish it "at the request of the High Sheriff and Grand Jury" on August 7th of the same year. He published it again, for the third time, under his *nom de pulpitre,* as the final sermon in the fourth volume of *The Sermons of Mr. Yorick,* remarking by way of apology that it had already appeared in a "certain moral work" but had been misconstrued by its readers. And yet within the fictional time of the narrative, Trim sets about reading the sermon on the very day of Tristram's birth, in 1718, some thirty years before Yorick's lamented death. As an instance of Sterne's deliberate intercutting of fictional times and historic time the case is hardly unique. It may remain, however, as emblem of the ambiguities of authorship (and paternity) that haunt the novel. Further, both the fictional reader and his fictional audience complicate the text with their own knotted narratives—of Trim's brother Tom, of Slop's Romish apologetics, and of the Shandy brothers' contrary readings hobbyhorsically pursued.

But the preacher's text itself is a commentary on text that further impinges on the act of reading and, behind that, on the very act of self-apprehension: "For we *trust* we have a good Conscience" (*Hebrews,* 13:18). Within the polysemous weave of Sterne's narrative, the reader is invited to read with the fictional readers, to supply the final identification of yet another author, and to participate in the complex game of literary creation out of the "dead letter" (or "l'être mort"). The sermon, then, is read in Yorick's absence and demonstrates the impossibility of a self-contained moral discourse, despite its title: conscience cannot supply the true referent of morality but is rather the voice of desire and self-interest. Revelation, established religion thus seems to be required, but this, too, like the sermon itself, must be *read* and so is subject to conditions that no referential discourse can master.

Within the text of Yorick's (Sterne's) sermon, with all its dubieties about the assurance of our own "conscience," there are yet other invitations to confirm or correct our self-awareness through reading: "How readest thou?" he asks by way of qualification of the individual conscience. The preacher's *tolle lege* invites the sinner to test his conscience, like that "British judge" appealed to in the chauvinistic peroration, against that "which he knows already written." The appeal to the historical, judicial audience is obvious, but so is the paradox of a Common Law that is not exactly "already written" as statute but rather is intertextually dispersed as a continuing process of opinion and commentary; a similar paradox attends biblical authority: in the "already written" where does text end and commentary begin? Thwarted like Yorick in the heroic appeal to referential language, the reader's attention must still engage in a reciprocal relationship with text, like the successful interpreter of the Common Law or of the Bible. The spirit of the reader giveth life, but the letter of the text readeth its interpreters.

Somewhat later in the narrative, after reviewing some of Walter Shandy's eccentric budget of reading, including "the great and learned Hafen Slawkenbergius" whose treacherous tale is yet to come, Tristram comes a little closer to the dangers of the chain of signifiers liberated in a text and to the actual motor of such associations. He advises his "reader," apparently young and virginal: "Now don't let Satan, my dear girl, in this chapter take advantage of any one spot of rising-ground to get astride of your imagination. . . ." (III, 36) This leads him, however, to introduce a reference to "Tickletoby's mare," newly escaped from Rabelais' text (4:13). Some consultation of precedent texts leads back to *Tappecue*, of which Tickletoby is the handy English translation, and this (the lexicographers advise us) is a cant term for penis. From here it is but a step to Lacan's position of the subject with respect to the phallus. (The phallus as universal signifier in Tristram Shandy is clear enough in Slawkenbergius' twice-told tale Anoses. The phallus for the Lacanian reader is, however, "always veiled," manifesting itself only *"dans des phanies,"* as he remarks in the Hamlet seminars. This may provide sufficient gloss to the exhortation to reading that follows the emergence of Tickletoby's mare, a set-piece that introduces one more self-referential gesture in the games of *Tristram Shandy*, the insertion of the (actual) marbled page:

> —Read, read, read, read, my unlearned reader! read,-or by the knowledge of the great saint *Paraleipomenon*——I'll tell you beforehand, you had better throw down the book at once; for without *much reading*, by which your reverence knows, I mean *much knowledge*, you will no more be able to penetrate the moral of the next marbled page (motly emblem of my work!) than the world with all its sagacity has been able to unravel the many opinions, transactions and truths which still lie mystically hid under the dark veil of the black one.
>
> (III, 36)

THE SIGN OF THE JESTER'S SKULL

they do be saying, (skull!) that was a planter for you. . . .
—James Joyce, *Finnegans Wake*, p. 25

That which is "hidden" in Sterne's novel lies in time somewhere between the infinite possibilities of the Mallarmean blank page (VI, 38) and the final, finitely determined "black one" that concludes Yorick's ambiguous career. All of the narrator's desperate will to live is concentrated on keeping the story going, the digressions exfoliating, before the final closure of that memorial black page. And yet, to continue the reading of the passage above (where "the black one" is conventionally taken to refer to Satan), it is the marbled page that becomes "motley emblem" of the work. For it is in the space between the printer's marbled pages of the physical book that the act of reading—and of constitution of a subject—transpires. More exactly, in terms of "Freud's masterplot," through detours and repetitions, the novel's conclusion finally attains its beginning in the words of the dead Yorick.

Within this potential space Sterne claims two consciousnesses must be at work in relation to a third element, language; and more— the repositioning of reader and author opens the operations of the repressed material to the game: a PacMan system of relationships between manifest and repressed discourses. Their shaping collaboration, within the shifting networks and misapprehensions of the novel, must remain both active and passive. Speaking of the gap between what any author can say and what his reader must supply, Sterne insists "the truest respect which you can pay to the reader's understanding is to halve this matter amicably, and leave [the reader] something to imagine, in his turn, as well as yourself." (II, 11) All the rest is more than half.

Sterne is too well aware that the reader's imagination can be specular, illusory, and digressive as well as veridical and progressive. What follows the marbled page is, in fact, the elaborately sophistical preamble to "Slawkenbergius' Tale." And the tale itself, after the bookish interruption between volumes III and IV, proceeds in the double key of its punning Latin and Shandy père's erratic English translation, serving to destroy the autonomy of the written word itself. The word "nose," like "whiskers" in the "dangerous chapter" of Book V or Toby's "proper end of woman," suffers a "wound." It eludes the "intended" use despite all the author's protestations and abortive attempts at definition: "For by the word Nose, throughout all this long chapter of noses, and in every other part of my work, where the word Nose occurs—I declare, by that word I mean a Nose, and nothing more or less." (The operative word here may be "nothing.") But for the obsessed imagination, whether of Walter Shandy or of the book's reader, the word "nose" can never again signify quite that.

The act of reading takes place, then, in time, a time in which the players move toward death, in which the symbolic order in which the "world" is "created" rests on absence and death: it is erected between the dead determinations or ellipses of the text and the living responses of the reader. As John Dewey observed, in a Shandean vein, without the act of recreation the text cannot be inhabited as a work of art. The reader supplies, from clues within the text, the temporal dimensions of anticipation and memory. But he must supply as well the search for coherence within apparent chaos, something to fill the "holes" in the text (whether the dashes or asterisks or missing chapters or interrupted conversations). Finally, he must participate in the play of time that controls the vectors of all the discourses within the novel—of Tristram writing desperately in an effort to outdistance death in Book V and Yorick completing the novel from the position of death itself. Yorick is the figure whose mortality marks the boundaries of the Shandean world.

The characters try to "speak of death" as they mourn the "hole"

opened by the death of another. Thus both Walter and Trim, the
one through the mediations of rhetoric, the other with the mute
sermon of the dropped hat, mourn the death of Bobby (V, 2; V,
7). But Yorick and Tristram are met at what Lacan calls "the cross-
roads" of the graveyard itself. At the beginning of Book VII Tristram, whose role as the subject however tenuous of the autobiography puts him under a special constraint (as Louis Marin observes), has an uncanny moment and a narrow escape:

> Now there is nothing in this world I abominate worse, than to be
> interrupted in a story—and I was that moment telling Eugenius a most
> tawdry one in my way, of a nun who fancied herself a shell-fish, and
> of a monk damned for eating a mussel, and was shewing him the
> grounds and justice of the procedure—
> —Did ever so grave a personage get into so vile a scrape?' quoth
> Death. Thou hast had a narrow escape, Tristram, said Eugenius, taking
> hold of my hand as I finished my story—
> But there is no living, Eugenius, replied I, at this rate; for as this son
> of a whore has found out my lodgings—
> —You call him rightly, said Eugenius,—for by sin, we are told, he
> entered the world—I care not which way he entered, quoth I, provided
> he be not in such a hurry to take me out with him—for I have forty
> volumes to write, and forty thousand things to say and do which no
> body in the world will say and do for me, except thyself; and as thou
> seest he has got me by the throat (for Eugenius could scarce hear me
> speak across the table), and that I am no match for him in the open
> field, had I not better, whilst these few scattered spirits remain, and
> these two spider legs of mine (holding one of them up to him) are able
> to support me—had I not better, Eugenius, fly for my life? 'Tis my
> advice, my dear Tristram, said Eugenius—Then by heaven! I will lead
> him a dance he little thinks of—for I will gallop, quoth I, without
> looking once behind me, to the banks of the Garonne; and if I hear
> him clattering at my heels—I'll scamper away to mount Vesuvius—
> from thence to Joppa, and from Joppa to the world's end; where, if he
> follows me, I pray God he may break his neck—

His encounter propels him off on a break-neck race with death
across the Continent, and alters accordingly throughout Book VII
the tempo of the prose. The volume ends with the temptation to
abandon both life and opinions to the communal dance he meets
"betwixt Nismes and Lunel." But he writes on against time, turning
the course of the narrative backward to the story of Uncle Toby's
amours. He writes on in the ceaseless effort to possess time and to
incorporate "the lost object."

Writing and reading are pitched in time and subject to the compulsion of repetition. There are moments toward the end of the narrative where the authorial voice breaks out into an apostrophe; there is no fixed point, no ground for a reader "outside" the narrative, so Sterne's cry is ours as well:

> Time wastes too fast: every letter I trace tells me with what rapidity Life follows my pen; the days and hours of it, more precious, my dear Jenny! than the rubies about thy neck, are flying over our heads like light clouds of a windy day, never to return more—every thing presses on—whilst thou art twisting that lock,—see! it grows grey.
>
> (IX, 8)

There are parallel passages in Sterne's correspondence; thus in a letter of 1756, written after three hemorrhages, he resolves like Tristram: "I find I must once more fly from death whilst I have strength. . . ."[5]

Sterne's narrative of the subject in the process of constituting itself thus becomes an extended meditation on the reciprocal relations that so bind both author and reader under the sign of mortality. The "real" and the "fictive" interpenetrate; identification and analysis alternate. And thereby the novel can become a model for a certain kind of critical involvement and complicity in a "comedy of desire" (motley counterpart to Lacan's reading of *Hamlet*).

As Nietzsche shrewdly observed in his portrait of Sterne ("Der freieste Schriftsteller"),[6] the secret of his art is a matter of *Zweideutigkeit,* a doubling back in *double entendre,* ambiguity, and rapid shifting of roles. He recognized Sterne's genius not only for implicating his readers in the game but for reversing parts with them in the dance of time; while we become spectators to our own performances:

> Sterne is the great master of *double entendre,* this phrase being naturally used in a far wider sense than is commonly done when one applies it to sexual relations. We may give up for lost the reader who always wants to know exactly what Sterne thinks about a matter, and whether he be making a serious or a smiling face (for he can do both with one wrinkling of his features; he can be and even wishes to be right and wrong at the same moment, to interweave profundity and farce). His digressions are at once continuations and further developments of the story, his maxims contain a satire on all that is sententious, his dislike of seriousness is bound up with a

disposition to take no matter merely externally and on the surface. So in the proper reader he arouses a feeling of uncertainty whether he be walking, lying, or standing, a feeling most closely akin to that of floating in the air. He, the most versatile of writers, communicates something of this versatility to his reader. Yes, Sterne unexpectedly changes the parts, and is often as much reader as author, his book being like a play within a play, a theatre audience before another theatre audience.

In this extraordinary versatility and in the ambiguous "wrinkling" (*Faltung*) of gaze with which he faces us lie two clues to the analytic power of Sterne's "mountebank" performance. This performance can only be completed, however, with the complicity of the reader.[7]

That the text must be relived, and thus completed, is the first assumption in Sterne's problematics of the novel. Yet as the text is being read, in all its meanderings, détours, and displacements, both author and readers are establishing a "position" that disposes those ambiguous relations, concatenating events, and intersecting times and places so deliberately skewed in the original. The reciprocating interplay of readings and readers, time and arrest, "imaginary" and "symbolic" gives us a model for the interpretative act and, thereby, the invention of a new time—that of the interpretation: *first*, a naive, open, and "participatory" reading, like that of the generous Trim, tracing—diachronically—the "digressive, progressive" course of the narrative; *then* a paradoxically synchronic "reading" of the "hidden" elements and reconstituted structures in their dialectical relations, not unlike Walter Shandy at work on the differentials of language; and *finally*, a synthetic rereading of both, like that of the author comprehending the life he has discovered, a movement turning in the familiar critical circle back to the marbled page that begins, ends, and emblematizes the book. Those other physically intercalated pages, at once signifiers and signifieds, the potential blank one and the completely determined black one, remain as troubling reminders of the two kinds of absence that always escape the asymptote of the critical reading.

The Johns Hopkins University

NOTES

1 These comments derive from a paper delivered at a 1982 M L A session chaired by Robert Con Davis on the topic "Jacques Lacan's Impact on Current Narrative

Theory." They are considerably abridged from a longer essay on Laurence Sterne that is part of a volume on "terminal cases" and the fictions of mortal endings.

2 Originally published in Petrograd, 1921; reprinted in *O teorii prozy* (Moscow, 1929²), p. 204.

3 The story of Tristram's thwarted conception (the impossibility of Walter's being his natural father) and of Yorick's implied paternity was developed at length in "Where Was Uncle Toby Wounded," a "presidential paper" delivered to the Tudor and Stuart Club, May 1968. At that time this thesis was still capable of provoking scandal. My former colleague Ronald Paulson generously summarized my argument three years later in "A Chapter from Smollett," in *Bicentennial Essays Presented to Lewis M. Knapp*, edited by G. S. Rousseau and P.-G. Boucé (New York, 1971), pp. 75-77. To date I have been unable to discover any earlier version of this solution to the paternity riddle nor why the simple arithmetic was hid under a veil for more than two centuries. (Sam Weber apparently came independently to the same conclusion in Berlin during the early 1970s.)

4 *The Fictional Father: Lacanian Readings of the Text* (Amherst, 1981), p. 9.

5 *Letters* (Oxford, 1935), p. 257.

6 *Menschliches, Allzumenschliches*, Zweiter Band, No. 113, *Werke*, I, ed. Karl Schlechta (München, 1966), pp. 780–82.

7 Mrs. Shandy stands, no doubt, at the outermost limit of any notion of "reading." Echoing or interrupting Walter's rhetoric, she both confirms and subverts his authorial narcissism. (And, again, by holding him to the language of the marriage contract she ultimately determines the thin "plot" of the novel.) In her refusal to respond, to interpret Walter's language, she effectively opens a fatal split between words and the subject that would animate them. Thus she plunges the central questions of authorship, paternity, discourse, and the primacy of consciousness over its language into the deepest incertitude, exposing (like Yorick in another register) the problem of the text and legibility to an irreparable doubt. It is therefore profoundly appropriate that her interruptions provoke both the inception and the conclusion of the narrative.

BEYOND OEDIPUS:
THE SPECIMEN STORY
OF PSYCHOANALYSIS

❧

Shoshana Felman

I

What is a Key-Narrative?

"We are forever telling stories about ourselves," writes Roy
Schafer, in an essay[1] that most suggestively defines the crux of the
relation—and of the differentiation—between psychoanalysis and
narration: between the daily practice (need) of telling stories and
the narrative experience that is at stake in a practical psychoanalysis:

> We are forever telling stories about ourselves. In telling these stories *to others*,
> we may . . . be said to perform straightforward narrative actions. In saying that
> we also tell them *to ourselves*, however, we are enclosing one story within an-
> other. . . . On this view, the self is a telling. . . .
>   Additionally, we are forever telling stories about others . . . we narrate others
> just as we narrate ourselves. . . . Consequently, telling "others" about "ourselves"
> is doubly narrative.
>   Often the stories we tell about ourselves are life historical or autobiographical;
> we locate them in the past. For example, we might say, "Until I was fifteen, I
> was proud of my father" or "I had a totally miserable childhood." These histories
> are present tellings. The same may be said of the histories we attribute to others.
> We change many aspects of these histories of self and others as we change, for
> better or worse, the implied or stated questions to which they are the answers.
> Personal development may be characterized as change in the questions it is ur-
> gent or essential to answer. As a project in personal development, personal
> analysis changes the leading questions that one addresses to the tale of one's life
> and the lives of important others.[2]

Freud changed, indeed, our understanding of the leading questions underlying his patients' stories. The constitution of psychoanalysis, however, was motivated not just in the patients' need to

tell their stories, nor even merely in Freud's way of changing the essential questions that those narrative complaints addressed, but in Freud's unprecedented *transformation of narration into theory*. In transforming, thus, not just the *questions* of the story but the very *status* of the narrative, in investing the idiosyncrasies of narrative with the generalizing power of a theoretical validity, Freud had a way of telling stories—of telling stories about others and of telling others stories about himself—which made history.

> My dear Wilhelm,
>   My self-analysis is the most important thing I have in hand, and promises to be of the greatest value to me, when it is finished. . . . If the analysis goes on as I expect, I shall write it all out systematically and lay the results before you. So far I have found nothing completely new, but all the complication to which I am used. . . . Only one idea of general value has occurred to me. I have found love of the mother and jealousy of the father in my own case too, and now believe it to be a general phenomenon of early childhood. . . . If that is the case, the gripping power of *Oedipus Rex* . . . becomes intelligible. The Greek myth seizes on a compulsion which everyone recognizes because he has felt traces of it in himself. Every member of the audience was once a budding Oedipus in phantasy, and this dream-fulfilment played out in reality causes everyone to recoil in horror, with the full measure of repression which separates his infantile from his present state.[3]

"Only one idea of general value has occurred to me. I have found love of the mother and jealousy of the father in my own case too." From the *Letters to Fliess* to *The Interpretation of Dreams*, what Freud is instituting is a radically new way of writing one's autobiography, by transforming personal narration into a path-breaking theoretical discovery. In the constitution of the theory, however, the discovery that emerges out of the narration is itself referred back to a story which confirms it: the literary drama of the destiny of Oedipus, which, in becoming thus a *reference narrative*—the specimen story of psychoanalysis—, situates the validating moment at which the psychoanalytic story-telling turns and returns back upon itself, in the unprecedented, Freudian narrative-discursive space in which narration becomes theory.

> This discovery is confirmed by a legend which has come down to us from classical antiquity: a legend whose profound and universal power to move can only be understood if the hypothesis I have put forward in regard to the psychology of children has an equally universal validity. What I have in mind is the legend of King Oedipus and Sophocles' drama which bears his name. . . .
>   The action of the play consists in nothing other than the process of revealing, with cunning delays and ever-mounting excitement—a process that can be likened to the work of a psycho-analysis—that Oedipus himself is the murderer of Laius, but further that he is the son of the murdered man and of Jocasta. . . .
>   If *Oedipus Rex* moves a modern audience no less than it did the contemporary Greek one . . . there must be something which makes a voice within us ready to

recognize the compelling force of destiny in the Oedipus. . . . His destiny moves
us because it might have been ours—because the oracle laid the same curse
upon us before our birth as upon him. It is the fate of all of us, perhaps, to
direct our first sexual impulse towards our mother and our first hatred and our
first murderous wish against our father. Our dreams convince us that this is so.
King Oedipus, who slew his father Laius and married his mother Jocasta, merely
shows us the fulfilment of our childhood wishes. . . . While the poet . . . brings
to light the guilt of Oedipus, he is at the same time compelling us to recognize
our own inner minds, in which those same impulses, though suppressed, are still
to be found.[4]

Freud's reference to the Oedipus as a key-narrative—the specimen story of psychoanalysis—is structured by three questions
which support his analytical interrogation:

1) *The question of the effectiveness of the story* (Why is the story so
compelling, moving? How to account for the story's *practical
effect* on the audience—its power to elicit affect, its symbolic
efficacy?)

2) *The question of the recognition* (The story has power over us
because it "is compelling us to *recognize*" something in ourselves. What is it that the story is compelling us to recognize?
What is at stake in the recognition?)

3) *The question of the validity of the hypothesis, of the theory* ("a legend
whose profound and universal power to move can only be
understood if the *hypothesis* I have put forward in regard to
the psychology of children has an *equally universal validity*").

Any further inquiry into, or rethinking of, the significance of the
Oedipus in psychoanalytic theory and practice, would have to take
into account the implications of those three questions: the question
of the narrative's *practical efficacy* (and hence, its potential for a
clinical efficacy: its practical *effect* on us, having to do not necessarily with what the story *means,* but with what it *does* to us); the
question of the meaning of the *theoretical recognition* (what do we
recognize when we recognize the Oedipus?); and the question not
just of the mere validity of Freud's hypothesis, but of the very *status
of the theoretical validation through a narrative,* that is, the question of
the relationship between truth and fiction in psychoanalysis.

I would suggest, now, that Lacan's reading of Freud renews, indeed, each of these questions in some crucial ways; and that an
exploration of this renewal—an exploration of the way in which
the Oedipus mythic reference holds the key to a Lacanian psychoanalytic understanding—may hold the key, in turn, to the crux of
Lacan's innovative and enriching insight into what it is that Freud

discovered, and consequently, into what it is psychoanalysis is all about.

The Psychoanalytic Story: Oedipus the King

Nowhere is there in Lacan's writings any systematic exposition of Lacan's specific understanding of the significance of the Oedipus. As is often the case, Lacan's insight has to be derived, through a reading labor, from an elliptical and fragmentary text, from sporadic comments, from episodic highlights of (often critical and corrective) interpretations, and from the omnipresent literary usage of the reference to the Oedipus in Lacan's own rhetoric and style. My attempt at a creative systematizaton of what may be called Lacan's revision of the Oedipus would organize itself, in a structure of its own, as a relation between (the refraction of an insight through) three dimensions: 1) *the purely theoretical dimension:* how does Lacan understand (or modify the traditional understanding of) the basic psychoanalytic concept of "the Oedipus complex"? 2) *The practical and clinical dimension:* what is, in Lacan's eyes, the practical relevance of the Oedipus *to the clinical event,* to the practical dealings with a patient? 3) *The literary dimension:* How does Lacan understand the way in which the text of Sophocles *informs* psychoanalytic knowledge?[5]

While Freud reads Sophocles's text in view of the consolidation—the confirmation—of his theory, Lacan re-reads the Greek text, after Freud, with an eye to its specific pertinence not to theory but to psychoanalytic *practice.* Freud, already, had compared the drama of the Oedipus to the process of a practical psychoanalysis ("The action of the play consists in nothing other than the process of revealing . . . *a process that can be likened to the work of a psychoanalysis"*). But while this comparison between the literary work and the work of the analysand leads Freud to the confirmation of his *theory*—a theory of wish, of wish-fulfilment and of primordial Oedipal desires (incestuous and patricidal), Lacan's different analytic emphasis on the relevance of Oedipus to the clinician's *practice,* is not so much on wish as on the *role of speech*—of language—in the play.

What Freud discovered in, or through, the Oedipus—the *unconscious nature of desire*—implies, in Lacan's view, a *structural relation between language and desire:* a desire that articulates itself, substitutively, in a symbolic metomymic language which, thereby, is no longer recognizable by the subject.

> It is always at the juncture of speech, at the level of its apparition, its emergence, ... that the manifestation of desire is produced. Desire emerges at the moment of its incarnation into speech—it is coincident with the emergence of symbolism.
>
> (S-II, 273)

No wonder, then, that *Oedipus Rex*, dramatizing as it does *the primal scene* of *desire*, in effect takes place on *the other scene* of *language*. "The unconscious", says Lacan, "is the discourse of the other." *Oedipus Rex* could be viewed as nothing other than a spectacular dramatization, a calculated pedagogical demonstration, of this formula. For Oedipus' unconscious is quite literally embodied by the discourse of the Other—of the oracle.

> Oedipus' unconscious is nothing other than this fundamental discourse whereby, long since, for all time, Oedipus' history is out there—written, and we know it, but Oedipus is ignorant of it, even as he is played out by it since the beginning. This goes way back—remember how the Oracle frightens his parents, and how he is consequently exposed, rejected. Everything takes place in function of the Oracle and of the fact that Oedipus is truly other than what he realizes as his history—he is the son of Laius and Jocasta, and he starts out his life ignorant of this fact. The whole pulsation of the drama of his destiny, from the beginning to the end, hinges on the veiling of this discourse, which is his reality without his knowing it.
>
> (S-II, 245)[6]

> The unconscious is this subject unknown to the self, misapprehended, misrecognized, by the ego.
>
> (S-II, 59)

The Oedipal question is thus at the center of each practical psychoanalysis, not necessarily as a question addressing the analysand's desire for his parents, but as a question addressing the analysand's misapprehension, misrecognition [*méconnaissance*] of his own history.

> The subject's question in no way refers to the results of any specific weaning, abandonmnent, or vital lack of love or affection; it concerns the subject's history inasmuch as the subject misapprehends, *misrecognizes* it; this is what the subject's actual conduct is expressing in spite of himself, insofar as he obscurely seeks to *recognize* this history. His life is guided by a problematics which is not that of his life-experience, but that of his destiny, that is—what is the meaning, the significance of his history? What does his life-story mean?
>
> An utterance is the matrix of the misrecognized part of the subject, and this is the specific level of the analytic symptom—a level which is de-centered with respect to the individual experience, since it is, precisely, what the historical text must integrate.
>
> (S-II, 58)

Analysis is, indeed, nothing other than this process of historical integration of the spoken—but misrecognized—part of the sub-

ject. To do this, the subject must—like Oedipus—*recognize* what
he *misrecognizes*, namely, his desire, and his history, inasmuch as
they are, both, unconscious (that is, insofar as his *life-history* differs
from what he can know, or own, as his *life-story*).

> What we teach the subject to *recognize* as his unconscious is his history—that is
> to say, we help him to complete the present historization of the facts that have
> already determined a certain number of historical 'turning-points' in his exis-
> tence. But if they have played this role, they did so already as facts of history,
> that is to say, in so far as they have been *recognized* in a certain sense or censored
> in a certain order.
>
> (E 261, N 52, TM)

As in Freud's case, the reference of the clinical practice of psychoanalysis to the literary drama of the Oedipus hinges on the central
question of the *recognition* (as opposed to what the subject had,
beforehand, censored or misrecognized, misapprehended, or repressed). Recognition is, indeed, for Freud as for Lacan, the crucial
psychoanalytic stake both of the clinical and of the literary work.

The nature of the recognition is, however, somewhat differently
conceived, in Freud's discussion of the Oedipus as validating psychoanalytic *theory*, and in Lacan's discussion of the Oedipus as illuminating psycho-analytic *practice*. In Freud's analysis, Oedipus
recognizes his desire (incest, patricide) as (unwittingly) fulfilled,
whereas Sophocles's reader recognizes in himself the same desire,
as repressed. The recognition is thus constative, or *cognitive*. In
Lacan's different emphasis, however, the psychoanalytic recognition is radically tied up with language, with the subject's analytic
speech-act, and as such, its value is less cognitive than *performative*[7]:
it is, itself, essentially a speech-act, whose symbolic action *modifies*
the subject's history, rather than cerebrally observing or recording
it, at last correctly.

> To bring the subject to *recognize* and to *name* his desire, this is the nature of the
> efficacious action of analysis. But it is not a question of recognizing something
> that would have already been there—a given—ready to be captured. In naming
> it, the subject creates, gives rise to something new, makes something new present
> in the world.
>
> (S-II, 267)

> Analysis can have for its goal only *the advent* of an authentic speech and the
> realization by the subject of his history, *in relation to a future*.
>
> (E 302, N 88, TM)

The analytical speech-act by which the subject recognizes, and per-
formatively names, his desire and his history (insofar as the misapprehension of the one has in effect structured the other), has to
be completed, consummated, by an ultimate analytic act of speech

which Lacan calls "the *assumption* of one's history", that is, the ultimate acceptance—and endorsement—of one's destiny, the acknowledgment of responsibility for the discourse of the Other in
oneself, but also the forgiving of this discourse.

> It is certainly this *assumption* of his history by the subject, in so far as it is con-
> stituted by the speech addressed to the other, that constitutes the ground for
> the new method that Freud called Psycho-analysis.
>
> (E 257, N 48)

Oedipus the King, however, in Lacan's eyes, while recognizing,
naming his desire and his history, does not truly *assume* them; at
the end of *Oedipus Rex*, Oedipus accepts his destiny, but does not
accept (forgive) himself. This is why Lacan would like to take us,
as he puts it (in a formula that once again is resonant with many
meanings), *beyond Oedipus:* that is, first of all beyond *Oedipus the
King* and into Sophocles' tragic sequel, *Oedipus at Colonus.*

> If the tragedy of *Oedipus Rex* is an exemplary literary work, psychoanalysts
> should also know this *beyond* which is realized by the tragedy of *Oedipus at Colonus.*
>
> (S-II, 245)

II

Beyond Oedipus: Oedipus at Colonus

It is only in the tragic sequel that the true *assumption* of his destiny by Oedipus takes place:

> In *Oedipus at Colonus*, Oedipus says the following sentence: *"Is it now that I am
> nothing, that I am made to be a man?"* This is the end of Oedipus' psychoanalysis—
> Oedipus' psychoanalysis ends only at Colonus. . . . This is the essential moment
> which gives its whole meaning to his history.
>
> (S-II, 250)

What Lacan refers to is the following scene, which I will now quote
twice, in two different translations:

Oedipus
And did you think the gods would yet deliver me?

Ismene
The present oracles give me that hope.

Oedipus
What oracles are they? What prophecy?

Ismene
The people of Thebes shall desire you, for their safety,
After your death, and even while you live.

Oedipus
What good can such as I bring any man?

Ismene
They say it is in you that they must grow to greatness.

Oedipus
Am I made man in the hour when I cease to be?

(Walting's translation[8])

. . . .

Oedipus
You have some hope than that they [the gods] are concerned
With my deliverance?

Ismene
          I have, father.
The latest sentences of the oracle. . .

Oedipus
How are they worded? What do they prophesy?

Ismene
The oracles declare their strength's in you—

Oedipus
When I am finished, I suppose I am strong!

(Grene's translation[9])

"Is it now that I am nothing that I am made to be a man?" What
is it, then, which makes for Oedipus' humanity and strength at the
very moment at which he is "finished", at the moment when, reduced to nothing, he embodies his forthcoming death? What is it
that Oedipus, beyond the *recognition* of his destiny, here *assumes*,
and which exemplifies "the end of his analysis"? He *assumes the
Other*—in himself, he assumes his own *relation* to the discourse of
the Other, "this subject beyond the subject" (S-II, 245); he assumes,
in other words, his radical de-centerment from his own ego, from
his own self-image (Oedipus the King) and his own (self-) consciousness. And it is this radical acceptance, and assumption, of his
own *self-expropriation* that embodies, for Lacan, the ultimate
meaning of Oedipus' analysis, as well as the profound Oedipal
significance of analysis as such.

This significance is historically consummated by Oedipus at the
moment when he awaits—and indeed *assumes*—his death. But this
is not just a coincidence: the assumption of one's death is inherent
to the analytical assumption.

> You will have to read *Oedipus at Colonus*. You will see that the last word of man's
> relation to this discourse which he does not know is—death.
>
> (S-II, 245)

Why death? Here Lacan is at his most hermetic, at his most
elliptical. I believe, however, that this ellipsis embodies one of his

most complex, profound and important psychoanalytic insights, and I will try—at my own risk—to shed some light on it by continuing, now, the analysis of *Oedipus at Colonus* "beyond" what Lacan explicitly articulates, by using some Lacanian highlights borrowed from other texts (other contexts). Let me first make an explanatory detour.

The Oedipus complex, in its traditional conception, encompasses two fantasized ("imaginary") visions of death: the father's death (imaginary murder), and the subject's own death in return (imaginary castration). The Oedipus complex is resolved through the child's identification with his father, constituting his superego; in Lacan's terms, the resolution takes place through the introjection of the Father's Name[10] (embodying the Law of incest prohibition), which becomes constitutive of the child's unconscious. As the first, archetypal linguistic symbol ("name") which represses, and replaces, or displaces, the desire for the mother, the father's name (and consequently, in the chain of linguistic or symbolic substitution, any word or symbol used metaphorically or metonymically, that is, all symbols and all words), in effect incorporates the child's assumption of his own death as a condition—and a metaphor— for his *renunciation.* Since symbolization is coincident with the constitution of the unconscious (the displacement of desire), "the last word of man's relation to this discourse which he does not know"— his unconscious—"is [thus] death": to symbolize is to incorporate death in language, *in order to survive.*

> So when we wish to attain in the subject what was before the serial articulations of speech, and what is primordial to the birth of symbols, we find it in death, from which his existence takes on all the meaning it has.
>
> (E 320, N 105)
>
> Thus the symbol manifests itself first of all as the murder of the thing, and this death constitutes in the subject the eternization of his desire.
>   The first symbol in which we recognize humanity in its vestigial traces is the grave, and the intermediary of death can be recognized in every relation through which man is born into the life of his history.
>
> (E 319, N 104, TM)

What, now, happens in *Oedipus at Colonus* which is new with respect to the story (to the *recognition story*) of *Oedipus the King* (besides the subject's final death)?

Precisely the fact that Oedipus *is born,* through the assumption of his death (of his radical self-expropriation), *into the life of his history. Oedipus at Colonus* is about the transformation of Oedipus' story into history: it does not tell the drama, it is *about the telling* (and retelling) of the drama. It is, in other words, about the *his-torization* of Oedipus' destiny, through the *symbolization*—the trans-mutation into speech—of the Oedipal desire.

> *Oedipus*
> My star was unspeakable.
>
> *Chorus*
>   Speak!
>
> *Oedipus*
> My child, what can I say to them?
>
> *Chorus*
> Answer us, stranger; what is your race,
> Who was your father?
>
> *Oedipus*
> God help me, what will become of me, child?
>
> *Antigone*
> *Tell them; there is no other way.*
>
>   (Scene 1, 89)

. . . .

> *Oedipus*
>   Or do you dread
> My strength? My actions? I think not, for I
> Suffered those deeds more than I acted them,
> As I might show if it were fitting here
> *To tell my father's and my mother's story* . . .
> For which you fear me, as I know too well.
>
>   (Scene 2, 91)

. . . .

> *Chorus*
> What evil things have slept since long ago
> It is not sweet to awaken;
> *And yet I long to be told*—
>
> *Oedipus*
>   What?
>
> *Chorus*
> Of that heartbreak for which there was no help,
> The pain you have had to suffer.
>
> *Oedipus*
> For kindness' sake, do not open
> My old wound, and my shame.
>
> *Chorus*
> *It is told everywhere, and never dies;*
> *I only want to hear it truly told.*
>
>   (Scene 2, 102)

. . . .

Oedipus
There is, then, nothing left for me to tell
But my desire; and then the tale is ended.

(Scene 3, 105)

. . . .

Messenger
Citizens, the briefest way to tell you
Would be to say that Oedipus is no more;
But what has happened cannot be told so simply—
It was no simple thing.

(Scene 8, 147)

Embodying the linguistic drama—the analytical speech-act—of Oedipus' assumption of his radical expropriation, *Oedipus at Colonus* tells, thus, not simply the story of the telling of the story of the Oedipus, the drama of symbolization and historization of the Oedipal desire, but *beyond that* ("beyond Oedipus"), as the final verses indicate, the story of *the transmutation of Oedipus' death* (in all senses of the word, literal and metaphoric) *into the symbolic language of the myth.*

> The fact that Oedipus is the Patronymic hero of the Oedipus complex is not a coincidence. It would have been possible to choose another hero, since all the heroes of Greek mythology have some relation to this myth, which they embody in different forms. . . . It is not without reason that Freud was guided towards this particular myth.
>   Oedipus, in his very life, is entirely this myth. He himself is nothing other than the passage of this myth into existence.
>
> (S-II, 267–268)
>
> It is natural that everything would fall on Oedipus, since Oedipus embodies the central knot of speech.
>
> (S-II, 269)

Freud at Colonus

At the same time that *Oedipus at Colonus* dramatizes the "eternization" of the Oedipal desire through its narrative symbolization, that is, Oedipus' birth into his symbolic *life,* into his historical, mythic *survival,* the later play also embodies something of the order of an Oedipal *death-instinct,* since Oedipus, himself the victim of a curse and of a consequent parental rejection, pronounces, in his turn, a mortal curse against his sons. Oedipus' destiny is thus marked by a repetition-compulsion, illustrating and rejoining, in Lacan's eyes, Freud's tragic intuition in *Beyond the Pleasure Principle.* Like the later Freud, the later Sophocles narrates, as his ultimate human (psychoanalytic) insight, *the conjunction between life and death.*

Oedipus at Colonus, whose entire being resides in the speech formulated by his destiny, concretizes the conjunction between death and life. He lives a life which is made of death, that sort of death which is exactly there, beneath life's surface. This is also where we are guided by this text in which Freud is telling us, 'Don't believe that life . . . is made of any force . . . of progress, life . . . is characterized by nothing other than . . . its capacity for death'. . . .

Freud's theory may appear . . . to account for everything, including what relates to death, in the framework of a closed libidinal economy, regulated by the pleasure principle and by the return to equilibrium. . . .

The meaning of *Beyond the Pleasure Principle* is that this explanation is insufficient. . . . What Freud teaches us through the notion of primordial masochism is that the last word of life, when life has been dispossessed of speech, can only be this ultimate curse which finds expression at the end of *Oedipus at Colonus.* Life does not want to heal. . . . What is, moreover, the significance of the healing, of the cure, if not the realization, by the subject, of a speech which comes from elsewhere, and by which he is traversed?

(S-II, 271–272)

What Lacan endeavors here is obviously not a simple reading of the literary Oedipus in terms of Freud's theory, but rather, a re-reading of Freud's theory in terms of the literary Oedipus. Lacan's emphasis, as usual, is *corrective* with respect to a certain psychoanalytical tradition that tends to disregard Freud's speculations in *Beyond the Pleasure Principle* as "overpessimistic" and "unscientific," not truly belonging in his theory. For Lacan, however, *Beyond the Pleasure Principle* is absolutely crucial to any understanding of psychoanalysis, since it embodies *the ultimate riddle* which Freud's insight has confronted-and attempted to convey:

. . . Freud has bequeathed us his testament on the negative therapeutic reaction.

The key to *this mystery,* it is said, is in the agency of a primordial masochism, that is, in a pure manifestation of that death instinct whose *enigma* Freud propounded for us at the climax of his experience.

We cannot turn up our noses at this problem, any more than I can postpone an examination of it here.

For I note this same *refusal to accept this culminating point of Freud's doctrine* by those who conduct their analysis on the basis of a conception of the *Ego* [ego psychology], and by those who, like Reich, go so far in the principle of seeking the ineffable organic expression beyond speech that . . . [they expect from analysis something like an] orgasmic induction.

(E 316, N 101, TM)

In reading Freud across *Oedipus at Colonus,* Lacan is doing much more than to suggest an affinity of subjects between Freud's and Sophocles's later works (the constitutive, structural relation between life and death: primordial masochism, death-instinct, repetition compulsion). Lacan is *using the relation* between *Oedipus at Colonus* and *Oedipus the King* (the undeniable relation, that is, of the later literary work to the specimen narrative of psychoanalysis) in order to illuminate and to make a claim for the importance of

Beyond the Pleasure Principle. Oedipus at Colonus, says Lacan, is taking us *beyond Oedipus,* in much the same was as Freud is taking us *Beyond the pleasure principle.* By this multi-levelled, densely resonant comparison, Lacan is elliptically, strategically suggesting two things:

1) That *Beyond the Pleasure Principle* stands to *The Interpretation of Dreams* (the work in which Freud narrates, for the first time, his discovery of the significance of *Oedipus the King*) in precisely the same relation in which *Oedipus at Colonus* stands to *Oedipus the King;*

2) That the significance of the *rejection* of Freud's later text by a certain psychoanalytical establishment (embodying the *consciousness* of the psychoanalytic movement, that is, its own perception of itself, its own self-image), is itself part of an Oedipal story: the story, once again, of the *misrecognition*—misapprehension and mis-reading—of a history and of a discourse.

> The unconscious is that part of the concrete discourse . . . which is not at the disposal of the subject in re-establishing the continuity of his conscious discourse.
> (E 258, N 490)

> The unconscious is that chapter of my history which is marked by a blank . . . : it is the censored chapter.
> (E 259, N50)

The Oedipal significance of *psychoanalysis' misrecognition of its own discourse,* of its own history, can only be seen from Colonus. In confining itself, however, to *Oedipus the King* and to Freud's con-comitant discovery of wish-fulfilment (as theorized in the *Interpretation of Dreams*), the psychoanalytic movement, far from going— as did Freud—*beyond Oedipus,* is still living only the last scene of *Oedipus the King,* in repeating consciousness' last gesture of denial: the *self-blinding.*

Lacan, on the other hand, strives to make the psychoanalytic movement *recognize* what it misrecognizes, and thus reintegrate the repressed—the censored Freudian text—into psychoanalytic his-tory—and theory.

Why is Freud's *Beyond the Pleasure Principle* so important? Why is it not possible to *dispense with* this final phase of Freud's thought, in much the same way as it is impossible to dispense with *Oedipus at Colonus?* Because, let us not forget, "Oedipus' analysis *ends* only at Colonus. . . . This is the essential moment which gives its whole meaning to his history" (S-II, 250). In what sense can *Beyond the Pleasure Principle* be said to give its whole *meaning* to psychoanalytic *history?* In the sense that what is *beyond* the wish for pleasure—the *compulsion to repeat*—radically displaces the conception both of history and of meaning, both of what and how history means and of how meaning comes to be, and is historicized. This radical displacement of the understanding both of meaning and of temporality (or history), far from being episodic, marginal, dispensable, is essential both to psychoanalytic theory (what has happened in the subject's past) and to psychoanalytic practice (what is happening in the subject's present: the concrete unfolding of unconscious history in the repetition of the transference [E 318, N 102]). Since the compulsion to repeat is, in Lacan's view, the compulsion to repeat *a signifier, Beyond the Pleasure Principle* holds the key not just to history or to transference but, specifically, to the *textual functioning* of signification, that is, to the insistence of the signifier in a signifying chain (that of a text, or of a life).

What is, then, psychoanalysis if not, precisely, a *life-usage of the death-instinct*—a practical, productive usage of the compulsion to repeat, through a *replaying* of the symbolic meaning of the *death* the subject has repeatedly experienced, and through a recognition and *assumption* of the meaning of this death (separation, loss) by the subject, as a symbolic means of his coming to terms not with death but, precisely, with his *life?*

> The game is already played, the dice are already thrown, with this one exception, that we can take them once more in our hand, and throw them once again.
> (S-II, 256)

This is what a practical psychoanalysis is all about; and this is what Freud tells us in his later speculative narrative, which seeks its way beyond the pleasure principle, beyond his earlier discovery of wish-fulfilment, beyond his earlier wish-fulfilling way of dreaming Sophocles.

"The Oedipus complex", says Lacan in one of those suggestive, richly understated statements (pronounced in an unpublished Seminar), "the Oedipus complex is—a dream of Freud." This apparently transparent sentence is, in effect, a complex re-statement of the way psychoanalysis is *staked* in the discovery that *The Interpretation of Dreams* narrates: a complex re-statement both of Freud's *discovery of the theory* of wish-fulfilment as the meaning—and the motivating force—of dreams, and of Freud's *discovery of the narrative* of Oedipus as validating the discovery of the theory. It was, in effect, through his self-analysis, out of his own dream about his father that revealed to Freud his own Oedipal complexity, that

Freud retreived the founding, psychoanalytic meaning of the literary Oedipus. "The Oedipus complex is a dream of Freud."

Now, a dream (to any psychoanalyst, at least) is not the opposite of truth; but neither is it truth that can be taken literally, at face value. A dream is what demands interpretation. And interpretation is what goes *beyond* the dream, even if interpretation is itself nothing other than another dream, that is, not a theory, but still another (free-associated) narrative, another *metaphorical* account of the discourse of the Other.

In this respect, it is noteworthy that *Beyond the Pleasure Principle* was at first conceived by Freud as, precisely, *a rethinking of his theory of dreams*. This is born out by a paper Freud gave at the International Psychoanalytic Congress at The Hague (1920) under the title, "Supplements to the Theory of Dreams," and in which he announces his forthcoming publication. Here is how the paper's goal is summed up in the "author's abstract":

> The speaker dealt with three points touching upon the theory of dreams. The first two . . . were concerned with *the thesis that dreams are wish-fulfilments* and *brought forward some necessary modifications of it.* . . .
> The speaker explained that, alongside the familiar wishful dreams and the anxiety dreams which could easily be included in the theory, there were grounds for recognizing the existence of a third category, to which he gave the name of "punishment dreams". . . .
> Another class of dreams, however, seemed to the speaker to present a more serious exception to the rule that dreams are wish-fulfilments. These were the so-called "traumatic" dreams. They occur in patients suffering from accidents, but they also occur during psychoanalyses of neurotics and bring back to them forgotten traumas of childhood. *In connection with the problem of fitting these dreams into the theory of wish-fulfilment, the speaker referred to a work shortly to be published under the title, "Beyond the Pleasure Principle."*
>
> (Standard, XVIII, 4)

Beyond the Pleasure Principle is thus itself a sort of (differential) *repetition* of *The Interpretation of Dreams,* in much the same way as *Oedipus at Colonus* is a (differential) repetition of *Oedipus the King*.

Indeed, like *Oedipus the King, The Interpretation of Dreams* is the story of a riddle—and of its solution. Oedipus solves, first, the riddle of the Sphinx (by the answer "man"), and then the riddle of who is responsible for Laius' murder (by the answer "I, Oedipus"). Freud solves the riddle of the meaning of the dream (by the answer: "wish-fulfilment"). While Oedipus goes from the general, theoretical solution ("man") to the singular, narrative solution ("me"), Freud goes from the narrative solution (self-analysis, me, Oedipus) to the theoretical solution (Man, wish-fulfilment).

The later text, however, in both Freud and Sophocles, is not a simple "supplement" or sequel to the early work, but its *problema-*

tization. Both later works address *the riddle generated by, precisely, the solution,* the question constituted by the very answer. Both later works embody the enigma of an excess, a subversive residue, to (from within) the earlier solution: the enigma of the traumatic dream,[11] in *Beyond the Pleasure Principle,* insofar as this compulsion to repeat manifested as death-instinct is not reducible to (goes *beyond*) wish-fulfilment; the enigma, in *Oedipus at Colonus,* of Oedipus' assumption of (the gift inherent in) his own death, of (the blessing incarnated in) his own radical *self-expropriation,* insofar as this enigma is not reducible to (goes *beyond*) Oedipus the King's ultimate *self-recognition,* amounting to the self-denial and the *self-appropriation* inherent, paradoxically enough, in the final gesture of self-blinding.

In both Freud and Sophocles, the final text narrates, thus, *the return of a riddle.* In much the same way as the author of *Beyond the Pleasure Principle* talks about (to borrow Lacan's terms)—

> this *mystery* . . . that death instinct whose *enigma* Freud propunded at the climax of his experience—
>
> (E 316, N 101, TM)

Oedipus at Colonus (very unlike Oedipus the King) talks about (to borrow Sophocles's terms)—

> These things [which] are mysteries, not to be explained.
>
> (Scene 7, 145)

And Oedipus, like Freud, is conveying this residual enigma *from the position of a teacher:* "Indeed, you know already all that I teach" (*Ibid.,* 146), says Oedipus to Theseus.

This final teaching is, however, dramatized in *Oedipus at Colonus* as a *blessing* Oedipus imparts by the mystery in which his death is destined to be wrapped. Now, a blessing is, not the gift of a solution (in the manner of Oedipus the King), but nonetheless a gift—of speech. At Colonus, Oedipus ends up presenting, then, not a solution but the very paradoxical *gift of an enigma:* the gift (of speech, the blessing) of the enigma of his own death. And in Sophocles's words, in which Oedipus announces, at Colonus, both the gift of his own death and (the gift of) the return of a riddle, we may assume Lacan is hearing Freud's own words beyond his pleasure principle, in that work in which Freud, in his turn, talks about death as a riddle:

> *Oedipus*
> I come to give you something, and the gift
> Is my own beaten self; no feast for the eyes;
> Yet in me is a more lasting grace than beauty.

Theseus
What grace is this you say you bring to us?

Oedipus
In time you'll learn, but not immediately.

Theseus
How long, then, must we wait to be enlightened?

Oedipus
Until I am dead, and you have buried me.

(Scene 3, 105-106)

The psychoanalytical establishment may have come to the conclusion that they no longer have "to wait to be enlightened," since
they may believe they have, indeed, in burying *Beyond the Pleasure
Principle, buried* Freud. If Freud, however, is like Oedipus, Oedipus
is, paradoxically enough, *not* buried—*not yet buried*—since the mystery (the riddle) of his mythic disparition is precisely such that
Oedipus does die (or disappears), but *without leaving a corpse.*

And it is Lacan who tells us, in the words of Sophocles' messenger, this essential thing, that *Freud is not yet buried:*

Messenger
Citizens, the briefest way to tell you
Would be to say that Oedipus is no more;
But *what has happened cannot be told so simply—*
It was no simple thing.

(Scene 8, 147)

While Freud, as Dream Interpreter, may have, indeed, said in the
very words of Oedipus,

There is, then, nothing left for me to tell
But my desire; *and then the tale is ended.*

(Scene 3, 105)

—and while psychoanalysts may take Freud at his word, believe,
in other words, that in the meaning of the wish-fulfilment, in the
meaning of Freud's story of desire, *the tale is ended—*, Lacan is there
to tell us that not only is the tale (Freud's, Oedipus') *not* ended,
but that Freud is bequeathing us *Beyond the Pleasure Principle* so as
to tell us nothing other than this ultimate discovery, this ultimate
enigma: that the tale has, in effect, *no end.*

Lacan at Colonus

Thus, it is psychoanalysis itself, and not its object, which is now
staked in the literary narrative, in the story of the Oedipus. From
the perspective of Colonus, Lacan is telling us, re-telling us, *the*

very story of psychoanalysis as *"what cannot be told so simply:* it was no simple thing." And the story of psychoanalysis is not just the "not simple" story Freud tells (and re-tells), but the very story of Freud's telling and re-telling, the narrative, in other words, of *Freud himself as narrator.* And Freud as narrator is also far from being—says Lacan—a *simple* narrator.

Indeed, this non-simplicity of the narration—of Freud's narration of his theory—is crucial to an understanding of the theory itself. If *Beyond the Pleasure Principle* is, like the Oedipus, not a simple story, it is to the extent that it is, first and foremost, a *strategic* story. And what we have to understand, what Lacan is urging us to *recognize* in Freud's account, is the thrust, precisely, of Freud's strategy as narrator: not just what the story teller *means to say,* but (once again) what the story teller in effect *is doing* with, and through, his story.

> In the final analysis, . . . we can talk adequately about the libido only in a *mythic* manner. . . . This is what is at stake in Freud's text. . . .
>
> At what point, at what moment, does Freud talk to us about a *beyond* of the pleasure principle? At a point where the psychoanalysts, engaged in the path that Freud has taught them, *believe they know.* Freud has told them that desire is sexual desire, and *they believe him.*
>
> (S-II, 265)
>
> The Freudian experience starts out with a notion which is exactly contrary to the theoretical perspective. It starts out by positing a universe of desire. . . .
>
> In the classical, theoretical perspective, there is between subject and object a co-fitting, a co-gnizance [: knowledge, that is, possible adaptation, possible adequation]. . . .
>
> It is in an altogether different register of relations that the Freudian experience is inscribed. Desire is a relation of a being to a lack. . . . The libido is the name of what animates the fundamental conflict at the heart of human action. . . . Insofar as the libido creates the different stages of the object [oral, anal, etc.], no object would ever again be *it* [:of no object can desire ever say: *that's it.*]. . . .
>
> Desire, a function central to the whole of human experience, is the desire of nothing nameable.
>
> (S-II, 260-262)
>
> When Freud maintains that sexual desire is at the heart of human desire, all his followers believe him, believe him so strongly that they persuade themselves that it's all so very *simple,* and that all there remains to do with it is science, the science of sexual desire. It would suffice to remove the obstacles, and it should work all by itself. It would suffice to tell the patient—you don't realize it, but the object is there. This is how, at first, the stake of interpretation is understood.
>
> But the fact is, it doesn't work. At this point—the turning point—it is said that the subject resists. Why? Because Freud has said so. But one has not understood what it means to *resist* any more than one has understood the meaning of *sexual desire.* One believes one has to push. At this point, the analyst himself succumbs to a delusion. I have shown you what the *insistance* means on the part of the suffering subject. Now, the analyst is putting himself at the same level,

he too *insists* in his own way, a way which is however much more stupid, because conscious. . . .

Resistance is . . . the current state of interpretation of the subject. It is the manner in which, at this moment, the subject interprets the point where he's at. This resistance is an abstract, ideal point. It's you who call that resistance. It only means that the subject cannot advance more quickly. . . .

There is only one resistance, the resistance of the analyst. The analyst resists when he does not understand what is happening in the treatment. He does not understand what is happening in the treatment when he believes that interpreting is showing to the subject that what he desires is such and such sexual object. He is mistaken. . . . It's he who is in a state of inertia and of resistance.

The psychoanalytic goal is, on the contrary, to teach the subject to name, to articulate, to pass into existence this desire which is, literally, beneath existence, and for that very reason, insists. . . .

To bring the subject to recognize and to name his desire, this is the nature of the efficacious action of analysis. But it is not a question of recognizing something that would have already been there—a given. . . .

Since, in a sort of balancing, we always place ourselves between the text of Freud and our practical experience, I urge you to return now to Freud's text, so as to realize that the *Beyond* [of the pleasure principle] situates desire, in effect, beyond any instinctual cycle, specifically definable by its conditions.

(S-II, 266-267)

"In the final analysis, we can talk adequately about the libido only in a mythic manner: this is what is at stake in Freud's text". In *Beyond the Pleasure Principle*, Freud creates a new myth—that of the "death-instinct"—so as to *demystify* the literal belief in, and the simplified interpretation of, his first myth of the Oedipus. Freud is thus, essentially, a demystifying narrator. But the narrative strategy of *demystification* takes place only through a new narrative *mythification*. In urging us to go *beyond* the myth, Freud also tells us that beyond the myth there is, forever, but another myth. And it is in this sense, among others, that "the tale" (Freud's, Oedipus', Lacan's) is never "ended."

But who is speaking here? *Whose irony* is it that here traverses the narration of the psychoanalytic story, and which *unends* the (Oedipal, or Freudian, or Lacanian) tale? Lacan's voice fuses here with Freud's in what Lacan would doubtless call, a [narrative] "in-mixture of the subjects"[12]: the story of Freud's strategy as psychoanalytic narrator is, simultaneously, the story of Lacan as psychoanalytic educator. So that if we ask, "whose story is it (Freud's? Lacan's? or Oedipus'?)?"—the answer is not clear. And if we ask, "whose narrative voice is carrying through this narrative performance (Freud's? Lacan's? or Sophocles'?)?"—the answer is clear. But if we ask, what is this narrative performance *doing*?—the answer is quite clear. If we ask, that is, in a Lacanian manner, the question, not of who is the true *owner* of the story (to whom does it belong?), nor of whom Lacan is *quoting* in the story, nor of what Lacan *means* by the story, but of what Lacan *is doing* with this story, the answer would be unambiguous: Lacan is *training analysts*. Lacan as narrator of Freud as narrator, Lacan as narrator of Sophocles as narrator, Lacan in everything he says of does, and in the very way he breathes (breathes texts and breathes psychoanalytic practice), is always, above all, a *training analyst*.

And this is why, no doubt, he picks Colonus as the truly psychoanalytic place: for if Colonus—and Colonus only—marks "the end of Oedipus' psychoanalysis," it is to the extent that Oedipus' tale of desire ends only through its own dramatic, narrative discovery that the tale has, in effect, no end: "the end of Oedipus' analysis," in other words, is the discovery that analysis, and in particular didactic self-analysis, is in effect *interminable*. In dramatizing Oedipus' assumption of his own death, of his own expropriating discourse of the Other, and his analytic passage *beyond* his ego, Colonus, as "the end of Oedipus' psychoanalysis," marks the moment at which the analysand becomes an analyst, ready to bestow, indeed, (precisely that by which Lacan has characterized the analyst's spoken intervention:) a *gift of speech*. Colonus echoes, thus, Lacan's preoccupation as a training analyst.

But if Colonus resonates so forcefully in Lacan's heart, strikes such a forceful chord in Lacan's insight, it is because Lacan, perhaps unconsciously, identifies with Oedipus at Colonus. While Freud identifies quite naturally with Oedipus the King or the conquistador, *the riddle-solver* (who is, incidentally, a father-killer and a mother-lover: *King to his own mother*), even as he knows that this stupendous riddle-solving in effect will bring about "the Plaque"[13], Lacan identifies quite naturally with Oedipus *the exile* (a survivor of the Plaque), since Lacan has been, precisely *as a training analyst,* expropriated, *excommunicated* from the International Psychoanalytical Association.

I am here, in the posture which is mine, in order to address always the same question—*what does psychoanalysis mean?* . . .

The place from which I am re-addressing this problem is in effect a place which has changed, which is no longer altogether inside, and of which one does not know whether it is outside.

This reminder is not anecdotic: . . . I hand you this, which is a fact—that my teaching, designated as such, has been the object of a quite extraordinary *censorship* declared by an organism which is called the *Executive Committee* of an international organization which is called *The International Psychoanalytical Association*. What is at stake is nothing less than the prohibition of my teaching, which must be considered as *null and void* insofar as it concerns the habilitation of psychoanalysts; and this proscription has been made the condition for the affiliation of the psychoanalytic society of which I am a member with the International Psychoanalytic Association. . . .

What is at stake is, therefore, something of the order of what is called . . . a *major excommunication*. . . .

I believe . . . that, not only by the echoes it evokes, but by the very structure it implies, this fact introduces something which is at the very principle of our interrogation concerning psychoanalytic practice.

(S-XI, 9)

Colonus thus embodies, among other things, not just Lacan's own exile, Lacan's own story of ex-propriation from the International Psychoanalytical Association, but Lacan's dramatic, tragic understanding that psychoanalysis is radically *about expropriation*, and his *assumption* of his story, his assumption, that is, all at once of his own *death* and of his own *myth*—of the *legacy* of this expropriation—as his truly destined psychoanalytic legacy and as his truly training psychoanalytic question: "Is it now that I am nothing, that I am made to be a man?"

"It was ordained: I recognize it now", says Oedipus at Colonus (Scene 1,81). It may be but my own dream, but I can hear, indeed, Lacan's voice in the very words of Oedipus the exile:

> *Oedipus*
> That stranger is I. As they say of the blind,
> Sounds are the things I see.
>
> (Scene 1, 85)

. . . .

> *Ismene*
> The oracles declare their strength's in you—
>
> *Oedipus*
> When I am finished, I suppose I am strong!
>
> (Scene 2, 96)

. . . .

> *Oedipus*
> I come to give you something, and the gift
> Is my own beaten self: no feast for the eyes;
> Yet in me is a more lasting grace than beauty.
>
> *Theseus*
> What grace is this you say you bring to us?
>
> *Oedipus*
> In time you'll learn, but not immediately.
>
> *Theseus*
> How long, then, must we wait to be enlightened?
>
> *Oedipus*
> Until I am dead, and you have buried me.
>
> (Scene 3, 106)

Psychoanalysis at Colonus

At the same time, then, that Lacan is talking about *Oedipus at Colonus,* he is telling and retelling, not just Freud's, and his own, psychoanalytic story, but the very story of psychoanalysis, *seen from Colonus:* the story of Freud's going beyond Freud, of Oedipus' going beyond Oedipus, the story of psychoanalysis' inherent, radical, and destined self-expropriation. Lacan thus recapitulates at once the meaning of the story in which Freud is taking us beyond his own solution to the riddle, and the narrative voice—or the narrative movement—by which Freud *expropriates,* in fact, not just his own solution, but *his own narrative.*

In subscribing to Freud's psychoanalytic *self-recognition* in the Oedipus, as the moment of psychoanalysis' self-appropriation, its coming into the possession of its ("scientific") knowledge, and in censoring *Beyond the Pleasure Principle* as "non-scientific," the psychoanalytical establishment has, precisely, tried to censor, to repress this final Freudian self-expropriation, and this ominous narrative annunciation, by the "father of the psychoanalytic movement," of an inherent *exile of psychoanalysis:* an exile from the presence-to-itself of psychoanalytic truth; an exile from a *non-mythical access* to truth; an exile, that is, from any final rest in a knowledge guaranteed by the self-possessed kingdom of a theory, and the constrained departure from this kingdom into an uncertain psychoanalytic *destiny of erring.*

Counter this rejection of Freud's text, counter this repression, not just of Freud's insight, but of the very revolution involved in Freud's narration (in the unprecedented, self-trespassing, self-expropriating status of his narrative), Lacan has raised his training, psychoanalytic voice; but this protestation is, then, censored in its turn. Whatever the polemical pretexts, or the political reasons, given by the Censors, it is clear that the profound (and perhaps unconscious) thrust of the repressive gesture is the same: to eradicate from psychoanalysis the threat of its own self-expropriation (to repeat the Oedipal gesture of self-blinding); to censor, thus, in Freud as well as in Lacan, the radically self-critical, and *self-transgressive,* movement of the psychoanalytic discourse; to pretend, or truly to believe, that this self-transgression and this self-expropriation, far from being *the* essential, revolutionary feature of the psychoanalytic discourse, is (nothing other than) a historic accident, one particular historic chapter, to be (easily) erased, eliminated.

However, the repeated psychoanalytic censorships illustrate only
the effectiveness (the working truth) of Freud's *Beyond the Pleasure
Principle* (or of Sophocles'/Lacan's *Oedipus at Colonus*): in dramatizing the compulsion to repeat in the very midst of the psychoanalytic institution, they bear witness to the very Freudian story,
illustrate the very Freudian myth of (something like) a *death-instinct*
of psychoanalysis itself: the (Oedipal) repetition of a curse in a
discourse that is destined to bestow speech as a blessing.

Through his call for "a return to Freud"—a *return to Colonus*—
Lacan himself embodies, in the history of the psychoanalytic movement, a return of the repressed. This is why, like Oedipus at Colonus, he too announces (and his entire style is but a symptom of
this announcement) the return of a riddle.

> *Theseus*
> What grace is this you say you bring to us?
>
> *Oedipus*
> In time you'll learn, but not immediately.
>
> *Theseus*
> How long, then, must we wait to be enlightened?
>
> *Oedipus*
> Until I am dead, and you have buried me.

Lacan's narrative is, however, at the same time a dramatic repetition, a reminder, of the radical *impossibility of ever burying* the
(speech of the) unconscious. The riddle, thus, persists. And so does
Lacan's story, whose subject, in all senses of the word, is, precisely,
the insistence of the riddle.

What, however, is a riddle, if not a narrative delay ("In time
you'll learn"), the narrative analytical *negociation* of some truth or
insight, and their metaphorical approximation *through a myth?* The
rejection of *Beyond the Pleasure Principle* under the pretext that, as
myth, it is "unscientific" ("just a myth"), involves, in Lacan's view,
a radical misunderstanding both of what a myth is all about and
of the status of the myth, as such, in Freud's narration and in
psychoanalytic theory. (But then again, the *misrecognition of a myth*
is what psychoanalysis—and Oedipus—are all about.)

> In the final analysis . . . we can talk adequately about the libido only in a *mythic*
> manner. . . . This is what is at stake in Freud's text.
>
> (S-II, 265)

In trying to decipher the significance of Freud's work, Lacan
insists not just on the significance of Freud's myths, but, even more

importantly, on the (too often overlooked) significance of Freud's
acknowledgement of his own myths:

> At this point I must note that in order to handle any Freudian concept, reading
> Freud cannot be considered superfluous, even for those concepts that are hom-
> onyms of current notions. This has been well demonstrated, I am opportunely
> reminded, by the misadventure that befell Freud's theory of the instincts, in a
> revision of Freud's position by an author less than alert to Freud's explicit state-
> ment of the mythical status of this theory.
>
> (E 246, N 39, TM)

Freud's own terms of acknowledgement of his own myth are, indeed, enlightening:

> The theory of the instincts is so to say our mythology. Instincts are mythical
> entities, magnificent in their indefiniteness. *In our work, we cannot* for a moment
> *disregard them, yet we are never sure* that we are seeing them clearly.
>
> (Standard, XXII, 95)

Myth, in Freud, is not a supplement to, or an accident of, theory:
it is not *external* to the theory; it is the very vehicle of theory, a
vehicle of *mediation between practice and theorization.* This complex
acknowledgement by Freud of the mythic status of his discourse is
reflected, echoed, meditated in Lacan's response:

> I would like to give you a more precise idea of the manner in which I plan to
> conduct this seminar.
>
> You have seen, in my last lectures, the beginning of *a reading of what one might
> call the psychoanalytic myth.* This reading goes in the direction, not so much of
> criticizing this myth, as of *measuring the scope of the reality* with which it comes to
> grips, and to which it gives its *mythical reply.*
>
> (S-I, 24)

The analytical experience, says Lacan, has been involved, since its
very origins, not simply with fiction, but with the "truthful" structural necessity of fiction, that is, with its symbolical non-arbitrari-
ness (E 12, 17). Like the analytical experience, the psychoanalytic
myth is constituted by *"that very truthful fictitious structure"* (E 449).
Insofar as it is mediated by a myth, the Freudian theory is not a
literal translation or reflection of reality, but its *symptom,* its *metaphorical* account. The myth is not pure fantasy, however, but a
narrative symbolic *logic* that accounts for a very real *mode of functioning,* a very real *structure of relations.* The myth is not reality; but
neither is it what it is commonly (mis-)understood to be—a simple
opposite of reality. Between reality and the psychoanalytic myth,
the relation is not one of opposition, but one of (analytic) *dialogue:*
the myth comes to grips with something in reality that it does not
fully apprehend, comprehend, or master, but to which it gives an

answer, a *symbolical reply*. The function of the myth in psychoanalytic theory is thus evocative of the function of interpretation in
the psychoanalytic dialogue: the Freudian mythical account can be
thought of as Freud's theoretical *gift of speech*.

What does that mean? In much the same way as the gift of
speech of analytical interpretation, within the situation of the dialogue, acts not by virtue of its accuracy but by virtue of its *resonance*
(whose impact is received in terms of the listener's structure),
works, that is, by virtue of its openness to a linguistic passage
through the Other, so does the psychoanalytic myth, *in resonating
in the Other*, produce a *truthful structure*. The psychoanalytic myth,
in other words, derives its *theoretical effectiveness* not from its truth-
value, but from its truth-encounter with the other, from its capacity
for *passing through the Other;* from its openness, that is, to an *expropriating passage* of one insight through another, of one story
through another: the passage, for example, of *Oedipus the King*
through *Oedipus at Colonus;* or the passage of the myth of "Instinct"
through this later and more troubling myth of "Death":

> As a moment's reflection shows, the notion of the *death instinct* involves a *basic
> irony,* since its meaning has to be sought in the conjunction of two contrary terms:
> instinct in its most comprehensive acceptation being the law that governs in its
> succession a cycle of behaviour whose goal is the accomplishment of a vital func-
> tion; and death appearing first of all as the destruction of life. . . .
> This notion must be approached through its *resonances* in what I shall call *the
> poetics of the Freudian corpus, the first way of access to the penetration of its meaning,*
> and the essential dimension, from the origins of the work to the apogee marked
> in it by this notion, for an understanding of its dialectical repercussions.
>   (E316-317, N 101-102)

> The psychoanalytic experience has discovered in man the imperative of the
> Word as the law that has formed him in its image. It manipulates the poetic
> function of language to give to his desire its symbolic mediation. May that ex-
> perience enable you to understand at last that *it is in the gift of speech that all the
> reality of its effects resides;* for it is by way of this gift that all reality has come to
> man and it is by his continued act that he maintains it.
> If the domain defined by this gift of speech [says Lacan to an audience of
> psychoanalysts] is to be sufficient for your action as also for your knowledge, it
> will also be sufficient for your devotion.
>   (E 322, N 106)

Lacan's involvement with the Freudian myth (viewed as *the literary gift of speech* accomplished by Freud's discourse, through the
dimension of narration and of narrative in psychoanalytic theory)
is, thus, radically involved with the *difference* Freud is introducing
into the conception and the practice of narration, a psychoanalytic
difference that Lacan himself is replicating, in his own way, in his
own theoretical and mythical gift of speech. Lacan's own involve-

ment with the psychoanalytic difference in narration has three aspects: 1) Lacan's narration (both the story that he tells and his narrative voice, or style) is very *different from the usual psychoanalytical narration* of Freud's accomplishment and theory; 2) Lacan's narration is *about* [not identity, ego psychology, but the psychoanalytic myth as the story of the introduction of a] *Difference;* 3) The psychoanalytical narration, in Lacan's conception (modeled as it is on analytic dialogue), is always, necessarily, *different from itself.* In the very way it is narrated, the psychoanalytic theory inscribes (is constituted by) a radical *self-difference.* And this self-difference, this *Spaltung* in (within) the theory, this unavoidable *breach of theory,* is embodied by the myth, *is* the myth. The myth is thus at once the Other of the theory and that which *gives* the theory to itself, that which, from within the literary gift of speech, founds the theory. And while there is no possible cognition of the myth—*no constative exhaustion of the myth by theory*—, there should be a *performative acknowledgement* ("recognition" and "assumption") *by the theory of its relation to the myth,* and of the irreducibility of the myth, as something in the theory which, paradoxically enough, both expropriates it from its truth, and at the same time founds it as "a fictitious truthful structure." The myth is structurally truthful, and psychoanalytically effective, valid, not just in function of, but in proportion to, its capacity for narrative expropriation.

And this is why, precisely, Freud has privileged the Oedipus above all other myths. In dramatizing language as the scene (the acting out) of the unconscious (in both its clinical and its literary implications), the Oedipus is achetypal of the psychoanalytic myth in that it is the story of the narrative expropriation of the story by itself, the story of, precisely, the *acknowledgement* of the misrecognition of the story by itself. Misleadingly, the Oedipus appears, at first, to be the myth of a possession (of a kingdom, of a woman, of the solution to a riddle, of one's own story). But as it turns out, the Oedipus is not the myth of the possession of a story, but the myth, precisely, of the dispossession by the story—the dispossession of the possessor of the story. Any *kingdom* or *possession* coming out of the psychoanalytic riddle-solving is, in fact, *incestuous,* and, as such, is bound to bring about a Plague. Psychoanalysis can only be a gift of speech from the exile of Colonus.

As a narrative of *this* discovery, as a narrative, that is, not just of *a* discovery but of the *discovery of difference,* the story of the Oedipus exemplifies the psychoanalytic myth in that it exemplifies the problematic status of psychoanalysis telling its own story of discovery and, while telling, acting out its own unconscious, that is, *doing* something through the telling that the telling fails to account for, and thus discovering and re-discovering the *difference* between what it's telling and what it's doing in the telling, as the scene of its own dismantling by the literary myth and of its own theoretical self-subversion. The Oedipus is privileged, thus, as a myth, not just because it is about the creation of the myth ("Oedipus himself is nothing other than the passage of this myth into existence"), but because it is, specifically, about the *subversively performative aspect* of this mythical creation. The story of the Oedipus is archetypal of the psychoanalytic myth in that it dramatizes speech not as cognitive but as (self-subversively) performative, in that it embodies this performative self-difference of (within) its own narration, this practical discrepancy, forever re-emerging, between its narrative or mythic *statement* and its narrative or mythical *performance*.

> How, indeed, could speech exhaust the meaning of speech, . . . except in the act that engenders it? Thus Goethe's reversal of its presence at the origins of things, "In the beginning was the act," finds itself reversed in its turn: it was certainly the *speech-act* that was in the beginning, and we live in its creation, but it is the action of our mind that continues this creation by constantly renewing it. And *we can only turn back on that action by allowing ourselves to continue to be driven by it even further.*
>
> I know only too well that this will be my own case, too, in trying now to turn back upon the act of speech.
>
> (E 271, N 61, TM)

Beyond Colonus: Truth and Science, or What Remains to be Narrated

If Freud's psychoanalysis is, then, a symbolical *reply* to a *reality* it tries to come to grips with; and if this symbolical reply is made of myth—of *radical myth* which, in Lacan's conception, is absolutely irreducible from psychoanalytic theory—, it is to the extent that, in its function as a gift of speech, the psychoanalytic myth embodies, and derives from, *a residue of action in the very process of cognition* of that action. In another sense, this is equally what Freud has talked about, in his reference to his theory of the instincts as "his mythology":

> Instincts are mythical entities, magnificent in their indefiniteness. *In our work we cannot* for a moment *disregard them,* but *we are never sure that we are seeing them clearly.*
>
> (XXII, 95)

Myth is something which we cannot be sure we are seeing clearly, but with which we *work*, because *it works*. Myth is thus a mediation between action and cognition, between theory and practice, a narrative negotiation of difference and self-difference in the very *practice* of a discourse which purports to be cognitive and theoretical. As we have seen in the Oedipus, myth is, first and foremost, practically *efficacious, both clinically and literarily.* And it is, perhaps, because it thus combines the performative power of the clinical event and the performative power of the literary resonance, *the unique performative encounter, that is, of the literary and the clinical dimensions,* that the Oedipus has worked so well as the specimen story of psychoanalysis: a specimen story which, however, in the very act of grounding psychoanalytic theory, also points to the irreducible, *expropriating residue* of action in cognition, of fiction (narrative) in truth, of practice (dialogue) in theory.

Action, fiction, practice, are thus bound together in the (Oedipal) irreducibility of myth from the science of psychoanalysis. For the acknowledgement of the radicality—the irreducibility—of the mythic element in psychoanalytic theory is by no means an abdication, in Lacan's case as in Freud's, of the *commitment to psychoanalysis as science.* "It may perhaps seem to you," writes Freud, "as though our theories are a kind of mythology and, in the present case, not even an agreeable one":

> *But does not every science come in the end to a kind of mythology like this?* Cannot the same be said of today's physics?
>
> (XXII, 211)

In following Freud's mythical *and* scientific path, Lacan's interrogation, as opposed to Freud's, concerns, here again, not the theory but the practice. Can the *practice* of psychoanalysis have a scientific claim? *Does the practice work* (and if so, how?), *out of a reference to a truth which is of the order of a science,* which can be accountable by science? Lacan replies in the affirmative. But his answer is, as usual, paradoxical and challenging in the way it (analytically)˙displaces our expectation as to what a science is, and where the science of psychoanalysis would reside. If science is involved, suggests Lacan, in the *practice* of psychoanalysis, it is not because the *analyst* is scientific, but because the *patient* is, or can be. But the patient is not, as we would expect, the *object* of the science of psychoanalysis, but its *subject.* The (scientific) question of psychoanalysis thus becomes *the question of the subject of a science.*

> To pose that the subject on whom we operate in psychoanalysis can be nothing other than *the subject of science,* may seem like a paradox.
>
> (E 859)

The "subject of science" is a subject who can be defined by the structure of his "relation to truth as cause" (E 873). This (psychoanalytic) truth as cause (a cause that is at once material, formal, and efficacious) is, in Lacan's conception, "the incidence of the signifier" (insofar as it has *caused* the subject's unconsious). And this scientific cause is what the subject—the analysand—is after.

> I would like to ask you, analysts, the question: yes or no, does the exercise of your profession have the meaning of affirming that the truth of neurotic suffering is—*to have truth as its cause* [to have a rational causality which, though symbolic, has both a reference to, and a bearing on, the Real]?
>
> (E 870)

> This is why it was important to promote before all else, and as a fact to be distinguished from the question of whether or not psychoanalysis is a science (whether or not its field is scientific),—this fact, precisely, that *its praxis implicates no other subject than the subject of science.*
>
> (E 863)

Contrary to received opinion, Lacan's preoccupation is not with theory *per se* (with games of "intellectualization"), but always, with his *practice* as a psychoanalytical clinician. He is, first and foremost, a practitioner; a practitioner who happens to be thinking—and rethinking—about what he is doing in his practice. His *theory* is nothing other than his training practice—his practice as an educator, as a training analyst—who introduces others to the pragmatic issues (questions) of the practice.

Now, this *commitment to the practice of psychoanalysis as science*, concomitant with the *acknowledgement that psychoanalytic theory is fundamentally and radically composed of myth*—that the knowledge, that is, which is theorized out of the practice cannot transgress its status as a *narrative expropriating its secured possession as a knowledge*—, has repercussions both in theory and in practice. It means that, to be truly scientific, the practice has to be conceived as antecedent to the knowledge: it has to be forgetful of the knowledge.

> Science, if you look into it, has no memory. It forgets the peripeties out of which it has been born; it has, in other words, a dimension of truth which psychoanalysis puts into practice.
>
> (E 869)

> [To be a good psychoanalyst is to find oneself] in the heart of a concrete history where a dialogue is engaged, in a register where no sort of truth can be found in the form of a knowledge which is generalizable and always true. To give the right reply to an event insofar as it is significant is . . . to give a good interpretation. And to give a good interpretation at the right timing is to be a good analyst.
>
> (S-II, 31)

Any operation in the field of analytic action is anterior to the constitution of
knowledge, which does not preclude the fact that in operating in this field, we
have constituted knowledge. . . .
    For this reason, the more we know, the greater the risks we run. Everything
that you are taught in a form more or less pre-digested in the so-called institutes
of psychoanalysis (sadistic, anal stages, etc.,)—is of course very useful, especially
for non-analysts. It would be stupid for a psychoanalyst systematically to neglect
it, but he should know that this is not the dimension in which he operates.
                                                                    (S-II, 30)

The peculiar scientific status of psychoanalytic practice is then such
that psychoanalysis (as an individual advent and process) is always
living and re-living the very moment of the *birth of knowledge:* the
moment, that is, of *the birth of science.* Like Oedipus at the beginning
of his mythical itinerary, psychoanalysis has *no use for the Oedipus
myth* insofar as it has entered, through the oracles, the domain of
public discourse. Like Oedipus, psychoanalysis has no use of a
preconceived knowledge of the mythic story, no use for the story
insofar as the story is, precisely, in advance, well known. *In practice,*
there is no such thing as a specimen story. The very notion of a
specimen story as applied to the reading or interpretation of another story is thus always a misreading, a mistake.

This mistake exists in every form of knowledge, insofar as knowledge is nothing
other than the cristallization of symbolical activity which it forgets, once constituted. In every knowledge already constituted there is thus a dimension of error,
which consists in the forgetting of the creative function of truth in its nascent
form.
                                                                    (S-II, 29)

Paradoxically enough, it is precisely insofar as it embodies *its own
forgetting* that the Oedipus myth is constitutive of the *science* of
psychoanalysis. And this science only takes itself complacently
(non-problematically) to be a science when it in effect *forgets* the
fictive, generative moment of its birth, when it forgets, in other
words, that it owes its creativity—the *production* of its knowledge—
to a myth. In this respect, psychoanalysis, which treats the Real by
means of the symbolic, is not so different, moreover, from any
other science (physics, for example). There is a fictive moment at
the genesis of every science, a generative fiction (a hypothesis) at
the foundation of every theory.
    To borrow a metaphor from physics, one could say that the
generative, fictive psychoanalytic myth is to the *science* of psychoanalysis what the Heisenberg principle is to contemporary physics:
the element of mythic narrative is something like an *uncertainty
principle* of psychoanalytic theory. It does not conflict with sci-

ence—it *generates it*—as long as it is not believed to be, erroneously, a *certainty principle*.

The question of science in psychoanalysis is, thus, for Lacan, not a question of cognition but a question of commitment. And the concomitant acknowledgement of the psychoanalytic myth is, on the other hand, not a question of complacency in myth, but a question of exigency in and beyond the myth.

Science is the drive to *go beyond*. The scientist's commitment is at once to acknowledge myth and to attempt to *go beyond the myth*. Only when this (mythical, narrative) movement of 'going beyond' stops, does science stop. Only when the myth is not acknowledged, is *believed to be a science*, does the myth prevail at the expense of science. It is precisely when we believe we are *beyond* the myth that we are (indulge in) fiction. There is no 'beyond' to myth—science is always, in one way or another, a new (generative) myth.

There is no *beyond* to the narrative movement of the myth. But the narrative movement of the myth is precisely that which always takes us—if we dare go with it—*beyond itself*.

"Many complain", writes Kafka[14], "that the words of the wise are always merely parables and of no use in daily life, which is the only life we have":

> When the sage says, *"go beyond,"* he does not mean that we should cross to some actual place, which we could do anyhow if the labor were worth it; he means some fabulous yonder, something unknown to us, something too that he cannot designate more precisely, and therefore, cannot help us here in the very least. All these parables really set out to say merely that the incomprehensible is incomprehensible, and we know that already. But the cares we have to struggle with every day: that is a different matter.
>
> Concerning this a man once said: Why such reluctance? If you only followed the parables you yourselves would become parables and with that rid of all your daily cares.
>
> Another said: I bet that is also a parable.
> The first said: You have won.
> The second said: But unfortunately only in parable.
> The first said: No, in reality: in parable you have lost.[15]

NOTES

1 Roy Schafer, "Narration in the Psychoanalytic Dialogue", in *On Narrative*, ed. W. J. T. Mitchell (Chicago and London: The University of Chicago Press, 1981).

2 *Ibid.*, p. 31.

3 Freud, Letter to Wilhelm Fliess of Oct. 15, 1897, in *The Origins of Psychoanalysis*, translated by E. Mosbacher and J. Strachey (New York: Basic Books, 1954, pp. 221-224).

4 Freud, *The Interpretation of Dreams*, in *The Standard Edition of the Complete Psychological Works of Sigmund Freud*, translated from the German under the General

Editorship of James Strachey (London: The Hogarth Press and the Institute of
Psychoanalysis, 1964, Vol. IV, pp. 261-263). Unless otherwise indicated, quotations from Freud's works will refer to this edition: following quotations, in
parenthesis, roman numerals will signal volume number, and arabic numerals
page number, of the Standard Edition.

5 For lack of space, I had to skip here a detailed analysis of the first and second
   dimensions. This essay will therefore concentrate on the third dimension, trying
   to implicate the first two through the third.

6 The following abbreviations are here used to refer to Lacan's works:
      S-I (followed by page number), for: J. Lacan, *Le Séminaire, livre I: Les Ecrits
   techniques de Freud* (Paris: Seuil, 1975);
      S-II (followed by page number), for: J. Lacan. *Le Séminaire, livre II: Le Moi
   dans la théorie de Freud et dans la technique psychoanalytique* (Paris: Seuil, 1978);
      S-XX (followed by page number), for: J. Lacan, *Le Séminaire, livre XX: Encore*
   (Paris: Seuil, 1975).
      All quoted passages from these (as yet untranslated) Seminars are here in my
   translation.
      S-XI (followed by page number), for: *Le Séminaire, livre XI: Les Quatre concepts
   fondamentaux de la psychoanalyse* (Paris: Seuil, 1973). The following abbreviation
   "N" (followed by page number) will refer to the corresponding English edition:
   The Four Fundamental Concepts of Psychoanalysis, translated by Alan Sheridan
   (New York: Norton, 1978).
      E (followed by page number), for: *Ecrits* (Paris: Seuil, 1966); the following
   abbreviation "N" (followed by page number) will designate the page reference
   in the corresponding Norton edition, *Ecrits: A Selection,* traslated by Alan Sheridan (New York: Norton, 1977). When the reference to the French edition of
   the *Ecrits* ("E") is not followed by a reference to the Norton English edition
   ("N"), the passage quoted is in my translation and has not been included in the
   "Selection" of the Norton edition.
      The abbreviation "TM"—"translation modified"—will signal my alterations
   of the official English translation of the work in question.
      As a rule, in the quoted passages, italics are mine, unless otherwise indicated.

7 I am using here the term "performative" in the sense established by J. L. Austin.
   Cf. "Performative Utterances", in *Philosophical Papers* (London and New York:
   Oxford University Press, 1970) and *How to Do Things with Words* (Cambridge/
   Mass.: Harvard University Press, 1975). For a different perspective on the re-
   lation between speech-acts and psychoanalysis (as well as on the theoretical
   relation between Austin and Lacan), see my book, *The Literary Speech-Act: Don
   Juan with J. L. Austin, or Seduction in Two Languages* (Ithaca: Cornell University
   Press, 1983). [Original edition in French: *Le Scandale du corps parlant: Don Juan
   avec Austin, ou La Séduction en deux langues,* Paris: Seuil, 1980.]

8 Sophocles, *Oedipus at Colonus,* in Sophocles, *The Theban Plays,* translated by E. F.
   Walting (Baltimore: Penguin Classics, 1947; reprinted 1965), Scene 2, p. 83.

9 Sophocles, *Oedipus at Colonus,* translated by David Grene, in Sophocles I, *The
   Complete Greek Tragedies,* ed. D. Grene and R. Lattimore (Chicago and London:
   The University of Chicago Press), Scene 2, p. 96. All subsequent quotations
   from *Oedipus at Colonus* will refer to this edition, by scene number followed by
   page number.

10 Cf. E 277-278, N 66-67: "Even when in fact it is represented by a single person,
   the paternal function concentrates in itself both imaginary and real relations,
   always more or less inadequate to the symbolic relation which constitutes it.
      It is in the *name of the father* that we must recognize the support of the symbolic
   function which, from the dawn of history, has identified his person with the
   figure of the law."

11 This insight was first suggested to me (in a course on the Oedipus myth which tried to come to grips with the present questions) by my student, Teddy Cohen, to whom I here address this purloined letter of my thanks.

12 E-415. Cf. my essay, "The Originality of Jacques Lacan, In *Poetics Today*, Vol. 2, Number 1b (Winter 1980/81), pp. 51-52.

13 Aboard the ship which transported him to the U.S. to give the "Clark lectures", Freud, apparently, said to Jung (who reported it to Lacan): "They don't know that we bring with us the Plague. . . ."

14 Franz Kafka, "On Parables", in *Parables and Paradoxes* (New York: Schocken Books, 1970), p. 11.

15 The present essay is (part of) a chapter from my forthcoming book, *Psychoanalysis in Contemporary Culture: Jacques Lacan and the Adventure of Insight*.

SELECTED BIBLIOGRAPHY

I. **By Jacques Lacan** (in chronological order)

Lacan, Jacques. *De la psychose paranoïaque dans ses rapports avec la personnalité.* Paris: Le François, 1932; Paris: Éditions du Seuil, 1975.

———. "La Famille." *Encyclopédie Française* 1938 ed. (Vo. VIII).

———. "Some Reflections on the Ego." *International Journal of Psycho-Analysis* 34(1953):11-17.

———, trans. " 'Logos' de M. Heidegger." *La Psychanalyse* 1(1956):59-79.

———, and Vladimir Granoff. "Fetishism: The Symbolic, the Imaginary, and the Real." In *Perversions, Psychodynamics, and Therapy.* Ed. M. Balint. New York: Gramercy Books, 1956, pp. 265-76.

———. "Les formations de l'inconscient." *Bulletin de Psychologie* 2 (1957-58):1-15.

———. "Le Désin et son interpretation": Le Séminaire VI, 1958-59. Unpublished typescript.

———. "L'éthique de la psychanalyse": Le Séminaire VII, 1959-60. Unpublished typescript.

———. "Hommage fait à Marguerite Duras, du Ravissement Lol V. Stein." *Cahiers M. Renard et J.-L. Barrault* 52(December 1965):9-13.

———. *Écrits.* Paris: Éditions du Seuil, 1966.

———. "Responses à des étudiants en philosophie sur l'objet de la psychanalyse." *Cahiers pour l'analyse* 3(1966):5-13.

———. *Scilicet* 1-8. Paris: Éditions du Seuil, 1968-76. Journal of the *école freudienne* with articles by Lacan and unsigned pieces by members of the *école.*

———. "L'envers de la psychanalyse": Le Séminaire XVIII, 1969-70. Unpublished typescript.

———. "Of Structure as an Inmixing of an Otherness Prerequisite to Any Subject Whatever." *The Language of Criticism and the Sciences of Man: The Structuralist Controversy.* Eds. Richard Macksey and Eugenio Donato. Baltimore and London: The Johns Hopkins Press, 1970.

———. "Radiophonie." *Scilicet* 2/3(1970):55-99.

———. *Écrits.* 2 vols. Paris: Éditions de Seuil, Collection "Points," 1970-71.

———. "The Seminar on 'The Purloined Letter.' " Trans. Jeffrey Mehlman. *Yale French Studies* 48(1972):39-72.

———. "Les non-dupes errent": Le Séminaire XXI, 1973-74. Unpublished typescript.

———. *Télévision.* Paris: Éditions du Seuil, 1974.

————. *Premiers Écrits sur la paranoia*. Paris: Éditions du Seuil, 1975.

————. *Encore:* Le Séminaire XX, 1972-73. Paris: Éditions du Seuil, 1975.

————. *Le Séminaire: Livre I. Les Écrits techniques de Freud*. Ed. Jacques-Alain Miller. Paris: Éditions du Seuil, 1975.

————. *Ornicar?* 1- . Paris: Dept. of Psycho-Analysis at the Univ. of Paris VIII (Vincennes), 1975- . Published versions of Lacan's seminars and research materials of the Dept.'s current projects.

————. *Le Scission de 1953: La communauté psychanalytique en France I*. Ed., Jacques-Alain Miller. Supplement to *Ornicar?* VII (1976).

————. "Desire and the Interpretation of Desire in *Hamlet*." *Yale French Studies* 55/56(1977):11-52.

————. *Écrits inspirés*. Besançon: Éditions Arep, 1977.

————. *Écrits: A Selection*. Trans. Alan Sheridan. New York: W. W. Norton and Co., Inc., 1977.

————. *The Four Fundamental Concepts of Psycho-Analysis*. Ed. Jacques-Alain Miller. Trans. Alan Sheridan. New York: W. W. Norton and Co., Inc., 1978.

————. *Le Séminaire: Livre II. Le Moi dans la théorie de Freud et dans la technique de la psychanalyse*. Ed. Jacques-Alain Miller. Paris: Éditions de Seuil, 1978.

————. *Le Séminaire: Livre III. Les Psychoses*. Ed. Jacques-Alain Miller. Paris: Éditions du Seuil, 1981.

————. *Speech and Language in Psychoanalysis*. Trans., Notes and Commentary by Anthony G. Wilden. Baltimore and London: The Johns Hopkins Univ. Press, 1982. (Revised reprinting of *The Language of the Self*, Johns Hopkins Univ. Press, 1968)

————, and the *école freudienne*. *Feminine Sexuality*. Eds. Juliet Mitchell and Jacqueline Rose. Trans. Jacqueline Rose. New York: W. W. Norton and Co., Inc., 1982.

————. "Joyce le symptôme." *L'Ane* (fall 1982).

II. **About Jacques Lacan and Narration** (in alphabetical order)

Althusser, Louis. "Freud and Lacan." *Lenin and Philosophy*. Trans. Ben Brewster. New York: Monthly Review Press, 1971.

Astle, Richard. "Dracula as Totemic Monster: Lacan, Freud, Oedipus and History." *SubStance* 25(1980):98-105.

Bär, E. "The Language of the Unconscious According to Jacques Lacan." *Semiotica* 3(1971):241-68.

————. "Understanding Lacan." *Psychoanalysis and Contemporary Science*, Vol. 3. Eds. L. Goldberger and V. H. Rosen. New York: International Universities Press, 1974.

Baudrillard, Jean. *Simulacres et simulation*. Paris: Edition Galilée, 1981.

Bellemin-Noël, Jean. *Vers l'inconscient du texte*. Paris: Presses Universitaires de France, 1979.

Benveniste, Emile. "Remarks on the Function of Language in Freudian Theory." *Problems in General Linguistics,* Vol. 1. Coral Gables: Univ. of Miami Press, 1971.

Bowie, Malcolm. "Jacques Lacan." *Structuralism and Since: From Lévi-Strauss to Derrida.* Ed. and Intro. John Sturrock. Oxford: Oxford Univ. Press, 1979.

Brenckman, John. "The Other and the One: Psychoanalysis, Reading, the *Symposium.*" *Yale French Studies* 55/56(1977):396-456.

Bruss, Neal H. "The Freudian Practitioner as 'an Ideal Speaker-Listener.'" *Semiotica* 19(1-2):131-47. 1977.

————. "Lacan and Literature: Imaginary Objects and Social Order." *Massachusetts Review* 22(1):62-92. 1981.

————. "Re-Stirring the Waters, or the Voice that Sees the World as Patients." *Massachusetts Review* 20(1979):337-54.

Certeau, Michel de. "Lacan: une éthique de la parole." *Débat* 22(1982):54-69.

————. "Le roman psychanalytique et son institution." *Confrontation: Géopsychanalyse* (1981):129-145.

Clément, Catherine. *Miroirs du sujet.* Paris: Plon, 1975.

————. *Vies et Légendes de Jacques Lacan.* Paris: Grasset, 1981.

Coward, Rosalind, and John Ellis. *Language and Materialism: Developments in Semiology and the Theory of the Subject.* London, Henley, and Boston: Routledge and Kegan Paul, 1977.

David-Menard, Monique. "Lacanians Against Lacan." *Social Text* 6(1982):86-111.

Davis, Robert Con, ed. *The Fictional Father: Lacanian Readings of the Text.* Amherst: Univ. of Massachusetts Press, 1981.

Deleuze, Gilles, and Felix Guatari. *Anti-Oedipus: Capitalism and Schizophrenia.* Trans. Robert Hurley, Mark Seem, and Peter R. Lane. New York: Viking, 1977.

————. *Différence et répétition.* Paris: Presses Universitaires de France, 1979.

Derrida, Jacques. *La Carte postale: de Socrate à Freud et au-delà.* Paris: Flammarion, 1980.

————. "Freud and the Scene of Writing." *Writing and Difference.* Trans., Notes, and Intro. by Alan Bass. Chicago: Univ. of Chicago Press, 1978.

————. *Positions.* Trans. and Annotated by Alan Bass. Chicago: Univ. of Chicago Press, 1981.

————. "The Purveyor of Truth." Trans. W. Domingo, J. Hulbert, M. Ron and M.-R. Logan. *Yale French Studies* 52(1975):31-113.

Descombes, Vincent, *L'Inconscient Malgré lui.* Paris: Editions de Minuit, 1977.

De Waelhens, A. *Schizophrenia: A Philosophical Reflection on Lacan's Structuralist Interpretation.* Trans. W.Ver Eecke. Pittsburgh: Duquesne Univ. Press, 1978.

————. *Le duc de Saint-Simon*. Bruxelles: Pub. des Fac. Univ. St. Louis, 1981.

Dragonetti, Roger. *La Vie de la lettre en Moyen Age (Le Conte du Graal)*. Paris: Éditions du Seuil, 1980.

Durand, Régis. *Melville: Signes et Métaphores*. Lausanne: L'Age d'Homme, 1980.

Ey, Henri, ed. *L'Inconscient*. Paris: Desclée de Brouwer, 1966.

Fages, J.-B. *Comprendre Jacques Lacan*. Toulouse: Privat, 1971.

Felman, Shoshana. *La Folie et la chose littéraire*. Paris: Éditions du Seuil, 1978.

————, ed. "Literature and Psychoanalysis. The Question of Reading— Otherwise." *Yale French Studies* 55/56(1977). (Reprinted under the same title by Johns Hopkins Univ. Press, 1982.)

————. "La méprise et sa chance." *L'Arc* 58(1974):40-48.

————. "The Originality of Jacques Lacan." *Poetics Today* 2(1980-81):45-57.

————. "To Open the Question." *Yale French Studies* 55/56(1977):5-10.

————. "On Reading Poetry: Reflections on the Limits and Possibilities of Psychoanalytic Approaches." *The Literary Freud: Mechanisms of Defense and the Poetic Will*. Ed. Joseph H. Smith. New Haven: Yale Univ. Press, 1980.

————. "Turning the Screw of Interpretation." *Yale French Studies* 55/56 (1977):94-207.

Fisher, Eileen. "The Discourse of the Other in Not I: A Confluence of Beckett and Lacan." *Theater* 10(3):101-03. 1979.

Flieger, Jerry Aline. "The Prison-House of Ideology: Critic as Inmate." *Diacritics* 12(3):47-56. 1982.

————. "Trial and Error: The Case of the Textual Unconscious." *Diacritics* 11(1):56-67. 1981.

Frank, Manfred. *Das Sagbare und das Unsagbare: Studien zu neuesten französischen Hermeneutik und Texttheorie*. Frankfurt/M: Suhrkamp, 1980.

"French Freud: Structural Studies in Psychoanalysis." *Yale French Studies* 48(1972). [edited by Jeffrey Mehlman]

Gallop, Jane. *The Daughter's Seduction: Feminism and Psychoanalysis*. Ithaca: Cornell Univ. Press, 1982.

————. "Impertinent Questions: Irigaray, Sade, Lacan." *SubStance* 26(1980):57-67.

————. "Lacan's 'Mirror Stage': Where to Begin." *SubStance* 37/38(1983):118-128.

Gasché, Rodolphe. "La Sorcière métapsychologique." *Digraphe* 3 (1974):83-122.

Georgin, Robert. *Lacan*. Cahiers Cistre No. 3. Lausanne: L'Age d'Homme, 1977.

Gorney, James E. "The Clinical Application of Lacan in the Psychoanalytic Situation." *The Psychoanalytic Review* 69(2):241-248. 1982.

"Graphesis: Perspectives in Literature and Philosophy." *Yale French Studies* 52(1975).

Green, André. *Un Oeil en trop: Le Complexe d'Oedipe dans la tragédie.* Paris: Éditions de Minuit, 1969.

————. "La Psychanalyse devant l'opposition de l'histoire et de la structure." *Critique* 14(1963):649-62.

————. "L'Objet(*a*) de J. Lacan, sa logique, et la théorie freudienne." *Cahiers pour l'Analyse* 3(May 1966):15-37.

————. "The Unbinding Process." *New Literary History* 12(1):11-39. 1980.

Grimaud, Michel. "Sur une métaphore métonymique hugolienne selon Jacques Lacan." *Littérature* 29(1978):98-104.

Grosrichard, A. *Structure du Serail. La fiction du despotisme asiatique dans l'occident classique.* Paris: Éditions du Seuil, 1979.

Hartman, Geoffrey H. "Monsieur Texte: On Jacques Derrida, His Glas." *Georgia Review* 29(4):759-97. 1975.

————, ed. *Psychoanalysis and the Question of the Text.* Baltimore: Johns Hopkins Univ. Press, 1978.

Heath, Stephen. "Difference." *Screen* 19(1978).

Hertz, Neil. "Freud and the Sandman." *Textual Strategies: Perspectives in Post-Structuralist Criticism*, ed. Josué V. Harari. Ithaca, NY: Cornell Univ. Press, 1979.

Hesnard, André. *De Freud à Lacan.* Paris: E.S.F., 1970.

Hottois, Gilbert. "La hantise contemporaine du langage. Essai sur la situation philosophique du discours lacanien." *Confrontations psychiatriques* 19(1981):163-188.

Hyde, Michael J. "Jacques Lacan's Psychoanalytic Theory of Speech and Language." *The Quarterly of Speech* 66(1):96-108. 1980.

Irigaray, Luce. "La 'Mecanique' des fluides." *L'Arc:* "Jacques Lacan" 58(1). 1974.

————. *Ce Sexe qui n'en est pas un.* Paris: Éditions de Minuit, 1977.

————. *Speculum de l'autre femme.* Paris: Éditions de Minuit, 1974.

Irwin, John T. *Doubling and Incest.* Baltimore: Johns Hopkins University Press, 1975.

Jameson, Fredric. "Imaginary and Symbolic in Lacan: Marxism, Psychoanalytic Criticism, and the Problem of the Subject." *Yale French Studies* 55/56(1977):338-95.

————. *The Political Unconscious: Narrative as a Socially Symbolic Act.* Ithaca: Cornell Univ. Press, 1981.

————. *The Prison-House of Language: A Critical Account of Structuralism and Russian Formalism.* Princeton: Princeton Univ. Press, 1972.

Johnson, Barbara. *The Critical Difference: Essays in the Contemporary Rhetoric of Reading.* Baltimore and London: The Johns Hopkins Univ. Press, 1980. See particularly "The Frame of Reference."

Kahane, Claire, and Janice Doane. "Psychoanalysis and American Fiction:

The Subversion of Q.E.D." *Studies in American Literature* 9(2):137-57. 1981.

Krem :r-Marietti, Angèle. *Lacan et la rhétorique de l'inconscient.* Paris: Aub.er-Montaigne, 1978.

Kristeva, Julia. *Desire in Language.* Ed. Leon S. Roudiez. Trans. Thomas Gora, Alice Jardine, and Leon S. Roudiez. New York: Columbia Univ. Press, 1980.

Kurzweil, Edith, and William Phillips, eds. *Literature and Psychoanalysis.* New York: Columbia Univ. Press, 1983.

Lacoste, Patrick. *Il écrit: une mise en scène de Freud.* Paris: Editions Galilée, 1981.

Lacoue-Labarthe, P., and J.-L. Nancy. *Le Titre de la lettre (Une Lecture de Lacan).* Paris: Éditions Galilée, 1973.

Laplanche, Jean. "Fantasme originaire, fantasmes des origines, origine du fantasme." *Les Temps modernes* 19(215):1833-68. 1964. [translation in *Inter. J. Psychoanalysis* 49 (1968)]

———. *Hölderlin et la question du père.* Paris: Presses Universitaires de France, 1961.

———, and J.-B. Pontalis. *The Language of Psycho-Analysis.* Trans. Donald Nicholson-Smith. Intro. Daniel Lagache. New York: W. W. Norton, and Co., 1973.

———. *Life and Death in Psychoanalysis.* Trans. and Intro. Jeffrey Mehlman. Baltimore and London: The Johns Hopkins Univ. Press, 1976.

———, and Serge Leclaire. "The Unconscious: A Psychoanalytic Study." Trans. Patrick Coleman. *Yale French Studies* 48(1972):118-75.

Leavy, Stanley A. "The Significance of Jacques Lacan." *Psychoanalytic Quarterly* 46(1977):201-19.

Leclaire, Serge. *Démasquer le réel: un essai sur l'objet en psychanalyse.* Paris: Éditions du Seuil, 1971.

———. *Psychanalyser.* Paris: Éditions du Seuil, 1968.

Leitch, Vincent B. *Deconstructive Criticism: An Advanced Introduction.* New York: Columbia Univ. Press, 1983.

MaCallum, Pamela. "Indeterminacy, Irreducibility and Authority in Modern Literary Theory." *Ariel* 13(1):73-84.

MacCabe, Colin. *James Joyce and the Revolution of the Word.* New York: Barnes and Noble, 1979.

———, ed. *The Talking Cure: Essays in Psychoanalysis and Language.* London: Macmillan, 1981.

MacCannell, Dean, and Juliet MacCannell. *The Time of the Sign: A Semiotic Interpretation of Modern Culture.* Bloomington: Indiana Univ. Press, 1982.

Mannoni, Octave. "A Brief Introduction to Jacques Lacan." *Contemporary Psychoanalysis* 8(1971):97-106.

———. *Clefs pour l'imaginaire ou l'Autre Scène.* Paris: Éditions du Seuil, 1970.

————. *Fictions freudiennes.* Paris: Éditions du Seuil, 1973.

————. *Freud.* Trans. Renaud Bruce. New York: Vintage Books, 1974.

————. *Freud: The Theory of the Unconscious.* London: New Left Books; New York: Random House, 1971.

Manoni, Maud. *La Théorie comme fiction.* Paris: Éditions du Seuil, 1979.

Mehlman, Jeffrey. "Entre psychanalyse et psychocritique." *Poétique* 3(1970):365-85.

————. "The 'Floating Signifier': From Lévi-Strauss to Lacan." *Yale French Studies* 48(1972):10-37.

————. "*Poe pourri:* Lacan's Purloined Letter." *Aesthetics Today.* Eds. Morris Philipson and Paul J. Gudel. New York: New American Library, 1980.

————. *A Structural Study of Autobiography: Proust, Leiris, Sartre, Lévi Strauss.* Ithaca and London: Cornell Univ. Press, 1974.

————. "The Suture of an Allusion: Lacan with Léon Bloy." *SubStance* 33/34(1981/1982):99-110.

Melz, Charles. *Blanchefleur et le saint homme ou la semblance des reliques: Etude comparée de littérature médiévale.* Paris: Éditions du Seuil, 1979.

Miel, Jan. "Jacques Lacan and the Structure of the Unconscious." *Yale French Studies* 36-37(1966):104-11.

Miller, Jacques-Alain. "Introduction à la transmission de la psychanalyse." *Lettres de L'École,* 25, Vol. 1. *La Transmission* (1). Bulletin Intérieur de l'école freudienne de Paris. Paris: Claude Conté, 1979.

————. "La Suture." *Cahiers pour l'Analyse* 1(1966):93-105.

Mitchell, Juliet. *Psycho-Analysis and Feminism: Freud, Reich, Laing and Women.* New York: Vintage Books, 1975.

Montrelay, Michèle. "Inquiry into Femininity." Trans. and Intro. Parveen Adams. *m/f* 1(1978):65-101.

Muller, John P. "The Analogy of Gap in Lacan's *Écrits: A Selection.*" *Psychohistory Review* 8(3):38-45. 1979.

————. "Ego and Subject in Lacan." *The Psychoanalytic Review* 69(2):234-240. 1982.

————, and William J. Richardson. *Lacan and Language: A Reader's Guide to "Écrits."* New York: International Universities Press, Inc., 1982.

————, and William J. Richardson. "Psychosis and Mourning in Lacan's *Hamlet.*" *New Literary History* 11(1):147-65. 1980.

————, and William J. Richardson. "Toward Reading Lacan: Pages for a Workbook." *Psychoanal. Contemp. Thought* 1(1978):323-372.

————, and William J. Richardson. "Toward Reading Lacan: Pages for a Workbook, Chapter 2 (Agressivity in Psychoanalysis)." *Psychoanal. Contemp. Thought* 1(1978):503-529.

Mykyta, Larysa. "Lacan, Literature and the Look: Woman in the Eye of Psychoanalysis." *SubStance* 39(1982):49-57.

Ortigues, Edmond. *Le Discours et le symbole.* Paris: Aubier, 1962.

Ortiques, Marie-Cécile, and Edmond Ortiques. *Oedipe Africain.* Paris: Plon, 1966.

Palmier, Jean-Michel. *Lacan.* Paris: Éditions Universitaires, 1970.

Pichon, Edouard. "La famille devant M. Lacan." *Revue Française de Psychanalyse* 11(1939):107-35.

Pontalis, J.-B. *Après Freud.* Paris: Gallimard, 1968.

———. *Entre le rêve et la douleur.* Paris: Gallimard, 1977.

———, ed. "Les Formations de l'inconscient." *Bulletin de Psychologie* 12(1958):250-56.

Ragland-Sullivan, Ellie. "Explicating Jacques Lacan: An Overview." *Univ. of Hartford Studies in Literature* 11(1979):140-56.

———. "Jacques Lacan: Feminism and the Problem of Gender Identity." *SubStance* 36 (1982):6-20.

———. "Lacan, Language, and Literary Criticism." *Literary Review* 24(4):562-77. 1981.

Rapaport, Herman. "Lacan Disbarred: Translation as Ellipsis." *Diacritics* 6(4):57-60. 1976.

Rey, Jean-Michel. *Parcours de Freud.* Paris: Editions Galilée, 1973.

Richardson, William J. "Lacan's View of Language and Being." *The Psychoanalytic Review* 69(2):229-233. 1982.

Rifflet-Lemaire, Anika. *Jacques Lacan.* Trans. David Macey. London, Boston, and Henley: Routledge and Kegan Paul, 1977.

Roland, Alan, ed. *Psychoanalysis, Creativity, and Literature: A French-American Inquiry.* New York: Columbia Univ. Press, 1978.

Rosolato, Guy. *Essai sur le symbolique.* Paris: Gallimard, 1969.

———. *La Relation d'inconnu.* Paris: Gallimard, 1981.

———. "Semantique et altérations du langage." *L'Evolution Psychiatrique* (1956):865-99.

———. "Le Symbolique." *La Psychanalyse* 5(1959):225-33.

Roudinesco, Elizabeth. *La Bataille de cent ans: Histoire de la psychanalyse en France.* Paris: Ramsay, 1982.

Roussel, J. "Introduction to Jacques Lacan." *New Left Review* 51(1968):63-77.

Roustaing, François. *Discipleship from Freud to Lacan.* Trans. Ned Lukacher. Baltimore and London: The Johns Hopkins Univ. Press, 1982.

———. *Psychoanalysis Never Lets Go.* Trans. Ned Luckacher. Baltimore and London: The Johns Hopkins Univ. Press, 1983.

Ryan, Marie-Laure. "Is There Life for Saussure after Structuralism?" *Diacritics* 9(4):28-44. 1979.

Ryan, Michael. *Marxism and Deconstruction: A Critical Introduction.* Baltimore and London: The Johns Hopkins Univ. Press, 1982.

Sadoff, Diane F. *Monsters of Affection: Dickens, Eliot, and Brontë on Fatherhood.* Baltimore: The Johns Hopkins Univ. Press, 1982.

Safouan, Moustapha. *Etudes sur Oedipe: Introduction à une théorie du sujet.* Paris: Éditions du Seuil, 1974.

———. *La sexualité féminine dans la doctrine freudienne.* Paris: Éditions du Seuil, 1976.

————. "De la structure en psychanalyse: contribution à une théorie du manque." *Qu'est-ce que le structuralisme?* Ed. François Wahl. Paris: Éditions du Seuil, 1968, pp. 239-98.

Schafer, Roy. "Narration in Psychoanalytic Dialogue." *On Narrative*. Ed. W. J. T. Mitchell. Chicago: University of Chicago Press, 1981.

Schleifer, Ronald. [Review-essay of] Robert Con Davis, ed. *The Fictional Father: Lacanian Readings of the Text. MLN* 96(5):1185-92. 1981.

Schlossman, Beryl. "James Joyce et le don des langues." *Tel Quel* 92 (1982):9-30.

————. *Joyce's Catholic Comedy of Language*. Madison: University of Wisconsin Press, 1983.

————. "L'Ecriture joycienne: juive ou catholique?" *L'Herne: James Joyce* (forthcoming)

————. "Signatures of the Wor(l)d." *Genre: The World as Text* (forthcoming)

————. "Finnegans Wake: The Passage Toward Pentecost." *James Joyce: A Symposium All His Own:* VIII International James Joyce Symposium, Dublin, June 14-19, 1982. (forthcoming)

Schneiderman, Stuart. "Afloat with Jacques Lacan." *Diacritics* 1(2):27-34. 1971.

————. "Lacan et la litterature." *Tel Quel* 84(1980):39-47.

————. *Jacques Lacan: The Death of an Intellectual Hero*. Cambridge, Mass.: Harvard Univ. Press, 1983.

————, ed. and trans. *Returning to Freud: Clinical Psychoanalysis and the School of Jacques Lacan*. New Haven and London: Yale Univ. Press, 1980.

Schwartz, Murray M., ed. "Psychology and Literature: Some Contemporary Directions." *New Literary History* 12(1). 1980.

Sédat, Jacques, ed. *Retour à Lacan*. Paris: Fayard, 1981.

Shullenberser, William. "Lacan and the Play of Desire in Poetry." *Massachusetts Studies in English* 7(1):33-40. 1978.

Sibony, Daniel. "*Hamlet:* A Writing-Effect." Trans. James Hulbert with Joshua Wilner. *Yale French Studies* 55/56(1977):53-93.

Smith, Joseph H., ed. *The Literary Freud: Mechanisms of Defense and the Poetic Will*. New Haven: Yale Univ. Press, 1980.

————. *Psychoanalysis and Language: Psychiatry and the Humanities*. New Haven: Yale Univ. Press, 1978.

Sollers, Philippe. "Freud's Hand." Trans. Barbara Johnson. *Yale French Studies* 55/56(1977):329-37.

Speziale-Bagliacca, Roberto. "Lacan l'ineludibile." *Nuova Corrente* 82-83(1980):97-129.

Spivak, Gayatri Chakravorty. "The Letter as Cutting Edge." *Yale French Studies* 55/56(1977):208-26.

Szafran, A. W. "Propos sur les concepts du langage et de l'inconscient chez Lacan et la tradition ésotérique." *Acta Psychiatrica Belgica* 73(4):484-96. 1973.

Turkle, Sherry. *Psychoanalytic Politics: Freud's French Revolution.* New York: Basic Books, 1978.

Viderman, Serge. *Le Céleste et le sublunaire.* Paris: Presses Universitaires de France, 1977.

Weber, Samuel. *Freud-Legende.* Olten & Freiburg/B: Walter-Verlag, 1979. Revised English transl.: *The Legend of Freud.* Minneapolis: Univ. of Minn. Press, 1982.

——. "The Divaricator: Remarks on Freud's *Witz.*" *Glyph* 1 (1977):1-27.

——. *Rückkehr zu Freud: Jacques Lacans Ent-stellung der Psychoanalyse.* Frankfurt/M: Ullstein Verlag, 1978.

——. "The Sideshow, or: Remarks on a Canny Moment." *MLN* 88(1973):1102-1133.

Wilden, Anthony. "Freud, Signorelli, and Lacan: The Repression of the Signifier." *American Imago* 23(4):332-66. 1966.

——. *System and Structure: Essays on Communication and Exchange.* London: Tavistock, 1972.

Wollheim, Richard. "The Cabinet of Dr. Lacan." *New York Review of Books* 21/22(1979):36-45.

Wordsworth, Ann. "Lacanalysis: Lacan for Critics." *Oxford Literary Review* 2(3):7-8. 1977.

Wright, Elizabeth. "Modern Psychoanalytic Criticism." *Modern Literary Theory.* Eds. Ann Jefferson and David Robey. Totowa, New Jersey: Barnes and Noble Books, 1982.

Young, Robert. "The Eye and Progress of His Sons: A Lacanian Reading of *The Prelude.*" *Oxford Literary Review* 3(3):78-98. 1979.

Zons, Raimer Stefan. "Ein Familienzentrum: Goethes 'Erlkönig'." *Fügen* I(1980):125-31.

BIBLIOGRAPHIC NOTE: Since Nov.-Dec. 1982 the New York Lacan Study Group has published a newsletter, edited by Stuart Schneiderman and Helena Schultz-Keil: *Lacan Study Notes* (5 Carmine St., New York, NY 10014; $10 per annum). It includes reviews and a continuing bibliography of publications related to Lacan. Helpful bibliographies are also included in the following earlier volumes: Josué Harari, ed., *Textual Strategies* (Ithaca" Cornell Univ. Press, 1979); Claudio Toscani, *La Metastasi analitica* (Milano: Edizioni Effe Emme, 1978)

ROBERT CON DAVIS AND RICHARD MACKSEY